GW01445339

DISORDE
EATERS

DISORDERLY EATERS

Texts in Self-Empowerment

edited by
Lilian R. Furst
and
Peter W. Graham

The Pennsylvania State University Press
University Park, Pennsylvania

In the chapter on pages 29–41, by J. Ellen Gainor, the quotations and illustrations from *Mrs. Piggle-Wiggle* are used by permission of HarperCollins Publishers and Brandt & Brandt. Text quotations copyright © 1957 by Betty MacDonald. Illustrations copyright © 1957 by Hilary Knight.

Library of Congress Cataloging-in-Publication Data

Disorderly eaters : texts in self-empowerment / edited by Lilian R.
  Furst and Peter W. Graham.
      p.   cm.
    ISBN 0-271-00815-6 (cloth)
    ISBN 0-271-00871-7 (paper)
    1. Food in literature. 2. Eating disorders in literature.
  3. Dinners and dining in literature. 4. Literature—History and
  criticism. I. Furst, Lilian R. II. Graham, Peter W.
  PN56.F59D57   1992
  809′.93355—dc20   91-28357
                                                             CIP

Copyright ©1992 The Pennsylvania State University
All rights reserved

Published by The Pennsylvania State University Press,
Suite C, Barbara Building, University Park, PA 16802-1003

Printed in the United States of America

It is the policy of The Pennsylvania State University Press to use acid-free paper for the first printing of all clothbound books. Publications on uncoated stock satisfy the minimum requirements of American National Standard for Information Sciences—Permanence of Paper for Printed Library Materials, ANSI Z39.48–1984.

Contents

INTRODUCTION

Lilian R. Furst

This volume explores literary portrayals of aberrant eating behaviors. Because no historical or geographic limitations were imposed, it was possible to examine a spectrum that ranges over Europe and the United States and spans from Euripides to Toni Morrison. The strength and interest of this collection stem from the variety of its contributions as well as from the originality of the individual chapters.

Both as a lexical phrase and as a sociomedical concept, "eating disorders" has become assimilated into current usage in the last twenty and more years. Familiarity with eating disorders in their most common forms of anorexia and/or bulimia has expanded far beyond the medical community. Parents of adolescents are aware of the potential danger, and many high school and college teachers have come into contact with the syndrome among their students. Although not literally contagious diseases, eating disorders have a tendency to spread by imitation, competition, or solidarity, particularly among a cohort of young people living in close quarters, as on a college campus. The notorious resistance of eating disorders to medical treatment makes them very real threats to the health, well-being, and future of those afflicted. Experimental therapies with new drugs are being tested, but it is not yet known whether changes in eating alter the brain's chemistry, or vice versa. Not least, the mystery that still surrounds eating disorders makes them a disturbing problem of our day.

In this context the burst of attention to eating disorders since about 1970, in popular culture as well as in professional circles, is not at all surprising. Joan Jacobs Brumberg, in the second chapter of *Fasting Girls*, [1] has given an impressive overview of the intense interest aroused by eating behaviors in the 1980s. Her survey encompasses articles in publications as heterogeneous as *Science Digest*, the *New York Times*, *People* magazine, *Mademoiselle*, and *Seventeen*, a movie (*Down and Out in Beverly Hills*, 1986), television shows, and novels. She also points to the impact made by the death in 1983 of the popular singer Karen Carpenter, who died of the effects of prolonged starvation. Equally significant is the success of a number of semipopular books, written from diverse angles but all aiming to educate the general public about the dynamics of eating disorders. Foremost among these is Hilde Bruch's *The Golden Cage: The Enigma of Anorexia Nervosa* (Cambridge, Mass.: Harvard University Press, 1978), a sympathetic address directly to her patients by the leading psychiatric expert. Very different in tone and perspective is Cherry Boone O'Neill's intimate confession, *Starving for Attention* (New York: Continuum, 1982), whose piquancy is heightened by the glamorous environment. John A. Sours, in *Starving to Death in a Sea of Plenty* (New York and London: Jason Aronson, 1980), tries to reinforce the instructional appeal of his investigations by appending a fictional story that illustrates his thesis. Several books, notably those by Kim Chernin and Susie Ohrbach,[2] have made the link between eating disorders and the women's movement. The compulsive nature of the entire subject and the ready market (or should one say *hunger?*) for it is perhaps best revealed by the fact that both Chernin and Orbach have each written two successive books on virtually the same topic.

During the same period the results of scientific inquiries into eating disorders have appeared with increasing frequency since Sten Theander's pioneering 1970 study of the medical and social histories of ninety-four female patients in southern Sweden.[3] In this respect too, Hilde Bruch marks a milestone with her *Eating Disorders: Obesity, Anorexia Nervosa, and the Person Within* (1973). The *International Journal of Eating Disorders*, founded in 1981, elicited an instantaneous response by attracting a large number of both submissions and subscribers. In 1985 bulimia was listed in *DSM-III-R* as a separate disease, though often associated with anorexia. In the same year, the Renfrew Center, the first residential facility specifically devoted to eating disorders, opened near Philadelphia. Two more major textbooks have recently appeared: *The Eating Disorders,* edited by Barton J. Blinder, Barry F. Chaitin, and Renée S. Goldstein, and *The Family Approach to Eating Disorders,* edited by W. Vandereycken, Elly Krog, and Joham Vanderlinden, both published in 1989 by the PMA Publishing Corporation in New York. The Summer-Fall 1991 issue of *Mosaic* is titled "Diet and Discourse: Eating, Drinking, and Literature," and *Modern Language Notes* 106 (September 1991) is devoted to "Cultural Representations of Food."

In all these works, whatever their audience or tone, eating disorders are understood as anorexia and/or bulimia. Undereating and overeating are indeed the most common forms of eating disorder, but other kinds of disorderly eating, such as cannibalism or a concentration on single foods endowed with magic capacities, are also being included in this volume. The underlying purpose of this wider view is to prompt a reconsideration of what the now hackneyed phrase "eating disorder" actually means. The word "disorder" implies a deviation from some acknowledged order or norm. The order of eating, as every anthropologist realizes, is one of the activities most highly conditioned by the culture in which it is sited. Which foods are desirable, acceptable, unacceptable, or even taboo varies as radically from culture to culture as it does from person to person. The old proverb could well be updated to "One man's meat is another woman's poison," less in order to underscore gender differences than simply as a reminder of personal likes and dislikes. Religious factors may also play a part, as, for instance, in the prohibition of beef as coming from a sacred animal among Muslims, and of pork and shellfish as "unclean" among Jews.

Without looking beyond Western culture, a clearly discernible order of eating can be seen in our three traditional meals, breakfast, lunch, and dinner, with certain foods deemed particularly suitable to each. For example, to eat cereals in the evening is an eccentricity because they are regarded as a breakfast food. Order becomes manifest again in the sequence of dishes within a meal: soup is a starter, followed by salad, the main course, and dessert. Yet the arbitrariness of even this order is apparent in the alternative position of the salad, usually taken after the main course in France and Italy but in Central Europe served with the main dish. The place of cheese is another controversial issue; in the United States it functions most often as an hors d'oeuvre, whereas in France and Italy it comes after the main course (sometimes with the salad), and in England after the dessert to end the meal with a savory. Trivial though these small disparities may seem in isolation, they amount to a tacitly established order of eating that is equated with normality. The traveler in a foreign country who orders by pointing to three successive items on a menu in a language he does not know, and who is brought exactly what he had unwittingly picked in this order—chocolate cake, a plate of radishes, and a bowl of soup—is given strange looks, unless perchance that happens to be the dominant pattern of eating in that place.

The order of our eating has come to be more and more dominated by the authority of nutrition as a science. Possibly because it is still a relatively new discipline, its fiats change drastically and quite rapidly. As a child and adolescent, I was constantly urged to eat more red meat as the only way to become strong; now I look back at my stubborn resistance as a blessing that may, perversely, have made me healthier in the long run, and I am relieved at the removal of that particular pressure. Others, however, replace it as we are urged in almost daily articles and reports to take more fiber, more oat bran (no longer "in"), more fish oil, and who can guess what the next panacea will be to lower the bad cholesterol and increase the good. Having switched to decaffeinated coffee to alleviate my insomnia, I now learn that certain methods of decaffeination are at least suspected of being carcinogenic and that decaffeinated coffee has been linked to higher levels of bad cholesterol. The joke that a new toll-free number, 1–800–What's-Good-For-You-Today, ought to be instituted is hardly a joke anymore.[4]

The growing prescription of an ever-narrower order of approved eating is bound to provoke rebellion. One novel style of eating, called "grazing," is frequently attributed to workaholic yuppies who nibble at giant chocolate-chip cookies, lick frozen yogurt, or eat whatever takes their fancy or comes their way without leaving their work stations for long. Is such behavior a disorder insofar as it departs from the norm of three square meals a day? For the grazers, as indeed for others too, the order of eating represents a means to assert not merely one's own personal preferences but beyond that, one's will and even one's autonomy. One of the central themes of this collection is that eating, like noneating, is a tool for power both over oneself and over one's surroundings. The individual, especially when forced into a coercive situation of any sort, can exercise control and a measure of choice by the mode and amount of food ingested. The order of eating thus becomes a very fundamental vehicle for self-expression, and simultaneously for manipulation.

The complex, subterranean connections between eating, control, and power seem to have been intuited by the medical profession well before they became formalized. Cases of deviant eating were generally recorded as insoluble puzzles in the absence of identifiable organic disease. The situation was complicated by the long-standing association of abstinence from food with sainthood. There is still considerable controversy about whether the so-called "miraculous maids" were forerunners of modern anorexics or whether they were impelled by entirely different motives.[5] Insofar as holy fasting is an attempt to set oneself apart by self-consecration to an uncommon ideal, it should be seen as the expression of an endeavor to take control over one's bodily functions and, by extension, over one's whole being. The British physician William W. Gull, who launched the term "anorexia nervosa" in a paper presented to a medical forum in London in 1868,[6] perceived the malady as a moral or mental aberration rooted in the nervous system but exacerbated by the patient's youth and life-style. While Gull, as a Victorian clinician, confined himself to a description of the physical symptoms without sounding their possible causes, he did insist that the patient's removal from the home environment was an essential element of the cure. Alternatively, or in addition, as feasible, a strong-minded nurse was to be hired to take charge of nutritional management and to govern the patient's regimen without heed either to the subject's inclinations or to the parents' misguided solicitude. It is quite evident that a grim power struggle for the right to control oneself formed the implicit agenda behind this scenario.

Long before the physicians and post-Freudian psychiatrists, however, creative writers, as shrewd observers of human behavior, were aware of the potential of disorderly eating as a coercive tool to empower the self and simultaneously to exert pressure on others. Just as the Romantics and their successors had an intuitive insight into the darker, unconscious drives of the psyche, so writers were to an astonishingly precise degree cognizant of the internal sources and external impact of disorderly eating. Their grasp of the psychological mechanisms of disordered eating, as revealed in the texts discussed in this volume, is nothing short of amazing, considering how very recently scientific study has come to a rational understanding of the mental and social processes involved.

Highly diversified though the texts analyzed here are, generically as well as temporally and geographically (they comprise dramas, narratives, lyric and epic poetry, and an autobiographical memoir), they are unified by a single recurrent theme that assumes a kaleidoscopic variety of forms. All reveal in one way or another the individual's lust for self-empowerment through choices consciously or unconsciously made in determining patterns of eating. The eating disorder thus becomes a vehicle for self-assertion as a rebellion against a dominant ethos unacceptable to the persona. Whether the outcome is ultimately positively triumphant or negatively destructive is in the last resort immaterial to the disorderly eater. What matters is the capacity for self-expression, so to speak, through the mute action of eating choices. It is the right to exercise that choice rather than the form it takes that is of crucial importance. This struggle for autonomous power over the self and, by extension, over others is nowadays recognized in anorexics as closely connected to the dynamics of family interaction.[7] The situations uncovered in the texts discussed in this volume suggest, however, that the conflict and need for self-assertion are equally pronounced beyond the confines of the family circle and may amount to a much larger and more significant stand against an entire social system, whose victims find their desperate outlet in a silent opposition to the normative customs of sustenance. Disorderly eating can thus represent the last protest left to the socially disempowered, and at the same time, paradoxically, a means for them to attain a kind of domination. What is interesting, and what our texts show, is the ingenious multiplicity of manifestations in which this syndrome can surface. The first chapter, "Cannibalism and Starvation: The Parameters of Eating Disorders in Literature," by Paulo Medeiros, is based on the premise that extremes of consumption/nonconsumption stem from the same desire to exercise the power of self over an uncongenial social system. To illustrate this hypothesis, Medeiros adduces examples as diverse as Kleist's drama *Penthesilea* (1808), Kafka's narrative *The Hunger Artist* (1922), and Louise Erdrich's short story "Saint Marie" (1984). In contrast to the tragic outcome in all these three instances, the case of Allen in Ellen Gainor's chapter, " 'The Slow-Eater-Tiny-Bite-Taker': An Eating Disorder in Betty MacDonald's *Mrs. Piggle-Wiggle* [1947]" ends happily, in keeping with its comic and didactic mode, through the intervention of a wise mind. Although the cure is achieved almost as if by magic, the underlying situation delineates Allen's self-assertion against family authority, albeit on the relatively small scale in consonance with his youth. The power game appears in a far more sinister guise in Mervyn Nicholson's "Magic Food, Compulsive Eating, and Power Poetics," which examines the seductive and destructive force of magical food compulsively ingested. Within this large context, Nicholson's specific focus is on the Circe theme, the ploys of what he denotes as the "Tricky Female," who exploits food as the vehicle for the sexual entrancement of the male.

Those chapters are followed by twelve others, each devoted to one or more texts, and arranged here in roughly chronological order. "*Medea* and *Beloved:* Self-Definition and Abortive Nurturing in Literary Treatments of the Infanticidal Mother," by Lillian Corti, spans time from Euripides to Toni

Morrison to show the role of fasting in the figure of the infanticidal mother whose power resides precisely in her control of eating functions. Gender distinctions are directly related to disorderly eating in the antithetical structures attached to men and women, analyzed by Nancy Gutierrez in her "Double Standard in the Flesh: Gender, Fasting, and Power in English Renaissance Drama." Fasting in men, she argues, is perceived as a physical, psychological, political, and social disempowerment, whereas asceticism, even unto death, is in women a self-empowerment through exemplary virtue. Joanna B. Gillespie's "Angel's Food: A Case of Fasting in Eighteenth-Century England" illustrates this too, while at the same time revealing the deep ambivalences in virtuous self-starvation. Drawing on the autobiographical memoir of a young middle-class woman, Gillespie shows how the woman pressures her family and achieves a degree of self-empowerment that is unusual for her time, station, and gender through voluntary fasting. The situation is close to that characteristic of today's anorexic family, except that here the fasting is religious in motivation.

That no fewer than six chapters are devoted to the nineteenth century is surely no coincidence. This is not only the period when eating disorders began to attract medical attention, but also the time when realism emerged as the dominant literary mode, encouraging the portrayal of commonplace happenings in everyday contexts. Admittedly, Peter Graham's "The Order and Disorder of Eating in Byron's *Don Juan*" from early in the century (1819-20) does not fit this paradigm, except as a satirical reversal. Graham appraises the exuberant extremes of Byron's epic, which ranges from cannibalism to sybaritic feasting to self-starvation, and postulates that patterns of eating may be beneficial, neutral, or harmful as the individual exercises power over himself or herself and others for good or evil through his or her eating choices. It is significant that, in keeping with contemporary medical opinion, the family is the forum for four of the other chapters on nineteenth-century texts. Paula Marantz Cohen, in "The Anorexic Syndrome and the Nineteenth-Century Domestic Novel," draws a parallel between the system governing the family and that implicit in the nineteenth-century domestic novel. In both she finds the daughter/heroine performing an analogous "regulating" role in the fine balance of power between the individual and the system. The two heroines in Charlotte Brontë's *Shirley* (1849), discussed by Deirdre Lashgari in "What Some Women Can't Swallow," both resort to hunger as protest and ultimately as a route to a romance resolution of their existential problems by attracting protective care-givers. My own chapter, "The Power of the Powerless," deals with three French disorderly eaters: Madame de Mortsauf in Balzac's *Le Lys dans la vallée* (1835), Emma in Flaubert's *Madame Bovary* (1857), and Gervaise in Zola's *L'Assommoir* (1877). Of disparate social class and at a temporal remove from each other, all three, equally powerless in their respective environments, nonetheless grasp for some degree of power through their disorderly eating. Even more complex power stratagems through disorderly eating are traced by Elsa Nettels in "New England Indigestion" in a number of novels by William Dean Howells, Elizabeth Stoddard, Mary Wilkins Freeman, and Edith Wharton. By contrast, Raymond A. Prier's "Consumption to the Last Drop: Huysmans' Dyspeptic Tale of Eating, *A Rebours*" deals with a male who has deliberately dissociated himself from all societal norms, including eating, and whose inversions almost result in his demise. The originality of Prier's piece lies in its suggestion that the style of Huysmans' 1884 novel, notorious for its eccentricities, in fact replicates the peristaltic movement of the digestive tract.

Of the three twentieth-century chapters, two are on German texts and on excessive eating. In "The Death of the Buddenbrooks: Four Rich Meals a Day," Martha Satz sees food as the compelling expression of the Buddenbrook family members' uneasy metaphysical relationship to life; the failure of their digestion is a concomitant and a manifestation of their decline and disempowerment. Barbara Lide, on the other hand, in "Dürrenmatt's Gastronomic Grotesqueries: Eating in a Dis-ordered World," finds in Dürrenmatt's plays and novels the energy of self-empowerment through grotesque overeating as a bulwark against a world out of joint. Finally, Gunilla Theander Kester's "The Forbidden Fruit and Female Disorderly Eating: Three Versions of Eve" provides a fitting conclusion by spanning female disorderly eating from the Old Testament book of Genesis through Milton's *Paradise Lost* up to Gayl Jones's 1976 novel *Eva's Man*, showing the extraordinary mythic continuities underlying the variations on the same theme.

A great many other examples might have been treated. Rabelais springs to mind immediately, as do several of Melville's stories, notably *Bartleby, Pierre*, and *White Jacket*, Henry James's *The Wings of the Dove*, Maupassant's *Deux amis, Boule de suif*, and *Yvette*, and Hemingway's *A Movable Feast*. In works by women writers, the incidence of disorderly eating is even higher, as it is among women in the population as a whole. The poetry of Emily Dickinson would yield much fascinating evidence, and the motif appears in Charlotte Perkins Gilman, Virginia Woolf, Katherine Mansfield, and May Sarton, and very prominently in Margaret Atwood's *The Edible Woman* and *Lady Oracle*, Barbara Pym's *Quartet in Autumn*, and Anne Tyler's *Dinner at the Homesick Restaurant*. Every reader could no doubt supplement this list with many other instances. Indeed, the problem for the present volume has not been one of finding suitable material but quite the opposite: how to select from the plethora of possibilities. When the topic was announced for a special session at the 1988 meeting of the Modern Language Association, more than 150 proposals were submitted. The offerings in this volume are the outcome of a deliberate decision to consider some of the less obvious examples of disorderly eating in literature, in preference to the more familiar ones.

To read a text as an instance of disorderly eating is to look at it from a different angle and to cast new light on it. This approach places the literary text in a somewhat unusual sociological context. It also creates a bridge between literature and medicine. While no claims can be made for clinical accuracy in these literary portrayals of eating disorders, they offer, nevertheless, intriguing paradigmatic case histories, in many instances from long before the medical sciences had taken note of these syndromes. And last but by no means least, in an era much concerned with eating disorders it is both illuminating and interesting to see the current problem foreshadowed and reflected in literary texts. The relevance of literature to life and the interdependence of disciplines is thereby forcefully confirmed.

Notes

1. Joan Jacobs Brumberg, *Fasting Girls: The Emergence of Anorexia Nervosa as a Modern Disease* (Cambridge, Mass.: Harvard University Press, 1988), 8–40.

2. Kim Chernin, *The Obsession: Reflections on the Tyranny of Slenderness* (New York: Harper & Row, 1981); *The Hungry Self: Women, Eating, and Identity* (New York: New York Times Books, 1985); Susie Ohrbach, *Fat Is a Feminist Issue: The Anti-Diet Guide to Permanent Weight Loss* (New York: Paddington Press, 1978); *Hunger Strike: The Anorectic's Struggle as a Metaphor for Our Age* (New York: W. W. Norton, 1986).

3. Sten Theander, *Anorexia Nervosa* (Copenhagen: Munksgaard, 1970).

4. Public Radio, *All Things Considered*, January 20, 1990.

5. See Rudolph M. Bell, *Holy Anorexia* (Chicago: University of Chicago Press, 1985); Caroline Walker Bynum, *Holy Fast, Holy Feast* (Berkeley and Los Angeles: University of California Press, 1987); Brumberg, *Fasting Girls*, 41–60.

6. Gull's paper was published in *Transactions of the Clinical Society of London* 7 (1874): 22–28. For further information on Gull, see Brumberg, *Fasting Girls*, 111–25.

7. Hilda Bruch, *The Eating Disorders: Obesity, Anorexia Nervosa, and the Person Within* (New York: Basic Books, 1973); and *The Family Approach to Eating Disorders*, ed. W. Vandereycken, Elly Krog, and Joham Vanderlinden (New York: PMA Publishing Corporation, 1989), 7ff.

CANNIBALISM AND STARVATION:
The Parameters of Eating Disorders in Literature

Paulo Medeiros

> "Well! What are you?" said the Pigeon. "I can see you're trying to invent something!"
>
> "I—I'm a little girl," said Alice. . . ."
>
> "A likely story indeed!" said the Pigeon, in a tone of the deepest contempt. "I've seen a good many little girls in my time, but never *one* with such a neck as that! No, no! You're a serpent; and there's no use denying it. I suppose you'll be telling me next that you never tasted an egg!"
>
> "I *have* tasted eggs, certainly," said Alice, . . . "but little girls eat eggs quite as much as serpents do, you know."
>
> "I don't believe it," said the Pigeon; "but if they do, why, then they're a kind of serpent."
>
> —Lewis Carroll, *Alice's Adventures in Wonderland*

For those grappling with the devastating effects of eating disorders, either in themselves or in loved ones, as well as for those who attempt to bring immediate help through therapy or counseling, the effort involved in relating such disorders to larger patterns of cultural organization through a speculative analysis of narratives might well appear suspect if not parasitical: suspect because an inquiry such as the one I propose presently offers no solution or palliative to the all-too-real problems posed by eating disorders; and parasitical because it can seem to derive its motivation from a prurient interest in suffering, or at best from an expropriation of tragic reality to serve as model for the understanding of fiction. Yet to avoid engaging in such speculation would be to ignore the fact that eating disorders, as much as they affect the bodies and minds of those who contend with them, often come about as the result of individuals' reactions to culture at the level of the family as well as at the larger levels of society and civilization. Eating disorders are not primarily about eating. Rather, as Hilde Bruch, Susie Orbach, and others, have demonstrated, eating disorders are the outcome of profound conflicts between individuals and their parents and society as they attempt to fashion (or to understand) themselves in relation (or in opposition) to prescribed roles and assumptions about adulthood, femininity, and sexuality.[1]

Eating disorders, whether in reality or through literary representation, present the stage for a conflict grounded on desire and power in which the individual process of identity-formation clashes with and rebels against traditional notions of what constitutes a human being. Under such notions, one may subsume key factors for identity, such as gender, kinship relationships, and ontology.

Pragmatically, the confrontation of any individual with society through the manipulation of the body seems to affect foremost that one individual who, by refusing to eat or by eating compulsively and inordinately, immediately threatens her or his life. Abstractly though, the threat must also be seen as affecting the fabric of society as a whole, not just because once considered collectively such individuals seriously drain resources, but also because as eating disorders become (and are generally perceived as) widespread they bring into question the way society itself functions or fails to function.[2] Implied in the notion of eating dis-order itself is the possibility of a rupture of established order, initially at the individual level but rapidly and increasingly more so at the societal level. Such a rupture is based on excess: either an excessive consumption of food well beyond the need for nourishment and the satisfaction of taste, or its opposite, the refusal to consume, which ultimately leads to self-consumption, as the body must draw on its own resources in its attempt to survive.

Paradigmatically, the conflict based on excess between forms of overeating and the refusal, or denial, to eat, is worked out in two ancient examples: that of Tantalus in Greek mythology and that of the first humans in the prelapsarian world as described in Genesis. Both involve the human characters in a dispute with divinities that centers on transgressive eating in which desire and power commingle with fatal results: on the one hand, Tantalus' theft of Olympian ambrosia leading to his eternal punishment in the form of absolute denial of both food and drink; and on the other, Adam and Eve's fateful tasting of the forbidden fruit, which brings about their expulsion from Eden so that they will not be able to eat from the tree of eternal life. Both stories serve to define the human condition in terms that cannot be dissociated from consumption, as Adam and Eve can be considered human only after the Fall, that is, after their transgressive consumption, and likewise, Tantalus' abortive attempt at securing eternal life through the food of the gods serves precisely to emphasize his mortality. Furthermore, beyond their importance in linking ontology with consumption, both examples, through their consequences, introduce the issue of inhuman consumption in the form of cannibalism. A resolution to the problem of human mortality is offered, in Christian terms, only by partaking of the flesh and blood of Christ in the consecrated Host—that is, by engaging, even if only at the symbolical level, in the ritual cannibalization of the human body of God.[3] Conversely, no escape from his damnation is allowed Tantalus; rather, the continuation of his story involves the dismemberment, and consequent eating by the gods, of the body of his son, Pelops.

Forbidden eating, the denial of a special food or of all food, the desire to transcend mortality through consumption, cannibalism, and starvation are keynotes around which the Western tradition, in both its Hellenistic and Judeo-Christian forms, has presented the questions of humanity and of the self in reference to society and to divinity. Modern narratives that concentrate on consumption while problematizing the humanity (and the respective concept of self) of their characters are thus fully enmeshed in a traditional project—even when seen as working away from it—that considers consumption and its modalities as an essential foundation for social order. In their divergent ways, Kleist's Penthesilea, Kafka's Hunger Artist, and Erdrich's Marie all struggle with the way society perceives them, their own identities, and the problem of death through their bodies and consumption.[4] Ultimately, whether their destinies prove to be fatal, tragic, ironic, or eternally unresolvable, each character comes to establish an unalienable identity, formed through desire (or its lack), which derives its power from its clashes with societal norms. The only way these characters can affirm themselves as individuals is through eating disorders.

Moreover, what these narratives, whether ancient or modern, have in common among themselves, and with the narratives of the lives of real people suffering from eating disorders (as presented by Hilde Bruch, for example), is the incredible power attributed to metonymical relationships. Through these relationships individuals are judged, and consequently come to see themselves, as belonging to a certain kind on the basis of their consumption and the shape of their bodies. Just as the Pigeon seizes on Alice's elongated neck and her admission to eating eggs to define her not as the little girl she is but as "a kind of serpent," anorexics often also are perceived (want to be perceived, and perceive themselves) as other than what they are (most often young women): as special, superhuman, or even subhuman, animal-like beings.

Consider "Elsa," age nineteen and weighing sixty-nine pounds, as Bruch describes her case and statements:

> "Sometimes I hear voices or feel things in my head, and sometimes I get frightening mental images." The voices seemed to be in conflict, some telling her "eat, eat, eat," and others, "don't, don't, don't." These food thoughts filled her mind so completely that they drowned out her former interests in various activities. . . . Even more terrifying was the continuous fear of being "not human" and the terror of "ceasing to exist."[5]

Indeed, even as anorexics start by clinging to their thinness as a coveted distinguishing feature to set them apart and above their peers, and afterward become incapable of perceiving themselves and others realistically,[6] often what strikes outside observers the most about anorexics is their inhuman aspect, their physical resemblance to animals or to mobile death-figures:

> When ["Alma"] came for consultation she looked like a walking skeleton, scantily dressed in shorts and a halter, with her legs sticking out like broomsticks, every rib showing, and her shoulder blades standing up like little wings. Her mother mentioned, "When I put my arms around her I feel nothing but bones, like a frightened little bird." . . . When ["Alma"] spoke or smiled . . . one could see every movement of the muscles around her mouth and eyes, like an animated representation of the skull.[7]

The opposite impression is made on Odysseus by the ghosts—Tantalus among them—whom he purposely set out to meet in hopes of finding his future fate from Tiresias. Misled by their lifelike appearance, Odysseus even repeatedly tries to embrace his dead mother, only to find that there is no substance to the figure of her body. As she explains, "[He] is only witnessing . . . the law of our mortal nature, when we come to die. We no longer have sinews keeping the bones and flesh together."[8] Yet the relationship between Odysseus' perception of the ghosts he meets and their disembodied nature is comparable to the other relationships that are the object of the present study, in that reality is misperceived because of bodily appearances. That the illusion can be achieved in its totality only when the ghosts speak with Odysseus, and that they can speak only after drinking from the black blood of the animals he has slaughtered for them, further reinforces the connection between excessive modalities of consumption and (illusory) representation: it is due to what they eat (or do not eat) and to their physical appearance that Alice can be said to be like a serpent, the anorexic like a bird or an animated skeleton, and the ghost of Odysseus's mother like her former, living self.

It is significant that Homer's account of Tantalus is already situated within a frame of excessive and supernatural consumption, the ghosts' desire for the black blood, which is presented as essential for speech, and thus as originator of representation itself. This is how Odysseus describes Tantalus' apparition:

> I also saw the awful agonies that Tantalus has to bear. The old man was standing in a pool of water which nearly reached his chin, and his thirst drove him to unceasing efforts; but he could never get a drop to drink. For whenever he stooped in his eagerness to lap the water, it disappeared. The pool was swallowed up, and all he saw at his feet was the dark earth, which some mysterious power had parched. Trees spread their foliage high over the pool and dangled fruits above his head—pear-trees and pomegranates, apple-trees with their glossy burden, sweet figs and luxuriant olives. But whenever the old man tried to grasp them in his hands, the wind would toss them up towards the shadowy clouds.[9]

In this first documented account of the myth, Homer concentrates on the punishment and the role accorded to desire as he presents in emblematic form a Tantalus forever wanting to drink and eat, constantly tempted by the seeming proximity of plenty of water and fruit and perpetually incapable of realizing his desire. The magnitude of Tantalus' predicament, starving amid plenty, is reinforced by the nature of his actions, which resulted in such punishment: the attempted theft of the food of the gods with its promise of immortality. Such a combination is also characteristic of many anorexics, who literally starve themselves as they are surrounded by great abundance and who often are motivated by the unconscious fear of growing up or of becoming old, if not by a direct wish for immortality.[10]

The major difference would appear to be that, although Tantalus is denied the food and drink he desires by some mysterious power that makes the water and fruits disappear, anorexics not only are the ones who deny themselves food but also strongly resist efforts by others to make them eat.

Their determination not to eat is often a cause of admiration and envy at first, and then a perplexing frustration once life becomes threatened. Yet anorexics, as much as they tend to boast about the self-control that allows them to withstand and even enjoy hunger, often do not perceive the denial of consumption as self-imposed. Instead, they see a prohibition against eating as formulated by a mysterious outside agency that, in spite of all efforts at naming it, remains as invisible and all-powerful as the invisible forces acting against Tantalus' desire. Elsa's case, where competing voices in her head compel her to eat at the same time that other voices forbid her to do so, uncannily approximates Tantalus' situation. In other cases, the prohibition on eating is exteriorized to the point of being attributed to someone else: a "little man who objects," "a dictator," or "a ghost, who surrounds" the anorexic.[11]

Another version of the myth of Tantalus, contained in Pindar's first Olympian Ode, moves from one pole of excessive consumption—the frustrated desire for the forbidden food of the gods—to the other: the gods' enjoyment of the human body (that of Pelops, son of Tantalus) as food:

> Son of Tantalos, against the ancients I will say
> that when your father summoned the gods
> to that stateliest feast at beloved Sipylos,
> and gave them to eat and received in turn,
> then he of the shining trident caught you up,
>
> his heart to desire broken, and with his horses and car of gold
> carried you up to the house of Zeus and his wide honor,
> where Ganymede at a later time
> came for the same desire in Zeus.
> But when you were gone, and men from your mother looked
>   long, nor brought you back,
> some of the spiteful neighbors whispered,
> how they took you and with a knife
> minced your limbs into bubbling water,
> and over the table divided and ate
> flesh of your body, even to the last morsel.[12]

Pindar's avowed intention is to provide an alternative to the ancient sayings whereby the gods partake of a cannibalistic feast in which a son is cooked and offered as food by his own father. Such a tale, Pindar maintains, cannot be true, and to entertain such notions would be blasphemous: "I cannot say that any god could gorge thus; I recoil. / Many a time disaster has come to the speakers of evil."[13] In place of the scandalous dinner, Pindar offers what appears, in his terms, to be a more decorous and believable story: the rape of Pelops by Neptune. He thus appears to substitute the gods' immoderate desire for consumption with their unbridled sexual appetite. Neptune's actions, even if excessive, are meant to be seen as fitting within an accepted pattern of divine behavior, also exemplified by the reference to Zeus' desire.

Nonetheless, instead of achieving a literal substitution of sexuality for consumption, Pindar calls attention to both acts and to their interchangeability. Rather than serving to convince the reader that the cannibalistic repast is a mere invention, Pindar's ode can be seen as having a definite role in the spread of the legend, especially when one considers that his text represents the first extant written account of the cannibalistic meal. Given the nature of Tantalus' crime—overstepping the boundaries of his humanity with the theft of Olympian food—having Pelops turn into an exquisite dish for the gods' delectation represents, on a structural level, a more satisfactory resolution. It at once posits human excessive consumption against divine excessive consumption, and inverts Tantalus' role, as he goes from being a thief to being the host—an inversion that, ironically, provides for his punishment as well.

It is at the structural level also that the myth of Tantalus and Pelops approximates the Fall and the consequent redemption through Holy Communion, since evidently, in detail as well as in purpose and intended outcome, the two narratives are dissimilar. But in their movement from transgressive consumption of forbidden food to an ensuing act of cannibalism, both Greek mythology and the Judeo-Christian tradition combine forms of excessive eating with ontological determination. Moreover, if one wants to consider the sexual component instead, as hinted in Pindar's alternate explanation for Pelops' disappearance, only the frequent equation of eating the forbidden fruit with the acquisition of carnal knowledge must be remembered.

Erotic attraction coalesces with cannibalism to form the climactic moment of Kleist's *Penthesilea:* the Queen of the Amazons, forced to fight her lover Achilles, not only defeats him but also rends him in pieces with her bites, a gruesome process in which her dogs aid her. The bestiality involved in the death of Achilles would shock any audience, but the peculiar form of loving cannibalism in which Penthesilea engages is far more scandalous than her abandonment of her lover's body to the dogs' jaws. Bite and kiss become interchangeable in Penthesilea's mind and actions, as she herself states, hesitantly at first, then more and more assuredly, as she confronts her priestesses:

> I ripped him?
> . . . .
> Or was it differently?
> . . . .
> Did I kiss him to death?
> . . . .
> No? I did not kiss him? Really torn to pieces? Speak!
> . . . .
> So it was an oversight. Kisses, bites
> that rimes, and who loves truly from the heart,
> can easily take one for the other.[14]

Penthesilea's excessive love for Achilles, who confronted her unarmed yet was known for his treacherous deceptions, is one reason for the play's tragic end. Another, and perhaps more important, reason is Penthesilea's determination not to be subjugated even when in love and to act literally. On the contrary, Achilles' decision to go into battle with Penthesilea without weapons is based on his desire to win her by deceit and on a false perception of Penthesilea's character, expressed in terms that are extremely ironic given the role of eating in the end of his life. As the Herald of his troops warns Achilles about Penthesilea's dogs and elephants, Achilles convinces himself they are docile, saying, "They feed from the hand, perhaps. . . . Oh! They are tame like her."[15] Penthesilea's actions turn Achilles' casual remark completely around. Instead of feeding obedient animals and a submissive woman from his hand, Achilles becomes the meal itself both for the dogs and for their master. The key element Penthesilea presents at first is the question of an "oversight" (*Versehen*, which also means "slip," "mistake," or "error") based on the linguistic proximity between kisses (*Küsse*) and bites (*Bisse*), allowing for the substitution of love for cannibalism.[16] Yet Penthesilea's slip of the tongue is more voluntary than accidental; she affirms her intention and her emphasis on the literalness of words as opposed to misleading metaphors while speaking to Achilles' defaced corpse:

> Like many, who hang at their lover's neck,
> It is well said: she loves him, oh so much,

That she could eat him from love;
. . . .
Well, you my love, I did not mislead.
Look here: when *I* hung at your neck,
I truly did it word for word;
I was not so crazy, as it clearly seemed.[17]

Penthesilea's declaration of lucidity prompts one of the Amazon princesses, Meroe, to classify her as most monstrous (*die Ungeheuerste,* 439), but even before such a radical statement Penthesilea's excessive consumption had earned her an inhuman epithet, when the Archpriestess substituted the generic "bitch" for Penthesilea's title of Queen (*Hündin,* 423). In the words of the Archpriestess, Penthesilea has ceased to be human because of her cannibalism, and it is with the pack of dogs—whom Penthesilea now calls sisters (*Schwestern,* 423)—that she finds her kind. Beyond expressing shock or contempt, the statement of the Archpriestess functions as a saving device to counterbalance the social imbalance brought about by Penthesilea's excessive consumption and literalness. It is as if with her words the Archpriestess could undo the fact that a special, royal human being had broken the bounds of societal norms. Ironically enough, what the Archpriestess does is exactly a reversal of Penthesilea's refusal of metaphor. By calling the Queen a "bitch" and placing her outside humanity, the Archpriestess uses language's metaphorical power to preserve a notion of social order in which cannibalism has no place.

However distasteful and threatening Penthesilea's actions may appear, they must also be seen as the radical expression of her conflicting emotions as Queen of the Amazons and as a woman who loves Achilles. By destroying him, she not only brings the conflict to a resolution but also does so in a way that upholds her predominance as warrior and, by extension, that of her subjects. Her frenzied tearing and eating of Achilles' body reveals the obsessive love she feels and at the same time excludes her from the community whose standards she otherwise upheld to the point of sacrificing her love. Penthesilea's ensuing suicide, which she describes as a voyage inward (*steig ich in meinen Busen nieder,* 440), is at once the final solution to her altered condition (Queen/bitch) and a way of affirming her self and her love in spite of societal constraints. The two Amazon princesses rightly seize this consequence when they state, as Penthesilea dies, that she "follows [Achilles] in reality" and that it was "good for her, since here her further stay was not" (441).

At the other pole of excess is Kafka's "Hunger Artist," who in his voluntary denial of any form of consumption most approximates the actual behavior of anorexics.[18] Kafka's story, like most of his writing, hinges on a paradox and the resulting *aporia* — in this case, the confession made by the Hunger Artist, just before he expires, that he never ate "because [he] could not find the food that [he] liked."[19] This crucial statement both questions the entire foundation for the nameless artist's existence — his capacity and wish to withstand hunger indefinitely — and negates his claim to artistic talent, because he appears to relegate all his actions to a fundamental experience of lack, the impossibility of finding food to his taste. Yet such a last denial of himself and of his art must be seen as an extension, perhaps in absolute form, of his previous practice of total denial of consumption (which brings about his death) and therefore as a final affirmation, in negative terms, of the Hunger Artist's project all along: a refusal to partake of food, parallel to the desire to set himself apart from society and even from humanity. The Hunger Artist tells his night watchers ("usually, strangely enough, butchers"), he "starved (*hungerte*) like none of them could."[20]

To this determination to prove his superiority through his control of appetite one could add at least two other characteristics, and all are common to anorexic behavior: (1) the exhibitionism inherent in the Hunger Artist's concept of art (*Schauhunger,* "exhibition fasting," 168), which makes his body an object for popular marvel either as an independent curiosity show or in conjunction with a circus; and (2) the determined attempt to resist any efforts to stop the fast and the ultimate surrender to outside force, leading to his almost involuntary feeding:[21]

> ...finally came two young ladies...[who] wanted to lead the Hunger Artist down a couple of steps out of the cage, to where a carefully chosen diet meal (*Krankenmahlzeit*) had been served on a small table. And at this moment the Hunger Artist always resisted. . . . Then came the food, from which the Impresario fed a little to the Hunger Artist during a faint-like half-sleep. . . . [22]

His refusal to stop fasting is typical of the anorexic's obsessive insistence. The Hunger Artist is deeply disappointed at the forced break of his fast at the end of forty days: "Why did one want to rob him of the fame, to go on fasting, not only to become the greatest Hunger Artist of all times, which he probably already was, but also to surpass himself up to incomprehensibility, since he felt no limits to his capacity to fast."[23]

The Hunger Artist's marginality is evident both in his being the object of a freak show and in his placement within a cage. The latter, with its suggestion of a subhuman existence, becomes even more pressing as the Hunger Artist's value as an attraction diminishes and he is forced to join a circus, his cage located at the entrance to the stables, where he is finally replaced by a panther. Yet the diminished attention of the public, which never understood him or his intent, is also what allows the Hunger Artist to pursue his goal of unlimited fasting. The Hunger Artist's absolute desire to refuse consumption is characterized best, in Gerhard Neumann's terms, as an "autarchic play of self-consumption": society ceases to matter as a force to resist or from which to draw attention and admiration.[24] Ultimately, the Hunger Artist can be seen not as subhuman and monstrous, and also not as superhuman in his resistance to hunger, but rather simply as extrahuman. His attempt to place himself outside the boundaries of society is also an attempt to surpass even his own boundary—literally, because by starving he reduces his own body so that he actually seems to have disappeared into the straw lining the bottom of his cage.[25] Consequently, and taking into consideration how the Hunger Artist in his uninterrupted fast becomes the sole audience for his art, Neumann concludes that the meaning brought about by such an "absolute sign," independent of any outside referent, is that of the "paradox of identity itself."[26]

To understand the paradox of identity one must realize that identity is but one term and that a corresponding concept of alterity, even when rejected, must always be present too. In "Saint Marie," Louise Erdrich offers the recollections of a woman who is acutely aware of her difference from the mainstream—as a child of both Native American and Caucasian descent— even as the others to whom she is made to feel marginal, either the Catholic nuns she partly admires or the drunks from the town bar, are themselves outcasts. In a sense, the story revolves around the confrontation between that woman, Marie, as a girl of fourteen, and Leopolda, one of the nuns. Leopolda at one point aptly summarizes Marie's position, from her perspective, while offering Marie two future possibilities, each connected with a form of alterity. " 'You're not vain,' she said. 'You're too honest, looking into the mirror for that. You're not smart. You don't have the ambition to get clear. You have two choices. One, you can marry a no-good Indian, bear his brats, die like a dog. Or two, you can give yourself to God' "[27]—either life as the wife of an Indian, which the nun perceives as a slip into subhuman, animal-like existence (or nonexistence: "die like a dog") or alienation from society in a sacrifice of the self for divinity.

Marie's fascination with the convent, and her obsession with Leopolda, however, do not stem from her belief that she is limited to those two options. Convinced of her physical attractiveness, she knows that the first way need not be true, and, as she clearly lets the nun know, she has no interest in the other way. Instead, Marie's actions are determined by a resolute desire for power, in the form of a wish to be adored as saint and completely reverse the existing hierarchy. This is also the wish to change from the absolute powerlessness she experienced as a child. Once she had been locked in a closet for having smiled in class. The disparity between her behavior and its consequences, combined with her fear of being confined and of physical punishment, made her see herself as a void: "I was nothing."[28] Marie's desire expresses itself primarily in terms that relate to excessive, transgressive consumption. Thus, at the outset she explains her wish in terms of a fundamental ambiguity: "But I wanted Sister Leopolda's heart. And here was the thing: sometimes I wanted her heart in love and admiration. Sometimes. And sometimes I wanted her heart to roast on a black stick." But even normal food, because generally unavailable, is inseparable from pleasure and desire:

> Inside [the larder] there was all kinds of good stuff. Things I'd tasted only once or twice in my life. I saw sticks of dried fruit, jars of orange peel, spice like cinnamon. I saw tins of crackers with ships painted on the side. I saw pickles. Jars of herring and the rind of pigs. There was cheese, a big brown block of it from the thick milk of goats. And besides that there was the everyday stuff, in great quantities, the flour and the coffee.
>
> It was the cheese that got to me. When I saw it my stomach hollowed. My tongue dripped. I loved that goat-milk cheese better than anything I'd ever ate. I stared at it. The rich curve in the buttery cloth.[29]

Leopolda holds the "giant key" to this unreachable repository of desirable, consumable materiality and therefore would naturally be seen as a figure of power to be overcome or replaced, especially as she embodies and verbalizes denial and prohibition that can be conquered only after her death. Marie's portrait of the nun is a classic description of an anorexic:

> She took my hand. Her fingers were like a bundle of broom straws, so thin and dry, but the strength of them was unnatural.... Her

strength was a kind of perverse miracle, for she got it from fasting herself thin. Because of this hunger practice her lips were a wounded brown and her skin deadly pale. Her eye sockets were two deep lashless hollows in a taut skull.[30]

Leopolda herself announces that consumption must be postponed until she dies: " 'When you inherit my keys,' she said sourly, slamming the door [of the larder] in my face, 'you can eat all you want of the priest's cheese. . . . If you're good you'll taste this cheese again. When I'm dead and gone.' "[31]

The kitchen is the center of action, and also where another form of perverse miracle happens: the false transformation of Marie into a saint so as to conceal Leopolda's violent cruelty. Baking bread provides the necessary backdrop as the two women engage themselves in a deadly struggle originated by Leopolda's attempt for absolute control of Marie's self by torture. A simple pretext, Marie's dropping of a cup, becomes an opportunity for an object lesson in suffering in which Leopolda metaphorically cooks Marie by pouring the content of a full kettle of boiling water over her skin, with the overt intent of driving the devil out from Marie: " 'I will boil him from your mind if you make a peep,' she said, 'by filling up your ear.' "[32] Such monstrous "cooking" gives rise in Marie to a vision of vengeance in which transgressive consumption, again, is the key, as she imagines herself walking through panes of glass, with Leopolda at her feet, "swallowing the glass after each step I took. . . . The glass she swallowed ground and cut until her starved insides were only a subtle dust."[33] Finally Marie seizes an opportunity, as Leopolda stands in front of the gaping oven, to reenact Gretel's liberating action, by kicking the nun (whom by now she perceives as possessed by the devil and therefore a kind of witch) into it.[34] Yet this too fails, as Leopolda, with the help of an iron poker, escapes from the oven, "the gate of a personal hell," quickly stabs Marie through a hand, and renders her unconscious.[35]

Marie's piercing wound, made with "that long sharp fork [Leopolda] used to tap the delicate crusts of loaves,"[36] would be inescapable evidence of the nun's cruelty, of her transgressive attempt to handle Marie as food for a second time, while no corresponding proof of Marie's desperate attempt at baking Leopolda herself could be produced. Nor would it appear credible that an apparently meek girl of fourteen years old had attempted to rid herself of her tormentor in such a way; the other nuns, in any case, could not be counted on to accept such a radical reversal of established order. In part, Marie's desperation had come from her correct assessment of how futile any attempts at explaining would be. The two French nuns who wander into the kitchen mistakenly see her simply as a docile girl ("Elle est docile"[37]), much the same way that Achilles misread Penthesilea. Marie's single wound to the hand is also misread. At Leopolda's instigation, what would be evidence for human transgression becomes undoubtable proof of divine favor. As Marie wakes up, she slowly realizes how Leopolda and the other nuns, in what appears to be a demented realization of Marie's secret desire, are prostrate in worship of her: Marie's stigma is (mis)understood as stigmata.

The key elements of the story come together when Marie's thought-processes run off in litany form, emphasizing both the process of identity change the girl undergoes and its connection with transgressive consumption:

> Marie! Marie! A girl thrown in a closet. Who was afraid of a rubber overboot. Who was half overcome. A girl who came in the back door where they threw their garbage. Marie! Who never found the cup. Who had to eat their cold mush. Marie! Leopolda had her face buried in her knuckles. Saint Marie of the Holy Slops! Saint Marie of the Bread Fork! Saint Marie of the Burnt Back and Scalded Butt![38]

It could be said that Marie has been able to evolve from her own perception of herself as nothing to an exalted, if painful, realization of her desire. Yet Marie's desire is accomplished only through Leopolda, so Marie's victory must be read instead as a defeat. The extent to which she is inescapably linked to the nun is even rendered explicit in the obvious juxtaposition of the two names, "Marie! Leopolda," separated only by a single exclamation mark.

This juxtaposition is also symptomatic of a far more important condition: whereas Kleist's play and Kafka's story represent opposite poles in the range of eating disorders, that distinction is blurred by Erdrich's narrative. Instead of being polarized, Marie and Leopolda appear interchangeable. Leopolda's anorexic characteristics have a counterpart in Marie's real hunger, just as the nun's act of boiling the girl causes Marie to push the nun into the fired oven. The resulting conflation at once voids each abnormal action or condition from specificity and emphasizes their common aspect of excess that threatens to disrupt established order irreparably. Thus, Leopolda's fictional explanation for Marie's wound is a desperate but successful measure aimed at preserving order. Leopolda's lie functions in much the same way as the metaphorical declaration of the Archpriestess that turns Penthesilea from

Queen to bitch. Furthermore, Leopolda's fiction not only restores order to the community, it retains Marie within it.

Instead of presenting an individual who must resort to one form of eating disorder or another so as to assert her individuality, Erdrich's narrative uses transgressive forms of consumption to show a society whose order depends on whether its members conform to interrelated, if false, roles. Unlike Penthesilea or the Hunger Artist, who succeed in isolating themselves absolutely from society and die, Marie goes on living and acquires the power she desired—but such a power is illusory, built on pretenses spun by her enemy, and Marie is confronted by that terrible knowledge, which in itself is one more secret bond between her and the nun. What Marie comes to realize, her attempts at cannibalistic baking notwithstanding, is how she has been drawn even tighter into the fiction of society and of the self, and that there is no escape to the human condition: "My skin was dust. Dust my lips. Dust the dirty spoons on the ends of my feet. . . . There is no limit to this dust!"[39]

Notes

1. Hilde Bruch's pioneering work, of which *The Golden Cage: The Enigma of Anorexia Nervosa* (Cambridge, Mass.: Harvard University Press, 1978) has become better known, remains extremely relevant. Her work has been complemented by other studies, especially Susie Orbach's *Hunger Strike: The Anorectic's Struggle as a Metaphor for Our Age* (New York: W. W. Norton, 1986), which considers extensively the effect of society's norms and constraints on the developing personalities of anorexics. Although women are not the only ones who become entangled in eating disorders—so that for some patients not femininity but masculinity might be an issue—both anorexia and bulimia occur far more frequently among women than among men. Obesity, on the other hand, appears to be keyed less to gender than to social class and ethnicity. See also Kelly D. Brownell and John P. Foreyt, eds., *Handbook of Eating Disorders: Physiology, Psychology, and Treatment of Obesity, Anorexia, and Bulimia* (New York: Basic Books, 1986).

2. Bruch refers to the proliferation of anorexia cases in terms of an epidemic (*Golden Cage*, vii–viii). Likewise, Orbach opens her book with a reference to the high number of women obsessed with eating and noneating, at once removing such an obsession from the realm of the pathological by insisting on its commonality, and emphasizing the extent to which it goes beyond the individual level (Orbach, *Hunger Strike*, 23).

3. The question of Jesus' Eucharistic teaching has long been a central issue of debate both within and outside a theological context. A concise yet detailed account of the history of the importance attributed to the Eucharist and its divergent interpretations is offered by Helmut Feld in *Das Verständnis des Abendmahls* (Darmstadt: Wissenschaftliche Buchgesellschaft, 1976). Louis Marin discusses extensively the literal logic of the Eucharistic utterance and its implications in *La Critique du discours: Sur la logique de "Port-Royal" et les "Pensées" de*

Pascal (Paris: Minuit, 1975). With regard to the subversiveness implied in the Eucharistic message, and to its view as cannibalism, see Gillian Feeley-Harnik's *The Lord's Table: Eucharist and Passover in Early Christianity* (Philadelphia: University of Pennsylvania Press, 1981). See also the discussion on the Eucharist (especially as it relates to Original Sin and the problematic of consumption) in Gerhard Neumann's "Das Essen und die Literatur," *Literaturwissenschaftliches Jahrbuch* 23 (1982): 173–88. Interestingly enough, Bruch includes an account by one of her anorexic patients in which the illness is described in terms of a rebellion against the human condition as defined in Genesis (and also in reference to Milton's *Paradise Lost*): "*Anorexia nervosa isn't an attempt to make yourself suffer; it's an attempt, from a postlapsarian vantage point, to recapture Eden by revealing it*" (75).

4. Heinrich von Kleist, *Penthesilea: Sämtliche Werke und Briefe*, ed. Helmut Sembdner, 2 vols. (Munich: Carl Hanser Verlag, 1952), 1:335–442; Franz Kafka, "Ein Hungerkünstler," *Sämtliche Erzählungen*, ed. Paul Raabe (Frankfurt: Fischer Verlag, 1970), 163–71; Louise Erdrich, "Saint Marie," *Love Medicine* (New York: Holt, Rinehart & Winston, 1984; Bantam Books, 1985), 40–57.

5. Bruch, *Golden Cage*, 12.

6. Ibid., 76–82.

7. Ibid., 2.

8. Homer, *The Odyssey*, trans. E. V. Rieu (Hamondsworth: Penguin, 1946), 177.

9. Ibid., 187.

10. Bruch, *Golden Cage*, 24–25, 64–69.

11. Ibid., 58.

12. *The Odes of Pindar*, trans. Richmond Lattimore, 2nd ed. (Chicago: University of Chicago Press, 1976), 2.

13. Ibid.

14. Kleist, *Penthesilea*, 438–39.

15. Ibid., 423.

16. In the present discussion about *Penthesilea*, and later also Kafka's "Hunger Artist," I am indebted to several studies Gerhard Neumann devoted to both subjects, especially his "Das Essen und die Literatur" (already cited) and, with special reference to Kafka's text, "Hungerkünstler und Menschenfresser: Zum Verhältnis von Kunst und kulturellem Ritual im Werk Franz Kafkas," *Archiv für Kulturgeschichte* 66 (1984): 347–88.

17. This passage, in the original, presents a further emphasis on the term "word." "It is well said" is only an approximate translation of "Sagt wohl das Wort," which literally means "well says the word." This initial emphasis on "word" plays with the subsequent "word for word" and, as Neumann has demonstrated (in "Das Essen und die Literatur"), with Penthesilea's own demise, as she dies of stab wounds produced by a dagger that seems to exist only in her words (440–41).

18. This is one of the few stories still published during Kafka's life so that a relative textual certainty exists. Yet, as Neumann stresses, an early draft found after Kafka's death contained a confrontation between the Hunger Artist and a cannibal, in which case the two poles of excess would be represented. See J.M.S. Pasley, "Asceticism and Cannibalism: Notes on an Unpublished Kafka Text," *Oxford German Studies* 1 (1966): 102–13, for the manuscript fragment and its first interpretation; see also Gerhard Neumann's "Das Essen und die Literatur" (189) and "Hungerkünstler und Menschenfresser: Zum Verhältnis von Kunst und kulturellem Ritual im Werk Franz Kafkas" where the relationship between the two figures is extensively discussed.

19. Kafka, "Ein Hungerkünstler," 171.

20. Ibid., 164, 165.

21. Bruch from the start directly links anorexia with exhibitionism in terms that recall the

Hunger Artist's predicament, even if no public, paid attraction is made of the patients. See, e.g., *Golden Cage*, 3; see also, in reference to the refusal to be fed, ibid., 96–111.

22. Kafka, "Ein Hungerkünstler," 166–67.

23. Ibid., 166.

24. Gerhard Neumann's expression comes as the conclusion to a part of his analysis of Kafka's text, in which the Hunger Artist's behavior is read in the light of Roger Caillois' *Les Jeux et les hommes: Le Masque et le vertige* (Paris: Gallimard, 1967), "Hungerkünstler und Menschenfresser," 362. Cf. Bruch's statement about her patients, "They all agree that at first it may have been nothing more than a half-playful effort at being thinner, even though they were not really overweight," and also that they took "extraordinary pride and pleasure . . . in being able to do something so hard. Suddenly it is easy and the conviction comes that it can go on forever" (77).

25. Ibid., 171.

26. Neumann, "Hungerkünstler und Menschenfresser," 365.

27. Erdrich, "Saint Marie," 45.

28. Ibid., 44.

29. Ibid., 46–47.

30. Erdrich, "Saint Marie," 45–46. On the correlation between the ascetic practices of nuns and anorexia, see Rudolph M. Bell, *Holy Anorexia* (Chicago: University of Chicago Press, 1985). Also, for a differentiated and complementary view emphasizing denial of consumption by medieval female saints as a form of subversive power in opposition to the institutionalized church, see Caroline Walker Bynum, *Holy Feast and Holy Fast: The Religious Significance of Food to Medieval Women* (Berkeley and Los Angeles: University of California Press, 1987).

31. Erdrich, "Saint Marie," 47.

32. Ibid., 49.

33. Ibid., 50.

34. The Grimms' tale of "Hansel and Gretel" provides an extraordinary example for the working out of a problematic of excessive consumption between the poles of absolute lack, the initial famine that moves the parents to abandon the two children in the forest, and forbidden abundance, the witch's cannibalistic intent to eat Hansel, a fate from which he is saved by Gretel's opportune shoving of the witch into the oven. See *The Grimms' German Folk Tales*, trans. Francis P. Magoun Jr., and Alexander H. Krappe (Carbondale and Evansville: Southern Illinois University Press; London and Amsterdam: Feffer & Simons, 1960), 57–63.

35. Erdrich, "Saint Marie," 53.

36. Ibid.

37. Ibid., 51.

38. Ibid., 54.

39. Ibid., 56.

"THE SLOW-EATER-TINY-BITE-TAKER":

An Eating Disorder in Betty MacDonald's *Mrs. Piggle-Wiggle*

J. Ellen Gainor

A striking literary depiction of an eating disorder resembling anorexia nervosa appears in Betty MacDonald's collection of children's stories, *Mrs. Piggle-Wiggle*.[1] Published in 1947, the book seems remarkably relevant today, particularly in its presentation of compulsive eating behavior. Although the identification of anorexia nervosa as a disturbingly prevalent disorder in our society postdates MacDonald's work, her startlingly accurate depiction of a child suffering from a condition like anorexia gives her story a new timeliness. From 1933 on, there is documentation of American mothers' concerns about their children's failure to eat. Related articles discuss physicians' implication of the family in their diagnoses of children with eating disorders, although these issues were not often linked to a specific condition.[2] MacDonald's story blends details from her personal observations of children with the kinds of concerns and information shared by many American women in the mid-twentieth century, and the composite bears a strong resemblance to more recent case studies of anorectic youths.

According to MacDonald's daughter Anne Canham, the story of "The

Slow-Eater-Tiny-Bite-Taker" is roughly based on the author's knowledge of a young boy named Allen who came to live with MacDonald's youngest sister Alison for a time. His mother, who accompanied him, was in the midst of a divorce and needed a place to stay while she settled her affairs and reorganized her life. At the time of his arrival, the child was extremely thin, would not eat, and seemed very depressed, although after being with the MacDonald family for a while he regained his appetite and a healthy disposition.[3] In the story, Allen lives in a more stable family but is obsessed with food. It is this obsession and the fictional circumstances of its development and cure that I explore here. MacDonald's narrative is distinctive not only for its identification of this problem in prepubescence, but also for its portrait of a male victim of an eating disorder that closely resembles anorexia nervosa. Although much less public and clinical attention has focused on male instances of this condition—the majority of cases occurring in women—male sufferers comprise approximately 10 percent of reported cases of anorexia nervosa.[4] A body of medical and psychoanalytic literature on males with the disorder does exist, and a number of case studies include instances of prepubescent onset.[5]

Arnold Andersen has noted the "essential similarity of psychopathological features in both males and females suffering from this disorder."[6] He explains that only "the terms used by young males with eating disorders to describe their motives for weight loss may differ from the terms used by females."[7] Yet clinicians must also understand the cultural and physiological differences between their male and female patients and take them into consideration when diagnosing and treating this condition. In her story, MacDonald presents a prescient sensitivity to the attitudes and concerns researchers have recently identified with young males, and the narrative's structure reproduces in condensed form the clinical pattern of an eating disorder in a male patient. Before turning to the story itself, I want briefly to establish some of the key features of anorexia nervosa in males that correspond to the details of MacDonald's work.

First, as Hilde Bruch observes, "anorexia nervosa is a misnomer; many patients do not lose their appetite but actively refrain from eating."[8] Eugene Falstein and colleagues expand on this point: "Generally there is no loss of appetite early, but aversion to food, fear of eating or voluntary restriction of food intake."[9] Thus a central criterion identified with cases of the disorder is "a distorted, implacable attitude towards eating, food, or weight that overrides hunger, admonitions, reassurance or threats."[10]

Clinicians have cataloged numerous variants on the composite profile of the male anorectic; patients present with a range of symptoms, including weight loss, fatigue, absence of secondary sexual characteristics, and personality dysfunctions. One of the more infrequent but interesting related disorders is "swallowing phobia," which physicians can identify "in patients who do not have fear of fatness but who do have fear of swallowing, often beginning with minor episodes of choking in the past and a recent recurrence."[11]

Far more common are the details related to body image. A general concern with body size—for example, being of "small stature"—may precede the onset of anorexia[12] and may coincide with "severe doubts about . . . adequacy and competence."[13] Many researchers note the involvement of their male patients in sports and exercise, both to lose weight and build muscle bulk. Although the approach to fitness may initially be excessive, this interest has been closely linked to the return to normalcy, to such an extent that "a lack of sporting interest during the illness [is] associated with poorer outcome."[14] Similarly, sports-related activity plays a major role in therapy. Males "often will benefit from an appropriate exercise program that is increased in vigor in proportion to their weight gain and improved overall health."[15]

In addition to the physical manifestations of the disorder, research has also focused on the socioeconomic and familial profile of anorectics, given the realization that certain factors recur in a number of cases. In her fascinating history of anorexia, Joan Jacobs Brumberg links the rise in numbers of cases in the past few decades to post–World War II prosperity.[16] The disease is limited to regions experiencing Westernization (for example, the United States, Western Europe, and Japan); instances have not been found in the Third World.[17] Furthermore, even within Westernized areas, members of the lower economic classes do not suffer from the condition,[18] which makes it a "disproportionately white . . . middle-class and upper-class" phenomenon.[19]

Researchers have analyzed the families of anorectics extensively and have found patterns in their structures and dynamics as well as in their class similarities. Family therapists describe the home environment of anorectics as "controlling, perfectionistic, and nonconfrontational"[20] and "success- and achievement-oriented."[21] A case study of one young male patient depicts his oppression "by his father's demands for prompt, perfect behavior. . . . In family therapy, he attempted to be more assertive and came to understand his anorectic illness as an attempt to feel effective as a person despite . . . difficult demands from his father."[22]

Yet other studies show that, despite this drive for perfection, the father "often play[s] a peripheral role" in the family,[23] and the male anorectic feels a greater affinity with and resemblance to the mother.[24] Brumberg observes, "When a parent *is* implicated in anorexia nervosa, it is almost always the mother,"[25] and many studies detail a complex, unhealthy relationship between mother and son. Brumberg describes the mothers as often "frustrated, depressed, perfectionistic, passive and dependent,"[26] while M. M. Fichter and C. Daser believe mothers of male anorectics turn to the male child to fulfill emotional needs.[27] Falstein and colleagues note "the great importance of food to the parents of patients with anorexia"[28] and observe that in "mother-child relationships, food constitutes a medium, heavily cathected with the forces of love and hate, as well as such related phenomena as rejection, acceptance, attention-getting, punishment, satiety, deprivation, sickness, health, growth, sadism, masochism, and finally, even life and death."[29]

Many theorists believe young people experiencing these problematic family relationships become anorectics in their attempt to take control of their lives through one of the few means available to them—control over their bodies, particularly through food intake. The period of late childhood through adolescence and early adulthood appears to be very stressful, as this is the time of transition from the relatively carefree days of youth to the responsibilities of maturity. During this developmental process, some patients feel restrained or pulled back by their families, while others find maturation itself overwhelming.

Hilde Bruch describes the resulting "excessive concern with the body and its size, and the rigid control over eating" as "late symptoms in the development of youngsters who have been engaged in a desperate fight against feeling enslaved and exploited, not competent to lead a life of their own. In their blind search for a sense of identity and selfhood, anorexic youngsters will not accept anything that their parents . . . have to offer."[30] Brumberg neatly summarizes the condition as follows: "Anorexia nervosa is seen as a pathological response to the developmental crisis of adolescence. Refusal of food is understood as an expression of the adolescent's struggle over autonomy, individuation, and sexual development."[31]

This last sentence captures the thrust of Betty MacDonald's story, "The Slow-Eater-Tiny-Bite-Taker Cure," which appears in her first collection of Mrs. Piggle-Wiggle tales. Each of the stories in the four volumes follows the same formula: MacDonald characterizes a child with some behavioral problem, and then, through the commonsensical or sometimes magical intervention of Mrs. Piggle-Wiggle, the child is cured and resumes normal activity.

Among other delightful episodes, MacDonald recounts how a child with bad table manners improves with the aid of a trained pig[32] and how children who whisper incessantly stop when given "whisper sticks"—magic candy that takes the voice away entirely to turn the tables on the whisperers.[33] One of the great strengths of MacDonald's stories—and a crucial element of the eating disorder tale in particular—is her egalitarian depiction of adults and children. The parents in her fiction are often no less to blame for the youngsters' faults than the children; the adults must also be "cured"—educated as to how to be good parents, so that the children can grow up to be healthy, happy individuals.

"The Slow-Eater-Tiny-Bite-Taker Cure" opens with an illustration of the boy Allen at the breakfast table.[34] MacDonald describes Allen as "a little boy" with "sturdy legs and a very shiny smile" (91). From the iconographic representation of Allen we can surmise that he is from at least a middle-class background. The chair on which he sits has a tastefully upholstered pad tied to the back, and he holds a large, probably cloth, napkin in his right hand. The table is set with a number of objects, including a large cereal bowl on a plate, a large glass probably containing milk, and slightly ornate salt and pepper shakers and a jam pot. Allen wears neat, adult-style clothing, unlike MacDonald's other young protagonists, who usually appear in more casual children's attire. Allen sports a dark blazer with light trim, white shirt, and patterned tie, his "curly brown hair" (91) neatly brushed back from his forehead (Figure 1).

Through the progression of events in the story we realize that Allen is an only child of a traditional American family, with a mother at home and a father who appears only at dinnertime, having little contact with Allen otherwise and little involvement in his upbringing other than as a disciplinary figure. As the story opens, MacDonald narrates the events of the morning when Allen's eating disorder first appears:

> One morning he sat down to breakfast, but instead of picking up his spoon and eating his mush and milk like a good little boy he took a fork and began eating his cereal grain by grain. . . . In a little while even a whole grain seemed too much so he broke each grain in two, taking only half grains on the fork tines. (91)

By calling attention to the movement away from his identity as "a good little boy," MacDonald's narration highlights Allen's calculated misbehavior in this first attempt to take control over food intake. These events seem

FIG. 1. Allen at the breakfast table. From *Mrs. Piggle-Wiggle*.

remarkably similar to details from more recently written anorexia fiction reported by Brumberg: "The books are notable for their graphic descriptions of the anorectic's food preoccupations (for instance, never allowing oneself to eat more than three curds of cottage cheese at one sitting)."[35]

Allen's mother is at first miffed by Allen's behavior. She speaks to him in an indulgent yet condescending manner, remarking, "My goodness, you are poky this morning dear" and "Now, then, eat properly and hurry or your egg will get cold" (91–92). After watching him manipulate his food for some time, however, she becomes angry and finally "whisked away his breakfast and sent him marching up to his room" (92), a nonconfrontational technique that nevertheless conveys a punitive attitude toward eating behavior. At lunchtime Allen floats and chases cracker crumbs in his soup for several hours, and

> at dinner that night, Allen cut his meat into such small pieces that his father looked over at him and said, "Perhaps you would like to borrow my magnifying glass? I am sure you are going to need it to see those infinitesimal bits of meat." (93)

MacDonald's subtle use of irony and sophisticated diction ("infinitesimal") in her characterization of the father's behavior to his son foregrounds the conflicting attitudes of the parents toward Allen—the mother infantilizing, the father expecting him to understand the intricacies of adult discourse. When his parents demand an explanation for this behavior Allen responds: "I guess I'm just a slow eater. I choke if I take larger bites" (93). This detail corresponds to the choking and/or swallowing phobia experienced by some anorectics who may not see weight as part of their conscious concerns.

Allen's father appears only at one other point in the story, at dinner the next evening, this time in a harsher, disciplinary role. When Allen asks to be excused from the table having barely touched his food, his father "started to say 'NO!'" but his mother intervenes and excuses him (98). MacDonald does not have the father participate in the subsequent curing process, an omission that corresponds to the theories of the centrality of the mother-son relationship in male anorexia.

MacDonald also puts Allen's situation in a larger social context of eating disorders by having his mother telephone the mothers of Allen's peers. Mrs. Crankminor helps us ascertain that Allen's problem is not physical; his mother reports to her that he has no temperature and claims to feel well (94). However, Wetherill Crankminor clearly has a related problem: "Yesterday morning before breakfast, he weighed one hundred and eighty-two pounds and his father has begun calling him Blimpy" (94). Once again a father appears as the sarcastic, negative force, but Allen's mother (perhaps mistakenly) perceives this as "a more serious problem than I have" (94) and decides to call another friend. Mrs. Wingsproggle's daughter Pergola, she learns, has been instructed to chew each bite of food "one hundred tie-ums [times]" (94), a detail that again implicates the parents in the problematic eating behavior of their children. Allen's mother correctly surmises that implementing Mrs. Wingsproggle's eating regimen would mean that her son "would die of slow starvation before a day had passed" (95). The humor and exaggeration of these conversations do not mask the seriousness of these children's problems, however, and the allusion to death by starvation is the very real corollary to Allen's fictional condition.

Finally, Patsy's mother suggests that Allen's mother call Mrs. Piggle-Wiggle, who reassures her that Allen will "be all right again in a day or two" and sends over the "Slow-Eater-Tiny-Bite-Taker dishes" to achieve his cure (96). Allen's mother tells Allen to run down to play at Patsy's house, to "put some roses in your cheeks" (97). The narrator continues: "However, instead of running down to Patsy's, he walked very, very slowly because he was tired from not having had enough to eat" (97). Both the encouragement to get exercise and the sensation of extreme fatigue are part of the anorectic experience, and both will be integral to the resolution of Allen's story.

When Allen's mother opens the basket from Mrs. Piggle-Wiggle, she discovers "four little sets of dishes" of decreasing size. The largest resembles a child's play set, while the tiniest includes implements that look like needles and pins (97). Mrs. Piggle-Wiggle instructs Allen's mother to use the dishes in decreasing order of size for the next four days and to serve proportionately sized meals on them. She warns that Allen "may lose some weight" but says "he will gain it right back" (96). She also mentions that she "may send for him on the last day and no matter how he feels, let him come to my house" (96).

This is the point in the story where MacDonald's parallel to the clinical profile of an anorectic male and his treatment diverges from standard contemporary medical practices. Although therapists use many different techniques, including counseling, and, if need be, hospitalization, with anorectic patients, depriving them of food to an even greater extent than they do themselves is not one of them. However, MacDonald's novel approach is not that far removed in principle from some of the elements of family therapy for these cases. The first step in Mrs. Piggle-Wiggle's cure in effect involves the mother, not the child. By having Allen's mother use the increasingly diminutive dishes, Mrs. Piggle-Wiggle forces her subconsciously to acknowledge the way she infantilizes her child. The smaller the place settings, the smaller the individual seems psychologically and emotionally. Yet as Figure 2 illustrates, Allen's physical size in proportion to the tiny dishes makes him appear gigantic, as Allen's mother must recognize. Thus Allen's mother must come to treat him in all regards as a "large" person— someone physically, intellectually, and emotionally more mature than he had been previously considered.

Allen's conflict also becomes very clear at this point, as we realize that the physical appearance he has assumed through his parents' guidance— that is, the little adult in the jacket and tie—does not correspond to the behavioral role in which his mother has cast him, that of a little boy. Nor is he yet capable, either emotionally or intellectually, of acting the part of a real adult, as his father's treatment of him demands. Allen's eating disorder is a manifestation of this tension; he tries, as does a mature person, to find a way to control his life, to match the external identity he feels he must fulfill, while at the same time he rejects the childish role he feels has been thrust on him. Allen's choice of the means of control—his food intake—exactly matches that of the anorectic in a similarly stressful environment.

FIG. 2. Allen and his mother. From *Mrs. Piggle-Wiggle*.

MacDonald describes how "happy" Allen is "about the tiny dishes" (98) and the small portions of food. "He cut the cornflakes into thirteen pieces and ate a part of one. He ate a speck of egg, a nibble of bacon and five drops of cocoa and then crawled in and lay on the couch" (98). Although regressive, this symmetry of Allen's immature feelings and gestures with the food quantity and dish size appeals to him, as it removes some of the factors associated with his sense of conflict. By the fourth day of near starvation he can barely eat or move at all, however, and when Mrs. Piggle-Wiggle calls Allen on the telephone he is so weak he cannot carry on a conversation with her. Instead Mrs. Piggle-Wiggle tells Allen's mother: "It is Allen's turn to exercise the spotted pony and I would like him to come over here right away" (101).

For Allen this news is terrifically exciting, as the opportunity to take care of Mrs. Piggle-Wiggle's animals is not to be missed. Mrs. Piggle-Wiggle is adored by all the neighborhood children, as her house is filled with all sorts of fascinating and magical objects left to her by her deceased husband, who was a pirate.[36] She also keeps a menagerie of unusual and talented animals, and an invitation to explore in her house or play with her animals is a highly prized occasion for the local youngsters. These rare moments also represent times of unusual responsibility, since Mrs. Piggle-Wiggle treats children as grownups and expects them to behave as such, although in a supportive way, very different from the mode of Allen's father. Thus Allen's job stands both for the physical activity central to the successful rehabilitation of the anorectic and for the kind of chance for self-reliance such a young person needs.

At the moment of the telephone call, however, Allen is in a severely deteriorated condition and can barely fulfill this obligation. Luckily, he can ride downhill to Mrs. Piggle-Wiggle's house in his wagon, where two other boys "lifted him ... and laid him across Spotty's back" (101). They "started slowly off down the street with Allen lying on his back like a bag of cornmeal," and although Allen "tried to sit up ... he was too weak" to do so (102). After a few embarrassing encounters with neighborhood mothers, who rushed out of their houses to ask Allen if he were ill, he realizes he is too tired to ride any longer, "so he guided the pony up to his own front gate. Then he rolled off his back onto the grass. He lay there like a wet sock, bawling" (102). As his mother dashes out to see if he is hurt, he is forced to explain that he has returned because of his extreme fatigue and weakness:

> It is just that I am so tired I cannot stay on his back. I rolled off and now I can't get back on and it's my turn to exercise him and I won't have another turn for a long, long tiiiiiiiiiiiIIIME! (102–3)

Allen's admission of his condition, with its direct relation to his inability to perform the activity he most desires, marks the turning point in his illness. He realizes that his eating behavior and its impact on him physically stand in direct conflict with his larger goals of personal responsibility and physical strength, and thus he must use a different technique to fulfill his ambitions. His mother responds in a direct, straightforward fashion:

> Now, see here, Allen. This all comes from your turning into a Slow-Eater-Tiny-Bite-Taker and if you want to ride Spotty this afternoon, you will have to come into the house and eat something. (103)

After helping him into the kitchen, Allen's mother proceeds to prepare lunch for the boy and serves it to him on Mrs. Piggle-Wiggle's dishes, this time in increasing order of size. This reversal indicates the symbolic maturation process acknowledged by both parent and child. Allen realizes he is still "very hungry" and asks for second helpings: "May I please have a *large* bowl of soup and a *large* glass of milk?" (104, emphasis added).

With a neat fillip, MacDonald ends the story with Allen and his mother together feeding Spotty "an apple and some lumps of sugar" (104), which shows the boy taking on another form of responsibility, one even more closely related to his own situation. After recognizing his own hunger, Allen can posit hunger in others, and he takes care of the animal as he can now take better care of himself, through the central medium of food. Then "Allen climbed on his back and rode proudly away, sitting up very straight and holding on to the reins with one hand" (104). But his mother calls him back, to ask him if he would mind taking the now unneeded basket of dishes with him.

> "Not at all," said Allen graciously. "Just hand me the basket. I'll put it here in front of me and hold it with this hand. You see, Mother, I only use one hand to steer now." (105)

Thus acknowledging and sharing this new authority and independent strength with her, he grasps the basket and kisses her in a loving gesture of reconciliation, and sets off again, still "in a very slow walk, toward Mrs. Piggle-Wiggle's house" (105).

This upbeat conclusion to MacDonald's tale, even with its realistic reminder of the slowness connected with Allen's recent recovery, corresponds to the tone of all her children's stories, which focus on the successful amelioration of problems. As a fictional account of a serious disorder, "The Slow-Eater-Tiny-Bite-Taker Cure" perhaps too quickly and easily resolves a conflicted situation that in reality could take months or years of treatment to improve. As a study of a child with an eating disorder, it resembles more closely the "mild cases with spontaneous recovery"[37] observed by some clinicians than the protracted cases, with poorer prognoses, that appear more frequently in the medical literature. Nevertheless, with its sensitivity to the familial difficulties inherent in these conditions, its understanding of the tensions over maturation and responsibility experienced by young children who manifest such behavior, and its practical illustration of ameliorative techniques, MacDonald's story merits attention and praise.

Notes

1. Betty MacDonald, *Mrs. Piggle-Wiggle* (Philadelphia: J. B. Lippincott Co., 1947). All page references are to this edition and are given in parentheses in the text. I am grateful to David A. Faulkner for his editorial assistance on this essay.

2. Joan Jacobs Brumberg, *Fasting Girls: The Emergence of Anorexia Nervosa as a Modern Disease* (Cambridge, Mass.: Harvard University Press, 1988), 339 n. 16.

3. I am grateful to Anne Canham for supplying some biographical information about her mother. There is little published criticism on Betty MacDonald, although many details about her life and her work can be gleaned from her adult fiction, which is often based on humorous experiences from her own life.

4. The first full-length study of this problem is edited by Arnold E. Andersen: *Males with Eating Disorders* (New York: Brunner/Mazel, 1990). Andersen's collection of essays presents an overview of these conditions in male patients and corroborates the evidence of earlier studies. Although the articles focus more on adult males, the book contains some useful references to younger subjects.

5. See, e.g., N. P. Sheppard, J. P. Malone, and A. Jackson, "Male Anorexia Nervosa: A Review of Nine Patients," *Irish Medical Journal* 77 (January 1984): 4-8.

6. Arnold E. Andersen, "Anorexia Nervosa and Bulimia in Adolescent Males," *Pediatric Annals* 13 (December 1984): 901.

7. Ibid.

8. Hilde Bruch, "Anorexia Nervosa in the Male," *Psychosomatic Medicine* 33 (January-February 1971): 31.

9. Eugene I. Falstein, Sherman C. Feinstein, and Ilse Judas, "Anorexia Nervosa in the Male Child," *American Journal of Orthopsychiatry* 26 (October 1956): 752.

10. Cherrie Galletly and B. James, "Anorexia Nervosa in a Male: Comment and Illustration," *New Zealand Medical Journal* 89 (March 14, 1979): 172.

11. Andersen, "Anorexia Nervosa," 904.

12. J. L. Margo, "Anorexia Nervosa in Males: A Comparison with Female Patients," *British Journal of Psychiatry* 151 (July 1987): 81.

13. Bruch, "Anorexia Nervosa," 45.

14. Tom Burns and A. H. Crisp, "Factors Affecting Prognosis in Male Anorexics," *Journal of Psychiatric Research* 19, nos. 2/3 (1985): 326.

15. Andersen, "Anorexia Nervosa," 904.

16. Brumberg, *Fasting Girls,* 10–11.

17. Ibid., 12–13.

18. Ibid.

19. Ibid., 12.

20. Ibid., 29.

21. Bruch, "Anorexia Nervosa," 42.

22. Andersen, "Anorexia Nervosa," 902.

23. M. M. Fichter and C. Daser, "Symptomatology, Psychosexual Development, and Gender Identity in 42 Anorexic Males," *Psychological Medicine* 17 (May 1987): 414.

24. Ibid., 413.

25. Brumberg, *Fasting Girls,* 29.

26. Ibid., 30.

27. Fichter and Daser, "Symptomatology," 415.

28. Falstein, "Anorexia Nervosa," 752–53.

29. Ibid., 765.

30. Hilde Bruch, *The Golden Cage: The Enigma of Anorexia Nervosa* (New York: Vintage Books, 1979), x.

31. Brumberg, *Fasting Girls,* 28.

32. Betty MacDonald, "The Bad-Table-Manners Cure," in *Mrs. Piggle-Wiggle's Magic* (Philadelphia: J. B. Lippincott Co., 1949), 39–57.

33. Betty MacDonald, "The Whisperer," in *Hello, Mrs. Piggle-Wiggle* (Philadelphia: J. B. Lippincott Co., 1957), 71–99.

34. The illustrations for this volume are by Hilary Knight. Because she was MacDonald's illustrator for three of the four collections (the pictures accompanying publication of the first editions), I am assuming a certain amount of collaboration between author and artist.

35. Brumberg, *Fasting Girls,* 16.

36. Betty MacDonald, "Mrs. Piggle-Wiggle, Herself," *Mrs. Piggle-Wiggle,* 11.

37. G. G. Hay and J. C. Leonard, "Anorexia Nervosa in Males," *The Lancet* 2 (September 15, 1979): 575.

MAGIC FOOD, COMPULSIVE EATING, AND POWER POETICS

Mervyn Nicholson

> She found me roots of relish sweet,
> And honey wild, and manna dew,
> And sure in language strange she said
> "I love thee true."
> —John Keats
> "La Belle Dame sans Merci" (1820)

In John Keats's "La Belle Dame sans Merci" a beautiful woman with faery powers destroys a knight. The knight is a vigorous male. He is mounted on a "pacing steed," the horse being an image (1) of masculinity, traditionally of (2) aristocracy, and therefore (3) of power. The richness of imagery in "Belle Dame" is typical of Keats, especially its appeal to senses other than the usual one of sight. For example, taste, a comparatively undeveloped sense in literature, is conspicuous. The beautiful lady finds at least three kinds of special food for the knight's delectation: roots, honey, and manna. Indeed, this is a poem about eating—and about *being* eaten.

Though brief, the menu unites both Greek and Hebrew traditions, implying the Greek Age of Gold with its happy vegetarian diet (roots, honey) and the Hebrew exodus, when the Israelites were fed miraculously with food from heaven (manna). This manna is not only from heaven; it is food that must be consumed at once. It cannot be hoarded—those who tried to keep it got into trouble with God. Manna is an object of *immediate* consumption, an image of desire unmediated by perplexities of brain or exigencies of place. At the same time, it is the pure bounty of power; it cannot be earned or controlled by subordinates. The Lady finds "manna dew" for the Knight because this is irresistible food: it is compulsive. What we notice here is that it is not food as such, but *control* of food, that is the key to the logic of food, eating, and eating disorders in literature.

This is an enormously complicated subject, a matter of what we may call power poetics and hence of literary theory itself. The power poetics of food is an entry to one of the most neglected areas of literary study—what might be called the logic of visualization, the way images and image-usage patterns constitute not merely texts but literary traditions and even the cultures that generate texts. Because little is known about the logic of visualization, food, which is so vital a unit of the imagination in culture generally as well as in literature, is a good focus for analysis. Eating disorders are directly related to this image-logic. Literary eating symbolism can no more be confined to a single text than eating can be understood in terms of a single meal. It is by definition intertextual.

Keats's poem also has, somewhat surprisingly, a third level of food symbolism, which differs from both classical Greek and Judeo-Christian traditions: a subtextual allusion to a specifically Romantic mythology. Behind this ballad lie the climactic lines of Samuel Taylor Coleridge's vatic "Kubla Khan" (1816), in which the poet becomes possessed by some kind of deity. Keats's "honey wild, and manna dew" conflates Coleridge's "honey-dew":

> And all should cry, Beware! Beware!
> His flashing eyes, his floating hair!
> Weave a circle round him thrice,
> And close your eyes with holy dread,
> *For he on honey-dew hath fed,*
> *And drunk the milk of Paradise.* (Emphasis added)

Coleridge lists "milk of Paradise" and something called "honey-dew"—agents, presumably, of divine metamorphosis. Special food makes you into a special person; divine food makes you a god or gives you godlike visions or powers. The fact that food appears as the climactic image in "Khan" suggests a Gravesian mushroom or drug cult—not unnaturally, given the links with opium here and for this poet generally. Both Coleridge and Keats associate food with metamorphosis, but whereas in Coleridge the speaker becomes a kind of god, in Keats he is entranced, and then in effect eviscerated.

Food symbolism, particularly in its special form of eating disorders, pivots on the theme of metamorphosis; eating (or abstaining) and shape-changing go together. Food may be defined as a substance the body can transform into the body itself. In other words it is the means and the substance of self-transformation. Hence, the control of food is the manipulation of the power of self, the material of identity. Metaphorically, what makes food food is that it is charged with life-energy, which in most cultures is identified with the divine. Food is god-substance. The control of it is, psychologically, the control of primal power.[1] Food and eating constitute our primary experience of life; to an infant the mouth is the center of the universe. What Freud's analysis of the "oral stage" and its polymorphous, diffused sexual sensibility indicates is that eating and sexuality are, in our originary phase of life, the same thing. It is clear that nothing is more basic—or more overdetermined in meaning—than food, eating, and the associated phenomena of eating disorders.

In Keats the beautiful female feeds the knight with special food, whereupon the knight becomes, effectively, food himself. In other words, there is an exchange act: false food (in effect poison) for real food. She trades food that is sweet—compulsively desirable—for the knight's life-energy. The poem ends with the knight sucked dry, an empty husk. Significantly, the knight, like the vatic poet in "Kubla Khan," has a vision:

> I saw pale kings and princes too,
> Pale warriors, death-pale were they all;
> They cried, "La Belle Dame sans Merci
> Hath thee in thrall!"

The kings, princes, warriors are "pale," indeed "death-pale." Their blood is drained, as if the Lady were a vampire. Medically they present as anorexic:

> I saw their starved lips in the gloam,
> With horrid warning gaped wide,
> And I awoke, and found me here,
> On the cold hill's side.

Keats emphasizes this anorexic look: they are not only drained of blood but "starved." Their lips are shriveled. They are eaten—and cannot eat.

The Lady clearly collects males: masculine, powerful, vigorous men—kings, princes, warriors. She reduces these, the most powerful members of society, to bloodless shades in a Homeric-style Hades. Her literary ancestress is Circe: Odysseus's visit, during which he grapples with her metamorphic powers (and her magic food), coincides with his visit to the underworld. He feeds blood to the shades of Hades, a magic food that gives them speech. He then returns to Circe before pursuing his *nostos,* as if she contained the underworld within her. But whereas in Homer Odysseus does not merely disarm her, but wins a working relation with her, in Keats the knight and company eat, then are eaten, and then are suspended in a life-in-death state of lost power. He is now a shade, doomed to wander like Elpenor. Her cave, like the withered landscape itself, suggests a sinister womb (or even more sinister belly) to which the man now belongs—a dead nature enclosing a ghost.

In the usual course the knight would "feed" on the Lady's sexual vitality. For him to enjoy her would not warrant special notice. Yet this Knight, totally obsessed in a form of life-in-death, is now unable to self-transform, and so unable to live. Recall that life-in-death in Coleridge is a female figure—half gorgeous, half monstrous—one who metaphorically feeds on her victims, as Coleridge's imagery of fear sipping vampirically on the lifeblood of the Mariner implies. Now Keats's Knight is one who cannot eat—unlike the squirrel whose granary is full, or birds who have escaped the withered vegetation for the abundance of southern lands. The natural life cycle rolls on, regardless of the individual male's fate within it.

What Keats crystallizes in this poem is an old convention. A lovely lady, offering special food/drink, seduces a powerful man, then destroys him. The food is a crucial motif in this complex: it poisons, intoxicates, or causes unreal hallucinations or delusions of grandeur or pleasure. The food either symbolizes sexual pleasure or accompanies it. Compulsive food is typically sweet food. In literature, sweetness and sugar, like the related beauty, are associated with deception ("pie in the sky when you die"). They are also associated with transience: "sweet not lasting," as Laertes says, trying to make Ophelia forget Hamlet (Ophelia is linked to sweet food throughout *Hamlet* —"Sweets to the sweet"). Such food, being compulsive, is associated with obsessive states of mind, and to be obsessed is to be enslaved, to lose the power of choice. Compulsive eating is symbolized by intensely desired food objects.

The figure at the center of this symbolism may be called the Tricky Female, usually a witch. In the familiar Grimms tale of Hansel and Gretel, the wicked witch attracts lost children with her sugar-candy house. The children eat the house, but they are in fact in the initial phase of being digested themselves by a witch who cages the male to fatten him, to make him (not his female sibling) "dead meat." Madam Mim in T. H. White's *Once and Future King* has the same need to cage and consume males. The compulsive food offered by the Tricky Female—a metaphor for her desirability—is really death itself.

Witches, while visualized as crones, often appear to men in the form of lovely maidens (like Carlos Fuentes's Aura or, for that matter, Edmund Spenser's Duessa)—that is, the witch has found a way to jump the gap from one end of the life cycle (old age) to the other (youth). Typically she achieves this immortality (immortality meaning not eternal life but indefinitely extended life) by absorbing the life-energy of men. When witches have power over a male, they proceed to suck him dry, as it were, leaving him drained of life-energy if not dead. Food = life, and life = change. Hence, to live forever is to be constantly changing, and to do that one must find and maintain the right food, a theme common in stories about immortals (Freya's apples in Norse mythology, for example).

The Tricky Female is deadly in a most complex manner. She does not merely destroy her victim physically. She also destroys his identity, the masculine force that constitutes his being. Keats's Dame crystallizes the figure of the Tricky Female, as well as, it seems, his own anxieties about female sexuality and about the food symbolism that permeates his work. But whatever his own anxieties (or however representative of men in general they may be), the Tricky Female is commonplace in literature, especially in romances, and in movies too. For example, in the film *The Maltese Falcon* an innocent-looking woman turns out to be a callous murderer who deceives men. The fearless hero, Sam Spade (played by Humphrey Bogart), unmasks her, revealing the murderous deathly nature concealed by her lovely body. She looks helpless, innocent, and, like so many maids in distress, intensely erotic, even seductive. Sarcastically calling her "Angel," he treats her at the end with firm brutality. As a Tricky Female, she is utterly unscrupulous and must be handled by someone deaf to her dangerous blandishments ("sweet talk"). This figure is a siren who lives by devouring males: a *Venus* fly-trap or black *widow*.[2]

Thus, love is visualized as an irresistible food. Distracted Ophelia has "sucked the honeyed music of [Hamlet's] vows" of love. Her images indicate that Hamlet is playing the part of Tricky Female, significantly reversing the usual gender roles; Ophelia has become a distracted lover who ate the forbidden food and now pays for this "love" first with her identity, then with her life. Love is ultimately death, because love generates beings that die, as Hamlet's "get thee to a nunnery" tirade indicates. Keats's description of

"Pleasure" in "Ode on Melancholy" (1820), "Turning to poison as the bee-mouth sips," encapsulates the love Yeats later called "the honey of generation," the compulsion to reproduce. Byron's nasty Lucifer calls it "a *sweet* degradation, / A most enervating and filthy cheat / To lure thee on to the renewal of / Fresh souls and bodies" (*Cain* 2.56–59 [1822], emphasis added). Love = compulsive food = the life cycle = death = poison.

In this context, the Tricky Female figure is conspicuous for several reasons. Women are of course associated with food, as food suppliers; they make and serve food to others. It is no accident that this role is low in status and associated with power-subordinate figures. But in the Tricky Female's case, the food/drink causes distortions of consciousness disabling those who eat it. The food she generates is compulsive; it is something one cannot resist and must have to live, a paradox in that it is (as John Milton puts it) "eating death." Here "gorging on food is no longer a way of satisfying hunger, but a terrifying, dominating compulsion."[3] Thus it is food that Blake calls "The fruit of deceit / Ruddy and sweet to eat." The Tricky Female and her food display a *reversal* in power relations: female power over males.

Again, it is not food as such but *control* of food that determines its symbolism. The woman takes control of the situation and uses food not as a means of supplying the male — and hence articulating her subordinate power status in relation to the male — but as a means of entrapping and, as Keats shows, enslaving him. Thus the male feeds the female, instead of the other way around, so that the Tricky Female represents a primal rebellion, a thing almost too terrible even to think about for patriarchal culture, a focus for anxiety so intense that it is almost paralyzing. It is not by accident that at the heart of traditional, established religion is a myth of a woman seizing a food object permitted only to a male God, and then seducing her natural male overlord to commit sin. Eve murders Adam with forbidden fruit.

When, in *Paradise Lost*, Eve greets Adam carrying the compulsive, magic food, Adam is in precisely the position of the Knight in my epigraph: "She found me roots of relish sweet, / And honey wild, and manna dew, / And sure in language strange she said / 'I love thee true.' " It is soon apparent that such "love" is the kind of love the devouring Worm has for the flower in William Blake's "The Sick Rose" (1794). It is simply, that is, predatory appetite: what Carroll's walrus and carpenter feel for their oyster victims, what Screwtape feels for his "patients" (whom he ultimately devours), or what the vengeful speaker of Blake's "Poison Tree" feels for the one who takes his lethal apple. "Love" for the Tricky Female is like the bait that lures a fish; food by which to draw the hapless male not only to lose his natural power over the female, but also to become the source of *her* power, as in the act of eating itself. This model of love has been a major strand in tradition, epitomized in the paintings of Edward Munch but at least as old as Saint Augustine. The woman loves by consuming the male "other," who thus literally becomes part of her, as an infant once was part of its mother.

Keats depicts man and woman riding together; the woman sings a special language — "language strange." The imagery suggests a male baby with mother. A mother not only feeds a baby physically but also nourishes it emotionally/mentally by singing lullabies; she talks the special dialect known as "baby-talk." (Notice that although the song is in a "language strange," it is a language the knight understands. He knows for "sure" its meaning: Love.) Medicine recognizes a neonatal phase, in which mother/infant are vitally linked as fetus is to womb; it devotes a whole branch to it — neonatology. From the standpoint of the male/aristocrat/power-figure, being a baby represents the worst possible situation: total dependency on a female figure (whose power, like that of all subordinates, ought to — must — be kept in check), a being whose body generated and once contained the self. Breast-feeding is an image of human union at least as potent as coitus, but whereas coitus is usually seen as putting the male in the power position (penis penetrating vagina), breast-feeding empowers the woman (breast penetrating mouth).

The central point of this group of motifs is contingency — a realization that the self is not and never can be utterly independent, in control. One cannot conceive the self in the way that religion conceived God, as someone utterly above nature and dependent on nothing but his own autonomous will. Human connection here is visualized differently. It is not one person controlling another, but mutual dependence: the mother feeds the child physically, the child feeds the mother emotionally — a point to return to.

The association of compulsive food and metamorphosis recurs in Keats, notably in other trance poems, such as "Ode to a Nightingale" and *The Fall of Hyperion,* where the speaker in a dream "drinks deliciously" and then finds consciousness "rapt" unwillingly away. The word choice is significant. "Rapt" displaces/implies rape and rapture, which both have the same Latin origin. Keats translated all the *Aeneid* as a boy, including the episode of Dido, who was killed by love and its deceits. The complex of motifs here can be summed up this way:

Power (that is, power as domination)
Food of compulsive desirability
Metamorphosis (where metamorphosis is a metaphor for loss of control or
    subordination)
Love (conceived in power terms as compulsive, as means of control)

Sexuality and eating are two aspects of the human life cycle—sexuality/
birth/growth/death/decay—and synecdoches or metonyms for a single existential process that absorbs/subsumes consciousness within itself, just as each
individual originally comes from sexual union, from the body of parents,
and eventually dissolves back into the material basis of living things, earth
itself. In traditional imagery, male authority is trapped in dependency on
the female body of nature. Deep anxiety, even panic, emerges here: male
fears about loss of power, fears that Freud translated into castration anxieties.
For consciousness as control-power is enclosed within the physical continuum of reproduction-in-time, of which food is a key symbol.

Eating disorders in literature are a function of the logic of food in literature,
which is, inescapably, a matter of power and power relations, of power
poetics—the way power relations constitute texts. In the primary configuration,
food is associated with those who are weak in the power grid. They provide
food to those who are stronger, who can coerce them to provide it. Indeed,
the weak often are food for the strong in the world of "dog eat dog." The
control of food is a male prerogative, as is evident from the etymology of
"lord," where the Old English hlaford means "bread-holder," that is, decider
of who eats what. Traditionally the provision of food is female. Women
produce food that men control—in other words, the weak serve the strong.
Olive Oyl is identified with food; Popeye eats food. The power relation of
male/female is manifested as Popeye's magic force embodied as a preferred
food. Food symbolism expresses the subordination of some groups in society
to others: women; originally also peasants; and of course animals. Hence
producing/providing food is a frequent marker of power-subordinate status.
Women, who traditionally feed others, actually are bodily, for infants, the
source of food. Food/eating-disorders are a matter of power, just as "women's
bodies are a locus of social control."[4]

One reason for the significance of food in power poetics is that it is the
power to exist. Without it, one dies. It is transformation-power, a theme
cleverly explored in the magic food of H. G. Wells's Food of the Gods (1905)
or John Wyndham's Trouble with Lichen (1960). But it is also power in that

it takes power to get food. Because food is by definition a being weaker than the one who does the eating, especially in the case of flesh, food derives from a struggle with other life-forms. The animal that people eat does not die by accident. It is slaughtered in a ghastly manner. It is subject entirely to human control-power. At every stage, power is encoded in the acquisition and distribution of food, as anthropology shows.

Any number of texts can illustrate the power poetics of food—Swift's "A Modest Proposal" (1729) is a classic example. James Thurber's fable "The Rabbits Who Caused All the Trouble" (1946) gives the basics in minimum time:

> Within the memory of the youngest child there was a family of rabbits who lived near a pack of wolves. The wolves announced that they did not like the way the rabbits were living. (The wolves were crazy about the way they themselves were living, because it was the only way to live.)

When an earthquake kills some wolves, the rabbits are blamed, "for it is well known that rabbits pound on the ground with their hind legs and cause earthquakes," and when lightning kills some wolves, "this was also blamed on the rabbits, for it is well known that lettuce-eaters cause lightning." The other animals ("who lived at a great distance") discourage the rabbits from escaping: " 'You must stay where you are and be brave. This is no world for escapists. If the wolves attack you, we will come to your aid, in all probability.' " After a flood kills more wolves, rabbits are again blamed, "for it is well known that carrot-nibblers with long ears cause floods. The wolves descended on the rabbits, for their own good, and imprisoned them in a dark cave, for their own protection." Thurber may have in mind Byron's "Destruction of Sennacherib": "The Assyrian came down like the wolf on the fold" (the predatory monarch being visualized as a wolf). The cave here is clearly the belly of the wolves; compare the similar cave in "La Belle Dame."

The rabbits are vegetarians ("lettuce-eaters," "carrot-nibblers")—that is, they are *by definition* harmless. But reality is constituted as a place of primal violence, as nature's catastrophes indicate. Hence only the violent thrive—those "fitted to survive," in Darwin's terms—meaning that they correlate with the violence nature displays. Furthermore, good and evil, the power to decide what is done and what ought to be done, and even the use of language, are all determined by one's place on the eater-eaten axis. Those who do the eating decide what is good and what is bad. They are the ones who determine the meaning of words themselves, as the wolves ironically indicate when they repeat the warning the other animals give the rabbits. Thus the wolves explain that the rabbits have been eaten.

> And since they had been eaten the affair was a purely internal matter. But the other animals warned that they might possibly unite against the wolves unless some reason was given for the destruction of the rabbits. So the wolves gave them one. "They were trying to escape," said the wolves, "and, as you know, this is no world for escapists."[5]

Food and eating are enclosed within the power relation of predator and prey. Thurber's moral, "Run, don't walk to the nearest desert island," reveals the panic that the fable expresses and that the power poetics of eating manifest. Especially in eating disorders, food implies the relation of predator and prey. It is interesting that this is the basic paradigm of power relations in society, as Machiavelli signals with his fox and lion emblems.

In this semiosis of power relations, anorexia nervosa is both an attempt to conform to the existing order of control and, more deeply, an intense protest against those relations: a protest fatal for a shocking number of people. Such a death is suicidal exactly in the way the death of a political protestor who fasts to death is suicidal. The anorexic woman withdraws from food not merely to fulfill a cultural ideal of thinness and self-control but also to defy and ridicule that cultural ideal and the control-power it articulates. Thus there is a close link between anorexia as religious observance and anorexia as pathology. Both imply an attempt to escape the eater-eaten cycle of the world of compulsion, of generating beings-that-die and feeding dying flesh with the dead flesh of animals.

For example, as Judith Van Herik puts it, in "[Simone] Weil's science of the supernatural, eating the food of this world strengthens precisely what must be killed, so that, in the other realm, the looking soul will eat light."[6] Note the way eating is a synecdoche for the life cycle and the fallen world of contingency in which the life cycle plays itself out. To reject food = rejecting the life cycle = rejecting the fallen world (i.e., sin and tyrannical power relations) = becoming one with God. In Weil's view, says Van Herik, "eating and being eaten in this world make one part of the natural system of impurity and force. Then one is inedible to God and unable to eat God, who is the only proper eaten and the only proper food. But if one refuses power, one may, by looking and waiting, become edible for God. Then God will feed the soul and use it to nourish others."[7] What Weil implies is that ultimately eating—and being eaten—are psychologically and symbolically the same act. If one eats, one will be eaten. To stop eating is to escape the body that worms destroy, to become in effect what Saint Paul called a "spiritual body."

By contrast, the eating disorder of compulsive eating—traditionally known as gluttony—is a displacement of pride: the appropriation of more food than a person requires or than the power structure allows. Undereating suggests self-abnegation; "gluttony" suggests self-aggrandizement. The original glutton was Eve, the first act of gluttony being her appropriation of forbidden fruit. The compulsion to eat that her act illustrates implies a magic food object, a forbidden fruit of knowledge, used to achieve a freer and more powerful existence. Medieval writing—for example, Chaucer, Langland, Gower, and the anonymous "Wynnere and Wastour"—is full of the danger of gluttony, one of the Seven Deadly Sins. Gluttony is lethal in Homer, as the fate of the sailors who eat the cattle of Helios and of the suitors who eat Odysseus's substance shows. Knowing when to eat and when to abstain is literally vital information. Stealing food is the archetypal crime; it is so prominent in the Bible that even Byron, in reworking the story of Cain and Abel, focuses on food. Byron's Cain offers the wrong food to God—fruits and vegetables, food of power-inferior status. Abel is smarter; his offer of throat-cut lambs is welcomed by God. Cain deprives God of his proper food—flesh, in the death of a living being—and is therefore effectively stealing from God. By so doing, he defies/threatens God's power. To this God, he is extremely dangerous. Eating disorders often display odd religious links.

Like addiction, compulsive eating signifies enslavement, a loss of independent identity that appears as obsession. Obsessiveness characterizes anorexia too.[8] Like every aspect of food symbolism, compulsive eating is overdetermined. It suggests not only enslavement but a yearning to change the self from one form to another, to gain the magic metamorphosis-power implicit in food, thereby escaping the abhorred identity that generates the compulsion in the first place. The compulsion to eat is actually repressed desire and so, like anorexia, is paradoxical. It expresses wishes, while denying them and displacing the pain of frustration. "The binge seems to numb all feeling" comment Lisa Thornton and Richard DeBlassie.[9] Ceasing to satisfy hunger, food becomes purely semiotic, a cipher standing for power. One has "difficulty discriminating between the internal stimuli associated with anxiety and those associated with hunger."[10] By (over)eating, one makes up a deficiency of emotion or spirit. The paradox involved has horrifying depths: overeating is compulsive but never satisfies.

Eating itself has a compulsive aspect, for one absolutely *must* eat if one is to continue living. Living and eating are in metaphoric relation: to live = to eat; to eat = to live. One lives to eat because one eats (in order) to live. This chiasmus is the topic of a charged discussion in the mad tea-party scene of *Alice in Wonderland,* which is a work full of food as a power token and the predator/prey relation as paradigm for power relations in general. Eating is a way of perpetuating identity and therefore has a compulsive force identical to that of the fear of death; if one stops eating one dies. So the underlying logic is that if one eats constantly one lives forever, just as a witch lives for ever by consuming the correct food. One tames or controls death (and its surrogate time) by compulsive eating. The "madness" of the March Hare and his Hatter ally is thus the terror of time running out; their compulsive eating underlines the panic. Eating disorders are not mere madness; they extend sanctioned eating practices, like dieting to keep weight down or eating simply to feel good. That is, they make explicit certain assumptions that are already implicit in social praxis.

It is no accident that the first thing we read about in Bram Stoker's *Dracula* (1897) is food. The novel is written in the key, so to speak, of food symbolism, food being the locus of power in a most complex way in this case. The imagery of predator/prey is the expanded social context of food, and Dracula naturally visualizes himself as predator, a wolf or vampire bat, for he is a predator; he epitomizes the hunting impulse that is characteristic of aristocrats. The aristocrat is constituted as a hunter, one who feeds on others. By consuming the life-essence of his female victims (blood), Dracula reproduces himself indefinitely, just as his female victims, now vampires, reproduce themselves by consuming male blood. The subtextual sexuality in acts of eating — exciting much critical comment — is actually indicated by the text itself. Reproduction is by eating, not by sex. Dracula is a displacement of the Tricky Female. The female vampires Harker meets display the Tricky Female symbolism discussed earlier. Harker is obsessed/entranced by their beauty. He yields eagerly to the "advances" of one whose "sweetness" of voice is emphasized, as is her sweetness of breath: "Sweet it was in one sense, honey-sweet, and sent the same tingling through the nerves as her voice, but with a bitter underlying the sweet, a bitter offensiveness, as one smells in blood."[11] Food is not a physiological object in literature, but a unit of imagination that in turn is generated less individually than socially, within a framework of power relations.

Ironically, the Count's food is compulsive. It indicates the dependence of the predator on his prey, a subtextual weakness. Dracula has reached a point where his food no longer satisfies and is modulating into a pure metaphor for ambition, in this case world-ruling domination. His periods of fasting are assimilated to traditional religion, for he requires sanctified earth to rest in. The Count is a metaphor for an obsolete religious vision, as implied by the novel's compensatory stickily religious traditionalism. Only a superstitious religion can dissolve a superstitious monster. *Dracula* shows how central food is to power relations and to religious feeling (especially concerning sacrifice). The possibility that the vampire legend is based on the rare disorder known as porphyria, which involves a craving for blood, suggests the powerful impact eating disorders have on culture.

The power poetics of compulsive eating are usefully summed up by C. S. Lewis's familiar *The Lion, the Witch, and the Wardrobe* (1950), in which a girl and a boy separately enter another world through a magic wardrobe. In the story lines of both, food is significant. Lucy, in the snowy woods of Narnia, meets a faun, which takes her to its cave and feeds her ("a nice brown egg, lightly boiled, . . . sardines on toast, and then buttered toast, and then toast with honey, and then a sugar-topped cake").[12] Metaphorically he is seducing her, as one might expect given his generic identity (faun); the appearance of food/drink is a natural appetizer to seduction. Then, conscience-stricken, he discloses that he is a spy paid to capture little girls, having never actually met one. He guiltily abandons his plot. For Lewis, the male version of the seduction story is invalid; males do not, so to speak, illegitimately prey on females. The food is wholesome food.

In the second case, a boy, Edmund, meets an evil queen in her sleigh, like Andersen's Snow Queen. She invites him into her sleigh and offers a delicious drink, then his favorite food. "Instantly there appeared a round box, tied with green silk ribbon, which, when opened, turned out to contain several pounds of the best Turkish Delight. Each piece was sweet and light to the very centre and Edmund had never tasted anything more delicious" (28). This food is typical of the Tricky Female, for that is what the Queen is. She is in effect seducing the male—taking control of him—and she does so by feeding him magic food:

> While he was eating the Queen kept asking him questions. At first Edmund tried to remember that it is rude to speak with one's mouth full, but soon he forgot about this and thought only of trying

> to shovel down as much Turkish Delight as he could, and the more he
> ate the more he wanted to eat, and he never asked himself why the
> Queen should be so inquisitive. She got him to tell her [everything].
> (28–29)

As he takes her food into his body, the Queen takes information out of the
boy. The two activities are really the same process. Her feeding him (with
food) is really his feeding her (with power). The accompaniment to this false
food is elaborate talk of love. Thus the Queen says she wishes to adopt
Edmund and to make him her consort. Later she tries to kill him in a ritual
sacrifice. She is in short a liar, a manipulator of language. False food = lying
language = loss of control = compulsion = death.

> At last the Turkish Delight was all finished and Edmund was
> looking very hard at the empty box and wishing that she would ask
> him whether he would like some more. Probably the Queen knew
> quite well what he was thinking; for she knew, though Edmund did
> not, that this was enchanted Turkish Delight and that anyone who
> had once tasted it would want more and more of it, and would even,
> if they were allowed, go on eating it till they killed themselves. But
> she did not offer him any more. (29)

She does, however, promise him more—*after* he has completed the task she
needs him for. He begs. "Just one piece of Turkish Delight" more, he pleads
(31). She refuses, and laughs in his face. The scene epitomizes the power
relations here. The Tricky Female controls the male by manipulating his
desire; he becomes her slave. The desire becomes compulsion.

As part of the same process, the boy becomes obsessed. He can think
of nothing but magic food ("he still wanted to taste that Turkish Delight
again more than he wanted anything else" [33]), and so he becomes
dependent totally on her, the sole source. Afterward, ordinary food fails to
satisfy. Eating her food is to become one with her. "He had the look of one
who has been with the Witch and eaten her food," comments a character
(68). To eat her food = to do her will. The power relations are neatly
constituted by addiction to a particular food item, a food that is both "simply
irresistible," as the Pepsi ads have claimed, and harmful too. (Advertising is
obsessed with the motif of the magic food-object the consumption of which
transforms the eater into a superior being: beer for males, and cake for
females, gives a person magic sex appeal—a modern variant on the elixir of

love motif. Candy is magic—the food of the gods of beauty, youth, and sex power.)

With remarkable consistency this Queen also plays the Tricky Female role in *The Magician's Nephew* (1955), where she tempts a boy to eat from the Tree of Life—without permission. Fortunately he refrains. To eat from the tree would mean entering the realm of life-in-death. Lewis dwells on how desirable the fruit is, how it is almost "irresistible." In his *Silver Chair* (1953), a similar evil female, again in the shape of a lovely lady, encourages two children and their companion to visit the "Gentle Giants"—who turn out to be cannibals, as her punning and deceitful language reveals. As Kate Ellis puts it, "Speech from a position of power *constitutes* social reality, rather than describing what is already there."[13] The control of language and the control of food correlate: both execute power. In children's literature the power symbolism of food is clear, dramatic, and extremely frequent. But it is also more important in literature generally than commonly recognized.

In Lewis, Lucy is seduced by a male who abandons his seduction; it is immoral. By contrast, Edmund is seduced by a Tricky Female who embodies evil. Food is used in both cases, but it is effectual only when employed by the female figure, as bait. Food is an extension of women. To fall under the spell of food is to fall on the ladder of power relations. Abstaining from food is not only virtuous but safe, and not only safe but empowering. The greatest danger is a subordinate figure who does not know her place in the scheme of things. The power of the powerful is above all the command of food. Subordination, by contrast, is supplying food, and ultimately, when the power relations are condensed a little further, to be food oneself. Power is thus paradoxically the manipulation of *other* people's power.

It is useful to compare *The Lion, the Witch, and the Wardrobe* with its source, E. Nesbit's "The Aunt and Amabel" in her collection *The Magic World* (1912). Nesbit, a Fabian socialist with both feminist and occult interests, is the immediate influence behind Lewis's Narnia books, both plot and image. In "The Aunt and Amabel" Amabel enters a magic land through a wardrobe and loving people welcome her. These "People Who Understand"[14] help to reconcile her and her aunt after Amabel had been punished for damaging a flowerbed. Amabel boards a train that supplies magically her favorite food (*"Whatyouwantoeat"*—*"Whatyouwantodrink"*). In Lewis the favored-food motif is part of a witch's program to seduce/enslave a young male; Nesbit uses the theme of the instant gratification of desire to articulate reconciliation. Magic food here is a communion motif. It marks a different complex, one that informs another of Keats's trance-poems, "The Eve of St. Agnes":

Freely giving
Releasing the past
Equalizing
Validating desire
Love as mutual trust (whether sexual or familial love)
Power (as liberation, not domination)

Lewis was a belligerently orthodox Christian. Human desire, and women, are devalued within a fixed hierarchy surmounted by an external, emphatically male God. In Nesbit, *human* (not divine) reconciliation is primary.[15] For her, the working model of such reconciliation is the relationship between mother and child — the mother who gives freely, the child who accepts gratefully. This provides a model for human relations, not a hierarchical order but mutual nurturance/dependency, emotional as well as physical. The compulsion to eat becomes the locus of interdependence, not a means of control operating externally, but opportunity for mutual support. Similarly, the Gospels visualize Jesus serving his followers and supplying them with food. He takes the power-subordinate role as a way to reconstitute divinity as a source of unlimited abundance, as a force of life-energy that serves, feeds, heals, and redeems, not as an external compulsion that feeds on inferiors.

This food has an apocalyptic context of symposium, communion, and paradise. The imagery of having the food one likes best when one wants it — food that is a crystal of life-power and hence a participation in the divine — is probably the kernel of paradisal visions. Compulsive food is typically sweet and false (in the sense of poisonous or harmful). By contrast, the delicious food of Paradise is not compulsive but a perfect attunement of the rhythm of life-in-time. It is interesting that C. S. Lewis also illustrates this perception of what good is, drawing on Romantic poetry, especially Shelley, in his superb science fiction fantasy of Paradise, *Voyage to Venus* (1944). In *Voyage to Venus*, compulsive eating is a paradigm of evil, a way to show how evil functions. Compulsive eating is a need to *repeat* satisfaction — that is, to manipulate one's experience as a kind of external owner. Evil may therefore be redefined: it is not disobeying authority but the itch to control. This compulsion is inherently self-defeating because by its very nature satisfaction cannot be controlled. The struggle to control stops life-in-time and so results in life-in-death, a state that is central to our topic, as Keats's poem immediately made clear. Clearly, compulsive eating is impossible in a true paradise, where food is freely available and there is no need to fight others for it or to hoard it. Paradisal food marks an end to compulsion, an end to struggle and unjust power relations. Furthermore, liberated from the anxieties of external contingency, the self attunes itself—as the infant does—to its own spontaneous needs and wishes, its own presence as life-in-time, the state Buddhists call "mindfulness" or "attention."

As a corollary, Hell is where eating is pure compulsion without satisfaction, as expressed by the myth of Tantalus, or where one is eaten, cannibalism being traditionally the most shocking theme in literature. In Dante, Satan is the incarnation of evil. It is significant that he is depicted as eating endlessly, clearly without satisfaction; the ultimate image of compulsive eating and the deepest that the logic of visualization takes us in this subject. No image is more appalling than to be eaten alive, hence the numinous horror of the shark (to a lesser extent of the grizzly bear). (In earlier culture, the horror would be the tiger or lion; and in myth it would be sea and land monsters, like the great fish that swallows Jonah, or Humbaba in the *Epic of Gilgamesh*.)

Paradisal food would be desired, but not compulsively. It would not require killing an animal. Coming from a plant, it would appear as a willing gift, not something extorted from the plant, and hence respecting the divine life in all things. (This is the feminist subtext of the passage in *Paradise Lost* that Keats replicates in "La Belle Dame.") Such food would be a liberation from eating disorders because it would be a liberation from power relations conceived as the controlling/consuming of others.

Notes

1. My "Food and Power," *Mosaic* 20 (Summer 1987): 37–55, explores food as a power token. The present chapter extends its analysis.

2. On the figure of the Tricky Female, see Barbara Fass, *La Belle Dame sans Merci and the Aesthetics of Romanticism* (Detroit: University of Michigan Press, 1974). See also my "Female Emancipation in Romantic Narrative," *Women's Studies* 18 (Summer/Fall 1990): 1–21, and "Romantic Desire," *San Jose Studies* 16 (Fall 1990): 65–79.

3. Hilde Bruch, *The Golden Cage: The Enigma of Anorexia* (New York: Random House, 1979), 10. Harrison Pope and James Hudson survey theories of compulsive eating in their *New Hope for Binge Eaters: Advances in the Understanding and Treatment of Bulimia* (New York: Harper & Row, 1984), 67–88; in psychoanalytic theory, eating disorders express unconscious anxieties of "oral impregnation" (ibid., 76–77). "Theorists of different orientations share the belief that at the core of disordered eating lie identity conflict, low self-esteem, powerlessness, lack of self-acceptance, and anger" (Maria Root, "Disordered Eating in Women of Color," *Sex Roles* 12 [December 1990]: 534); powerlessness is the key. Ironically, "despite research efforts

over many years and enormous sums of money, . . . both the cause and the control of obesity remain obscure" (Sandra Harber, "Obesity: The Psychology of a Multifaceted Volitional Disorder," in *Behavior in Excess: An Examination of Volitional Disorders,* ed. S. Joseph Mule [New York: The Free Press, 1981], 209). Real understanding of overeating may be unacceptable—hence impossible—to existing power relations/values.

4. Joan Jacobs Brumberg, *Fasting Girls: The Emergence of Anorexia Nervosa as a Modern Disease* (Cambridge, Mass.: Harvard University Press, 1988), 35. The paradoxes of anorexia are explored by Angelyn Spignesi, *Starving Women* (Dallas: Spring Publications, 1983). Fasting as (1) religious expression and (2) sign of power-subordination is ancient. "To the Jews, fasting is an intimate part of their compact with God, an expression of mourning, an expression of acceptance, an expression of . . . oneness with all other Jews" (Eric Rogers, *Fasting: The Phenomenon of Self-Denial* [New York: Thomas Nelson, 1976], 40). "In the history of female fasting behavior, the nineteenth century was a crucial divide. . . . Food refusal was transformed from a legitimate act of personal piety into a symptom of disease" (Brumberg, *Fasting Girls,* 98; see also Elaine Showalter, *The Female Malady: Women, Madness, and English Culture, 1830–1980* [New York: Pantheon, 1985]). The transfer of anorexia from religion to pathology coheres with the medicalization of women in the nineteenth century—e.g., the "rest cure," clinical clitorodectomy, and the displacement of midwife by obstetrician; see Barbara Ehrenreich and Deirdre English, *For Her Own Good* (New York: Doubleday, 1978).

5. *The Thurber Carnival* (New York: Dell, 1946), 265.

6. Judith Van Herik, "Simone Weil's Religious Imagery: How Looking Becomes Eating," in *Immaculate and Powerful: The Female in Sacred Image and Social Reality,* ed. Clarissa Atkinson et al. (Boston: Beacon Press, 1985), 274.

7. Ibid., 278.

8. See Marilyn Lawrence, *The Anorexic Experience* (London: W. H. Freeman, 1984), 21–25.

9. Lisa Thornton and Richard DeBlassie, "Treating Bulimia," *Adolescence* 24 (December 1989): 634.

10. A. W. Logue, *The Psychology of Eating and Drinking* (New York: W. H. Freeman, 1986), 174. "Most bulimics experience cognitive distortions relating to food" (Thornton and DeBlassie, "Treating Bulimia," 631). A common symptom of eating disorders is body-image distortion (see my "Food and Power," 37).

11. Bram Stoker, *Dracula* (1897; New York: Oxford University Press, 1983), 38.

12. C. S. Lewis, *The Lion, the Witch, and the Wardrobe* (Harmondsworth: Penguin, 1960), 12. Subsequent references to this work are given in the text. Compare E. Nesbit, "The Aunt and Amabel," in *The Magic World* (New York: Penguin, 1980).

13. Kate Ellis, "Fatal Attraction," *Journal of Sex Research* 27 (1990): 115.

14. Nesbit, "The Aunt and Amabel," 231.

15. I analyze the complex relation here in "What C. S. Lewis Took from E. Nesbit," *Children's Literature Quarterly,* in press.

MEDEA AND BELOVED:

Self-Definition and Abortive Nurturing in Literary Treatments of the Infanticidal Mother

Lillian Corti

Toni Morrison's award-winning novel *Beloved* and the *Medea* by Euripides are both based on stories about women who kill their own children. Although the novel deals with a historical event and the tragedy deals with mythical material, both works are set in social contexts in which slavery is practiced.[1] Each depicts the psychological experience of the protagonist as one in which the self is attacked by a part of itself. Like Medea, the character Sethe seems to be "invaded" by a figure from her own past and sometimes seems unprepared to chart a path from the present to the future. In both characters, self-definition is achieved when the conflict with the "invader" is resolved and the protagonist can move ahead into a new life. And in both cases the course of the crisis is articulated in terms of alimentary disorders.

Medea and *Beloved* are each works in which social patterns of disruptive nurturing are inseparable from the problem of diffuse ego boundaries in the individual. The differences between the ancient and modern treatments of thematic elements may be considerable, but they are relative in quality, not absolute. Whereas in the course of the Euripidean drama Medea goes from a melancholy state of fasting to an exuberant anticipation of feasting, the act of infanticide in the novel is preceded by a celebratory feast and followed eventually by a period of wasting away which has the quality of expiatory grief. The crises of conscience both Medea and Sethe suffer seem related to the effects of mourning, but Medea resorts to violence as a way out of her misery, and Sethe is engulfed by a tide of grief that becomes swollen and chronic in the wake of violence. The differences between the two works encourage speculation on the exigencies of form: the art of Euripides may seem to reflect the structured order of the masters, while that of Morrison reflects the relaxed effusions of the liberated slaves. But such neat categories are problematic.

The order of tragedy is not so controlled as one might think, and the freedom of prose narrative is not so unlimited either. Euripides was criticized in antiquity for the episodic and spectacular quality of his drama,[2] and the nineteenth-century slave narratives that Morrison studied in preparing to write *Beloved* were so likely to be criticized as "improbable" and "inflammatory" by contemporary readers that the writers of those autobiographical accounts subjected themselves to a rigorous process of self-censorship in order to avoid offending an essentially white middle-class reading public. Morrison's insistence that her own job is to rip away "that veil drawn over 'proceedings too terrible to relate' "[3] suggests a comparison between the role of the writer and the role of such tragic figures as Tiresias or Cassandra. The distance between ancient form and modern expression is great but not insurmountable.

The texture of Morrison's fiction leaves little doubt that she is quite conversant with the world of ancient tragedy. The image of the sow eating her own litter, described by the girl, Denver,[4] recalls the image of the pregnant hare being devoured by the eagle in the choral ode of the *Agamemnon*[5] as surely as the image of the infant Denver taking "her mother's milk right along with the blood of her sister" recalls the blood-stained milk of Clytemnestra's dreadful dream (Aeschylus, *Libation Bearers*, 533). The roles of Stamp Paid and Baby Suggs seem curiously reminiscent of Euripides' Tutor and of his Nurse. Like Medea or Agamemnon—or, for that matter, any tragic "hero"—Sethe could be charged with bringing her misery on herself through "her outrageous claims, her self-sufficiency" (171). Her "hubris" is resented by the women of Cincinnati, who play a role comparable to that of Euripides' chorus of Corinthian women. Sometimes they participate in the tragic action, sometimes they comment on it. In any case, documentation of textual resonances of tragedy in Morrison's novel would be an exercise in superfluity. The affinity between *Medea* and *Beloved* depends on the most essential of formal considerations: the two works share the same basic plot.

Aristotle called plot "the first essential and the soul of a tragedy" and insisted that "character comes second" (*Poetics,* 1450a). Although, in keeping with the conventions of fiction, the portrait of Sethe is developed in much greater detail than that of Medea, Morrison is no more inclined than Euripides to dismiss the crime of infanticide as a function of individual peculiarity. Instead, the elements of character—in the novel as well as in the tragedy—are arranged so that they illuminate what John Jones calls "the lost human relevancies of action."[6] Discussing the moral quality of tragic action, Jones says that "revealing a moral choice means, for Aristotle, declaring the moral character of an act in a situation where the act itself does not make this clear" (33). On the basis of such evidence as Sethe's claim that the first beating she took was the last (202), it might be quite possible to eke out an argument that her suffering is the result of her "hubris." Such a tactic would have the dubious effect of sanctioning opinions expressed by the women of Cincinnati, who are implicated in Sethe's "crime." But the real meaning of Sethe's refusal to be beaten can be grasped only with reference to the "tragic" action to which it refers. Spoken eighteen years after she killed a child who was about to be taken back into slavery, these words reveal a riveting degree of moral resolution; it is as if Sethe were to say that she would do it all again. Unlike Euripides' Jason or Morrison's schoolteacher, who whimper and complain about disasters they caused, Sethe and Medea display the ability to accept responsibility for the consequences of their actions. Despite the obvious disparity in rank between Morrison's former slaves and the exalted figures of tragedy, Medea and Sethe both conform to Aristotle's conception of the tragic hero in that they are mortals "who are neither outstanding in virtue and righteousness" and in that they fall into misfortune neither through wickedness nor through vice (*Poetics,* 1453a). In either case, the act of infanticide results not so much from "excess" on the part of the character who commits it as it does from the institutional "deficiencies" of societies founded on the operation of abortive nurturing.

If there is anything that does not distinguish either Sethe or Medea from her peers it is the fact of having killed a child. The banality of child-murder is perhaps most evident in the world of *Beloved.* Sethe owes her very life to the circumstance that she is the only one of the many children born to her mother that the woman chose to keep. Loath to nurture infants conceived as a result of forced relations with various white masters, Sethe's mother kept only the child she conceived by a black man. In this, Sethe's mother resembles the woman Ella, of whom we are told "her puberty was spent in a house where she was shared by father and son, whom she called 'the lowest yet' " (256) and that she had delivered but would not nurse a hairy white thing, fathered by the "lowest yet," which "lived five days never making a sound" (259). We are given to understand, moreover, that these accounts of slavewomen unwilling to raise children for hated masters are only the tip of the iceberg. More horrible than any particular incident of child murder is the scrap of "red ribbon knotted around a curl of wet wooly hair, clinging to its bit of scalp," which Stamp Paid fishes out of the river in the course of an ordinary workday (180). A world where such trophies may be found for the trouble of bending over is by definition a world in which children can be killed with impunity.

The world of the ancient Greeks was indeed one in which children were regularly killed or left to die. The most famous of all ancient tragedies is that of Oedipus, who was set out to die soon after he was born. When, after the murder of his sons, Jason indignantly taunts Medea with the declaration that "there is no Greek woman who would have dared such deeds,"[7] the statement is replete with dramatic irony because the text of the *Medea* is full of references to other mythical tales in which parents murder their children. The most conspicuous example is that of Ino (1248), who tried to kill her stepchildren and later killed her own son in a fit of madness.[8] The choral tribute to Erechtheus (824–25) recalls an Athenian king who sacrificed a daughter for military gain much as Agamemnon is said to have sacrificed Iphigeneia. With regard to murdered infants in particular, infanticide was not officially condemned as murder until 374 A.D.,[9] and Lloyd de Mause observes: "The image of Medea hovers over childhood in antiquity, for here myth only reflects reality."[10]

In *Beloved,* as in *Medea,* child murder is a spectacular individual reaction to flagrantly abusive customs. The act of infanticide is, in both cases, provoked by a previous interruption of the chain of nourishment that normally links the mother to the community as surely as it links the child to the mother. Not only has Sethe's milk been stolen in the "alimentary" rape performed on her by the nephews of schoolteacher, but she herself has also been deprived of her own mother's milk and given to a wet-nurse—whose job it was to nurse her, providing the woman still had enough milk left when she had finished feeding the master's children: "The little whitebabies got it first and I got what was left. Or none. There was no nursing milk to call my own" (200). The pain Sethe endures at the hands of the nephews leads her to the murder her own infant daughter because it confirms her resolve that "nobody will ever get my milk no more except my children" (200), but she does not completely understand the extent of what was done to her and to her children until years later, when she learns from Paul D. that her husband witnessed her humiliation and probably died because of it. Sethe's children have been deprived not only of their mother's milk but also of their father's support.

In that they have lost their father, the situation of Sethe's children resembles that of Medea's sons, about whom their mother complains: "Their father chooses to make no provision for them" (343). Although Jason insists that he is repudiating his wife so that his family may "live well, / And not be short of anything" (559–60), his claim is unconvincing. He expresses doubts of his own about whether the king will allow his children to remain in town (941), and his fiancée turns away in disgust when the little boys show up for a visit. The gratuitous antipathy of the princess toward Jason's sons lends credence to Medea's insistence that the lives of the children cannot be vouchsafed by leaving them in Corinth to be the "prey of her enemies' insolence" (1060–61).

The general problem of stepparents is implicit in the question of who will provide for Medea's children when she goes into exile. Such details as the allusion to Ino and the description of Creusa recall widespread misgivings among the ancient Greeks about the wisdom of entrusting children to the care of a spouse who was not their actual parent. The most self-sacrificing of all Greek wives was Alcestis, who on her deathbed warned her husband in no uncertain terms against the dangers of remarrying: "For the new-come step-mother hates the children born / to a first wife, no viper could be deadlier" (*Alcestis*, 309–10). Stepfathers as well as stepmothers represented a threat to the children of a former union. The survival of a Greek child was so much dependent on the willingness of a man to provide support that marriage was regarded as a "yoke" to be born by the father.[11] The general reluctance of men to bear the "yoke" for another man's children is witnessed by myths in which children of a first marriage are killed by a woman's second husband. Thus, after killing Clytemnestra's first husband in battle, Agamemnon also killed the child of that first marriage; Clytemnestra's first experience of her ill-fated second marriage was to watch her captor smash the infant's brains against a rock (*Iphigeneia in Aulis*, 1150–52). On the subject of second "marriages," it is worth noting that Sethe's lover, Paul D., is in a position analogous to that of the ancient stepfather, and his relationship with Sethe's daughters is hardly idyllic. He has been in Sethe's kitchen for only a matter of minutes when he is attacked by the ghost of her dead baby. He launches a rigorous counterattack, but soon after he routs the possessive poltergeist the incarnate otherworldly competition for the bounty of Sethe's love shows up in the person of Beloved.

An embodiment of the suffering Sethe endured in slavery, Beloved is also a walking collection of "eating disorders." Before actually appearing in the flesh, she has manifested her presence primarily as a kind of nagging indigestion that is evident in occasional "gusts of sour air" (4). Beloved shows up in front of 124 Bluestone Road in the grip of an unslakeable thirst, which corresponds to an overwhelming incontinence on Sethe's part (51). In the weeks that follow, Beloved eats and sleeps a good deal, continually craves sweets and liquids, generates piles of wash by soiling her undergarments and bedclothes, and inspires Denver to practice the maternal arts of "nursing" her sister and doing her laundry (54). None of these "disorders" would be worthy of the name if they occurred in an infant, but in an adult they might be indications of anything from infection to diabetes. Thus Beloved's "condition" has the interesting effect of suggesting that certain "eating disorders" are integral to the state of infancy. Moreover, it is a malady for which mothers and sisters have notably greater tolerance than "stepfathers." Sethe and Denver may engage in sympathetic speculation about whether Beloved suffers from "cholera" or "starvation," but Paul D. chafes with impatience over the girl's excesses:

> It was as though sweet things were what she was born for. Honey as well as the wax it came in, sugar sandwiches, the sludgy molasses gone hard and brutal in the can, lemonade, taffy, and any type of dessert Sethe brought home from the restaurant. She gnawed a cane stick to flax and kept the strings in her mouth long after the syrup had been sucked away. Denver laughed, Sethe smiled and Paul D. said it made him sick to his stomach. (55)

From the cornucopia of foods and compendium of eating disorders Morrison supplies, it is a long way to the single, measured phrase of the Euripidean Nurse: "She lies without food and gives herself up to suffering" (24). Medea languishes, at the beginning of the tragedy, in a kind of self-imposed deprivation that seems diametrically opposed to the greedy excesses of Beloved, whose appetite for such commodities as air, water, and food soon extends to an acquired interest in having sex with her mother's lover. But there is no question of an equivalence between the character Beloved and the ancient protagonist Medea. As an issue of the event that Stamp Paid calls "the Misery," Beloved would seem comparable to the Aeschylean Furies, whose function it is to punish those who have spilled the blood of kin. The effects of her presence are described to the reader before she ever shows up as "the baby's fury, rage" (5). A more appropriate analogy with Medea's dejection at the beginning of the tragedy may be found in the image of Sethe, as seen through Denver's eyes, when she has worn herself down to skin and bone by grieving for the child she has killed: "The flesh between her mother's forefinger and thumb was thin as china silk and there wasn't a piece of clothing in the house that didn't sag on her" (239). We would do well to consider the reciprocal excesses of fasting and feasting that eventually bind Sethe and Beloved to one another, in the light of Hilde Bruch's assertion that the "organization of awareness of hunger . . . is the outcome of reciprocal transactional processes within the interpersonal field."[12]

In her book-length study *Eating Disorders: Obesity, Anorexia, and the Person Within*, Bruch traces pathological failures and excesses of appetite to disturbances in the relationships between children and their primary nurturers. Although the images of obesity and anorexia seem relevant to the couple, Beloved/Sethe, in which the expanding girth of one member entails the wasting away of the other, the parasitic and destructive quality of Beloved's attachment to her wretched mother suggests that the interpersonal dimensions of the general theme of eating disorders in *Beloved* converge in a particularly extreme manifestation of the theme—cannibalism.

The idea of cannibalism, as such, is conspicuously introduced, along with the word, by "schoolteacher," who comes to take Sethe and her children back to Sweet Home. The clever fellow comes up with the accusation of cannibalism in a last-ditch effort to make sense out of the dreadful act that his own activity has clearly caused: "All testimony to the results of a little so-called freedom imposed on people who needed every care and guidance in the world to keep them from the cannibal life they preferred" (151). As a projection of his own predatory procedure, schoolteacher's attribution of cannibalism to the Negroes is comparable to Jason's claim that Medea is a barbarian. While the word *barbaros* originally referred to any person who was not a Greek, and the assumption of ethnocentrism is therefore inherent in the term, Euripides seems to call the very premises of the distinction between Greek and barbarian into question. Even as he endangers the lives of his wife and children, Jason tells Medea she ought to be thankful to him for taking her to live among Greeks instead of leaving her in a barbarian home (566). The term "barbarian," like the word "cannibal," functions as a declaration of cultural superiority that authorizes the most sordid kinds of exploitation. It is precisely the smug assumptions inherent in such epithets that provoke the dreadful acts Medea and Sethe commit. Schoolteacher articulates the essence of these assumptions with notable emphasis: "They would seem to recognize the futility of outsmarting a whiteman" (148). The word "whiteman"—used like "coloredpeople" throughout the novel as a whole term with no division between adjective and noun—suggests that a "whiteman" is a breed apart from a "coloredperson," in the same way that Jason's "Greeks" assume that they are a "race" separate from "barbarians." The brutality and irresponsibility of those who enjoy the privileges of whitemen and Greeks in *Beloved* and *Medea* cast a ferociously ironic light on such terms as "cannibal" and "barbarian."

Just as Euripides tends to ask, "Who are the barbarians?" so, Morrison asks who the cannibals in the world of *Beloved* are. The theme of cannibalism is an organizing principle in this novel where black men and women are gobbled up by the rice fields, the slaughterhouses, and the restaurants that feed a hungry white nation while Sethe brings her family scraps from the white man's table. Old men and women like Stamp Paid and Baby Suggs complain of "exhausted marrow" (177, 180, 181) as if some rough beast had sucked the living tissue from their bones and left them lying around like so many empty casings. For Denver, who for years is too intimidated to leave the house, the entire world outside 124 seems to be waiting to devour her. Only hunger finally prompts her to venture forth, "ready to be swallowed up in the world" (243). The ugliest example of the people-devouring creatures who inhabit the world of *Beloved* is the Ku Klux Klan: "Desperately thirsty for black blood, without which it could not live, the dragon swam the Ohio at will" (66).

Not unlike Medea, who saved Jason from the dragon in the land of Colchis, Sethe insists on sheltering her own from the Klan-dragon. In either case, the project is laden with alimentary overtones: Medea immobilizes the dragon by feeding it a potion, and Sethe's dedication to the enterprise of nurturing Beloved is valorized by the existence of the Klan. Paul D.'s notion of "placing" the girl is foiled as much by his own apprehension about the "dragon" as it is by Sethe's insistence that feeding the girl is no problem (67). In fact, the "dragon" is only one element in a constellation of magical concerns that characterize the texts of both *Medea* and *Beloved.* The most important of these is the witch. The game of "die-witch" played by Howard and Buglar is not only a reaction to the "Misery" of which their mother is, for them, the visible agent, but also a salient aspect of the affinity between the ancient sorceress, Medea, and the modern child-murderer.

Like the hungry Furies and the bloodthirsty dragon, the witch is a cannibalistic figure. From the Baba-Yaga of Slavic folk literature who puts children in ovens and eats them,[13] to the *vehini-hai* of the Marquesans who "brews poisons" and "continually desires to eat the flesh of children,"[14] the witch has been associated with concoction of dangerous comestibles and consumption of fellow creatures. To be sure, the terror Sethe inspires in her children cannot be dismissed as an imaginary projection of the "bad mother." The two dreams that torment the ghost Beloved are dreams about exploding and about being swallowed (133). These fears are directly related to the violence she suffered at her mother's hands: when her throat was cut her blood exploded outward, and when she died the earth swallowed her up. For the world of *Beloved* is, like that of *Medea,* a place where the land is regarded as a great mother; of Paul D. we are told that "he hid in its breast, fingered its earth for food, clung to its banks to lap water and tried not to love it" (268). Furthermore, sorcery is associated not solely with the negative powers of the female figure in these works; magic is also inseparable from the positive operation of maternal love.

D. W. Winnicott has suggested that the association of magic with the operation of maternal care may actually be relative to the efficiency with which the nurturer performs: "If . . . she knows too well what the infant needs, this is magic and forms no basis for an object relationship."[15] This assertion of a connection between maternal efficiency and deficient object relations is worth exploring with regard to the paradoxical problem of mothers who kill their children even though, or *because,* they love them. The idea of prodigious nurturing capacity is certainly implicit in the ancient myth. If little is said about the way Medea treats her children before the Corinthian debacle, we may conclude that Medea's competence in this area is not questioned. All the legendary feats for which she is noted have a nurturing aspect. Whether she is putting dragons to sleep, strengthening heroes for battle, rejuvenating old men, vanquishing enemies, or restoring fertility to barren royalty, Medea accomplishes her magic by dint of substances she prepares and prescribes for internal consumption or external application. Morrison's Sethe resembles Medea most in her formidable nurturing capacities.

The escaped slavewoman's talent for feeding her own is phenomenal. Arriving in Cincinnati with the fresh wounds of a terrible beating, feet swollen and bleeding from a horrendous overland journey in the terminal days of pregnancy, poorly clad, starving, feverish, burdened with the infant born on the way, Sethe joyfully resumes the task of nursing her babies, recalling later: "When I got there, I had milk enough for all" (198). Supporting herself and her daughter on her earnings as a cook, and welcoming Paul D. and Beloved into her home, she plans a feast to celebrate the happiness they bring her: "There was no question but that she could do it. Just like the day she arrived at 124 — sure enough, she had milk enough for all" (100). The ghost of Sethe's dead baby is indeed the issue of an overwhelming grief commensurate with her mother's boundless love. When Denver remarks that the baby casts a powerful spell, Sethe replies, "No more powerful than the way I loved her" (4). In the light of Sethe's seemingly miraculous ability to feed her children in the absence of social support, the ancient assumption of the magical potential of maternal love seems to gain new meaning.

Although the term "magical" seems appropriate enough for describing the activities of "dragons," "witches," and "ghosts," many of the supernatural phenomena in *Medea* and *Beloved* are a function of economic exigencies. A skeptic might be tempted to suggest that the word "cheap" would serve as well as "magical" to describe the advantages of maternal providence. For the purposes of men like Jason and schoolteacher, such talents as Medea and Sethe display are not only "magical" but also *profitable*. According to Paul D.'s observation, the slavewoman was especially valued as "property that reproduced itself without cost" (228). While we might assume that nobody would want to nurture children in exile, indigence, or slavery, Sethe and Medea are expected to do just that. Their tormentors are encouraged to believe that such self-sacrifice on the part of mothers is "natural" because it is common. The miraculous "nature" and the extraordinary economy of maternal love actually depend on the assumption of an identity of interests between mother and child which exists between no other mortal creatures.

The textual identification of the mother with her child is implicit in the works of Euripides and Morrison under examination here. In the play, Medea often seems to be pursued by the gods as relentlessly as her children are pursued by their mother (362–63). In the novel, the "greedy ghost" (209) of Sethe's murdered child corresponds to the mind of her mother, of whom we are told that her head "is like a greedy child" in its ability to take in wretched stories as if it were a gluttonous waif who eats until it "can't hold another bite" (70). Just as Sethe's love is the instrument of magical provision for her children, so her children are sources of magic for her: "The best thing she was, was her children. Whites might dirty *her* all right, but not her best thing, her beautiful, magical best thing — the part of her that was clean" (251). These texts seem to illustrate certain clinical observations on the functional identification of maternal and infantile interests: "Just as the child does not recognize the separate identity of the mother, so the mother looks upon her child as a part of herself whose interests are identical with her own."[16] But Euripides and Morrison expose the limitations of this principle as well as its obvious "advantages."

The act of child murder is the most notorious result of identifying the mother's interests with those of the child, but the effects of life with a "force of nature" take their toll on the survivors of "the Misery" as well as on its casualties in Morrison's novel; we are given to understand that Denver is a "ridiculously dependent child" (57). Her fragility seems directly proportionate to her mother's ferocious insistence on protecting her; on this score, Paul D. learns more than he wants to know the first time he and Denver get into each other's hair. A quarrel with Denver is as good as a quarrel with her mother. When Paul D. asks Sethe, rather defensively, "What's going to happen when you die?" Sethe parries with a remarkable assertion: "Nothing! I'll protect her while I'm live and I'll protect her when I ain't" (45).

An invented character who is essential to the resolution of the fictional plot, Paul D. provides something of what Aegeus seems to represent for Medea in the ancient tragedy—a way out of an intolerable situation. That rarest of entities in any context, Paul D. is a good man, willing and able to nurture other people. Just as Sethe is "licked, tasted, eaten by Beloved's eyes" (57), so do her own eyes enjoy looking into Paul D.'s face (46) as if the emotional resources going out to her hungry children might be replenished by the intimate bond that is textually expressed in terms of visual "nourishment." Although Paul D. is a devoted lover and a supportive friend, his relationship with Sethe is most interesting in that it demonstrates the impossibility of the kinds of expectations often imposed on maternal figures.

Having accepted with philosophical resignation the evidence of Sethe's selfless love for her daughter, and even her presumption to protect her loved ones beyond the grave, Paul D. nevertheless recoils with horror at the "news" that Sethe has killed a child. He accuses her, in so many words, of being an animal. Knowing what he does about the fate of the various slaves at Sweet Home, he nevertheless finds it more unthinkable that she would kill her child than that she should return to slavery with her children. In his amazement he thinks: "This here new Sethe didn't know where the world stopped and she began" (164). But that is precisely the point. The "new" Sethe is exactly like the "old" Sethe!

Like the ideal traditional mother, Sethe is supposed to have perfect empathy with her children and treat them as if they were part of herself, yet she is also supposed to hand them over like so many sacks of potatoes when somebody deems that to be expedient. When Paul D. leaves her and she retreats into a world of private grief, Sethe wonders, "Would he give his privates to a stranger in return for a carving?" (203). Her question is an apt expression of the basic problem. The logic of the expectation that a woman will identify her own interests with those of her children is inconsistent with the requirement that she expose them to suffering she herself could not bear to endure. Paul D.'s rejection of Sethe on the basis of such "logic" is analogous to an incident Harriet Beecher Stowe relates in *Uncle Tom's Cabin* in the chapter entitled "Select Incidents of Lawful Trade," in which the trader Haley is surprised when a mother whose child has been stolen and sold proves so "unreasonable" as to commit suicide.[17] In either case, the mother is expected to have perfect empathy with her child during the nurturing process, and then is expected to relinquish her bond completely as soon as "rational" order requires it.

It is interesting to consider the persistent hypothesis of "identical interests" uniting the primary nurturer with the child in the light of Bruch's observation that a variety of eating disorders may develop in individuals with "diffuse ego boundaries" who "feel helpless under the influence of external forces" (Bruch, 56). That the crisis of conscience destroying Medea's appetite and inspiring her with longing for death (97) is a state in which she suffers the domination of an introjected force experienced as if it were *external* seems apparent in the agonizing soliloquy in which she repeatedly resolves to kill the children and then changes her mind. In this scene, Medea pleads with her own vindictive inclinations as if she were talking to another person: "Do not, O my heart, you must not do these things!" (1056). The word "heart" evidently stands here for the Greek *thumos,* [18] which may also mean spirit or anger or passion. In this passage, Medea's *thumos* seems to exercise an ultimately irresistible resistance to her sensual expressions of desire to indulge her own love for the children by sparing them (1069–77). Medea cringes before this "angry spirit" as if it encompassed the judgmental functions of identifications with parental figures. Her retreat before this internal urgency recalls Freud's description of the superego as being "representative of our relation to our parents."[19] The tenacity of this "angry spirit" suggests that it is the most thoroughly integrated part of herself, as well as the part most profoundly rooted in her past. It eventually wins out over the "sweet presence" (1099) of her children's lives. Thus it might be said of Medea, as of Sethe, that she "does not know where the world stops and she begins."

At the beginning of *Beloved,* Sethe seems as little inclined as Medea, in the opening lines of the tragedy, to chart a course into the future. Insisting that "today is always here, . . . tomorrow never" (60), she gives herself up to the absorbing labor of feeding her family. Consumed by such mechanical tasks as cleaning vegetables and kneading dough, she manages to avoid all conscious thoughts of the future, thinking as she prepares the bread in the restaurant that there is nothing better than "working dough" to start "the day's serious work of beating back the past" (73). Haunted by the ghost of the "Misery," she manages to avoid all conscious awareness of both past and future until Paul D. arrives on the scene and "the notion of a future with him, or for that matter without him, begins to stroke her mind" (42). Very soon after he moves in, Beloved shows up. Her arrival heralds a period of captivity to the past that threatens to engulf all who live at 124 Bluestone Road. It does not end until the women of Cincinnati tire of the "invasion" and mobilize to evict the intruder. Conspicuous among the women who finally rally to Sethe's cause is Ella, of whom we are told that she "didn't like the idea of past errors taking possession of the present" (256).

The involvement of the women of Cincinnati in Sethe's ordeal is worth noting. Although the chorus of Corinthian women is also involved in the action of the *Medea,* at least to the extent of knowing her murderous plan and doing nothing to prevent her from carrying it out, the women of Cincinnati differ from the ancient chorus in that they do not always sympathize with the protagonist. Their disapproval of the bounteous feast that Baby Suggs gives in celebration of Sethe's escape from slavery is so pronounced that they do not warn Sethe and her mother-in-law of the approaching slavecatchers. Although they do not anticipate the murder of the children, their silence, like the silence of the Corinthian women, has the effect of approving the act that precipitates the murder. If their initial involvement in Sethe's case is an indication of the communal dimensions of responsibility for certain crimes, their participation in Sethe's "liberation" from the past lends to the conclusion of the novel a mellow, comic quality that contrasts markedly with the stark outlines of the tragic denouement.

Medea's internal conflict is resolved by a process of identification with the introjected antagonist who opposes her own best impulses. This is evident both in her fulfillment of the requirement of revenge and in the nature of her escape from the scene of the crime. Seated in the dragon-chariot supplied by her grandfather, Helios, Medea has purchased her passage to the future with the bodies of her children, in whose honor she plans to institute an annual memorial festival at the temple of Hera:

> In this land of Corinth
> I shall establish a holy feast and sacrifice
> Each year to atone for the blood guilt. (1381–83)

Medea's escape from the self-destructive fasting of her crisis is contingent on the promise of perpetual intervals of feasting, which may, ironically, seem at odds with the ideal of moderation articulated by the Nurse (126–27).

Morrison suggests in several ways that Sethe has a better chance of achieving the ancient ideal of moderation than the tragic heroine. Not only is Sethe's delivery from her ghostly captor accomplished by a community of women who seem as sensible as the Euripidean Nurse, but Sethe's reaction to the "deus ex machina" that shows up at her gate is very different from Medea's reaction. When Edward Bodwin drives up in a cart on the way to search for playthings he buried long ago in the yard at 124 Bluestone Road, Sethe runs out of the house with an icepick in her hand and attacks. Although Edward Bodwin has been a benefactor to several generations of women in this house, the sight of a white man driving up to her door is in Sethe's mind so linked with the "Misery" that she panics and rushes out yelling, as she had done eighteen years earlier, "No no Nonono" (163, 262). The incident is an ironic comment on the way even the most well-meaning white people make themselves scarce in the day-to-day lives of poor black people. The fact that Sethe attacks the "whiteman" rather than petitioning him for help demonstrates a certain continuity of character. Whereas Medea's escape in the chariot of the gods symbolizes her incorporation of the brutal imperatives that have tormented her into her own scheme of values, Sethe—starving, middle-aged, and wild with grief—remains not disposed to compromise with the "enemy." Sethe remains true to herself in a way that Medea does not. While Medea proceeds into the future riding in a pompous conveyance that is quite worthy of her arrogant oppressors, Sethe resolves her internal conflict by expelling the omnivorous intruder and joining forces with a nurturing companion. Paul D. comforts the exhausted Sethe, insisting: "We need some kind of tomorrow." As if in answer to her claim that her children are the best part of herself, he assures her of her own personal value: "You your best thing, Sethe, you are" (273). As Sethe recovers, her worst fears for herself are quelled and the miserable nightmare disappears: "The girl who waited to be loved and cry shame erupts into her separate parts, to make it easy for the chewing laughter to swallow her all away" (274). The girl "who waited to be loved" was not only the hungry child Sethe buried but also her own youthful self.

I would like to conclude by noting that the "eating disorders" with which these works are concerned are of a communal order. Medea's plan to establish a ritual feast at Corinth may appear to have a meta-tragic quality if we recall that tragedies were celebrated as part of the regular annual festival in honor of the god Dionysus. Intervals of ritual feasting in traditional agricultural societies can be understood only in the context of the ever-present threat of famine in such societies. The Euripidean Nurse addresses just this point when she questions the utility of wasting the therapeutic benefit of tragic art on occasions when it is least needed—that is, in scenes of festival abundance. Speaking of the "bitter grief" to which tragedy should be the antidote, she asks:

> Yet how good
> If music could cure men of this! But why raise
> To no purpose the voice at a banquet? For *there* is
> Already abundance of pleasure for men
> With a joy of its own. (199–203)

It is as if Euripides were to observe, through the Nurse, that the tragic wisdom so much in evidence during the festive season were otherwise in abysmally short supply among his fellow citizens, who were, on the eve of the first production of the *Medea*, in 431 B.C., preparing to embark on a ruinous military campaign. The Peloponnesian War would drag on for nearly thirty years, ravaging Athens in the process.

The alternation of famine and festival is essential to the rhythm of *Beloved*, in which runaway slaves hide in caves and "fight owls for food" and a witless "coloredwoman" is "jailed and hanged for stealing ducks she believed were her own babies" (66). The name "Sweet Home" is a ferociously ironic appellation for a place where slaves who live on a diet of bread, beans, hominy, and vegetables are beaten for stealing meat. Although the worst event of Sethe's life as a slave occurs in Cincinnati, the city is nevertheless the site of festivals—the celebration given by Baby Suggs in honor of Sethe, the carnival where Paul D. takes Sethe and Denver on the day Beloved shows up, the feast Sethe prepares for her family as a demonstration of her love for Paul D. Indeed, the way Beloved flourishes while Sethe wastes away may seem to suggest an analogy, on the level of character, with the ancient opposition of periods of feasting and fasting. Embodying extremes of plenty and want, these figures may also call to mind the economic inequities that have survived the abolition of legal slavery. But the idea of "eating disorder" as emblematic of social disruption is most apparent in the texture of Morrison's novel.

Among the dreadful images that tend to recur in this text is that of Halle—the husband Sethe loses—sitting by the churn with butter smeared on his face. The face of a man grieving beyond reasonable expression, a face covered up, with eyes staring impassively, is a face that recalls the masks of ancient tragedy. The image of Halle's face smeared with butter is, moreover, always linked to that of Paul D. biting on the iron bit he was forced to wear. The double image is first introduced by Paul D. himself, who tells Sethe: "Last time I saw him he was sitting by the churn. He had butter all over his face." He also tells her: "I had a bit in my mouth" (69). The image is repeated with ever-increasing economy: "Halle's face smeared with butter and the clabber too; his own mouth jammed full of iron" (96). It finally becomes an abbreviated sign of horror that is felt but not explained because it is quite literally "too terrible to relate"—"the taste of iron, the sight of butter" (113). Symbols of a perverted distribution of resources in which people are given to eat that which is inedible and in which edible substance is wasted in lavish display, "the taste of iron, the sight of butter" articulates the insanity of a wretched social "order" in terms of eating disorder.

Notes

1. See Phillip Vellacott, *Ironic Drama: A Study of Euripides' Method and Meaning* (London: Cambridge University Press, 1975), 104. The author argues that Euripidean drama presents "two worlds living side by side: the world of free males and the world of women and slaves."

2. Aristotle, *On Poetry and Style,* ed. G.M.A. Grube (New York: Bobbs-Merrill, 1958), 31, 60, 1454a-b, 1461b.

3. Toni Morrisön, *Inventing the Truth. The Art and Craft of Memoir,* ed. William Zinsser (Boston: Houghton Mifflin Co., 1987), 110.

4. Toni Morrison, *Beloved* (New York: New American Library, 1988), 12. Unless otherwise indicated, all citations of *Beloved* refer to this edition. Page numbers are noted parenthetically in the text.

5. Aeschylus, *Oresteia,* trans. Richmond Lattimore, *The Complete Greek Tragedies,* ed. David Grene and Richmond Lattimore (Chicago: University of Chicago Press, 1953), 38, 114-21. Unless otherwise indicated, all references to ancient tragedies refer to translations in this series. Numbers indicated parenthetically refer to lines of poetry.

6. John Jones, *On Aristotle and Greek Tragedy* (New York: Oxford University Press, 1962), 33.

7. Euripides, *Medea*, trans. Rex Warner, *The Complete Greek Tragedies*, ed. David Grene and Richmond Lattimore (New York: Washington Square Press, 1967), 113, line 1339. Unless otherwise indicated, citations from *Medea* refer to lines from this text.

8. Edward Tripp, *The Meridian Handbook of Classical Mythology* (New York: Meridian, 1970), 318.

9. H. Bennett, "The Exposure of Infants in Ancient Rome," *Classical Journal* 18 (1923): 341-51.

10. Lloyd de Mause, *The History of Childhood: The Untold Story of Child Abuse* (New York: Peter Bedrick Books, 1974), 51.

11. Euripides, *Medea*. In her speech to the Corinthian women (242), Medea speaks of the husband who "lightly bears the yoke" (*zugon*), and in the episode with Aegeus she is told that he is "joined to his wife in marriage" (673). A more literal translation of the latter statement would yield "yet unyoked of marriage." The term used by the king is *azuges*, which clearly shows a root in common with the word Medea uses. See Euripides, *Medea*, ed. Alan Elliott (Oxford: Oxford University Press, 1979), 15, 38.

12. Hilde Bruch, *Eating Disorders: Obesity, Anorexia Nervosa, and the Person Within* (New York: Basic Books, 1973), 5.

13. David Bakan, *The Slaughter of the Innocents* (San Francisco: Jossey Bass, 1971), 66.

14. Helene Deutsch, *Psychology of Women* (New York: Grune & Stratton, 1945), 2:41.

15. D. W. Winnicott, as quoted by Nancy Chodorow in *The Reproduction of Mothering: Psychoanalysis and the Sociology of Gender* (Berkeley and Los Angeles: University of California Press, 1978), 84.

16. Alice Balint, as quoted in ibid., 85.

17. Harriet Beecher Stowe, *Uncle Tom's Cabin* (New York: Bantam, 1981), 114-30.

18. *Medea*, ed. Alan Elliott (Oxford, 1979), 1056.

19. Sigmund Freud, *The Standard Edition of the Complete Psychological Works of Sigmund Freud*, vol. 19: *The Ego and the Id*, trans. from the German under the general editorship of James Strachey in collaboration with Anna Freud (London: Hogarth Press, 1966-74), 36.

DOUBLE STANDARD IN THE FLESH:
Gender, Fasting, and Power in
English Renaissance Drama

Nancy A. Gutierrez

In her brief but compelling *Tragic Ways of Killing a Woman,* Nicole Loraux
persuasively suggests that gender not only determines the method of death
of Greek tragic characters, but also the cultural meaning ascribed to women
and men, and especially to women.[1] This seems to hold true for the
depiction of fasting in English Renaissance drama. Women characters undertake fasting, fully intending to die, as a way of proving themselves chaste
and loyal wives. In the world of the play, their behavior is admirable and
exemplary.

The situation changes radically when male characters fast. Whether male
characters fast as ascetic-minded scholars or as languishing courtly lovers,
they do not intend to die, and in both cases the male playwright portrays
such a decision for ascetism as abnormal and unnatural, a decision that must
be corrected, because it *dis*empowers its male practitioner either psychologically or politically and socially, if not physically.[2]

This double standard in the dramatic depictions of fasting men and
women in English Renaissance drama is even more striking in light of the

Reformation and humanist regimen of opposing excessive asceticism and advocating moderation in diet. This is a reversal of the ascetic practices of the very early Middle Ages, practices that were believed to release the soul from its earthly chains so that a closer relationship with God could be achieved.[3] In fact, Renaissance moralists explicitly discouraged extreme abstinence for the very reason that it inhibited proper worship. An *inner* abstinence was more worthy, a kind of self-regulation that resulted in spiritual rather than physical self-denial.[4] For example, William Perkins advocated a "kind of fast . . . to be vsed of all Christians, at all times"—that is "the practise of temperance and sobrietie, whereby the appetite is restrained, in the vse of meates and drinkes, that it doe not exceede moderation."[5]

This attitude toward food as advocated in religious manuals is paralleled in the more secular humanist program. For example, in his colloquies "The Godly Feast" and "The Fish Diet," Erasmus advocates a moderate diet and rejects unthinking and often unhealthy obedience to fasting laws because such legalism has nothing to do with Christian compassion. Thomas Elyot, in arguing against gluttony and for "sobriety" in his education manual for boys, adds that such a regimen enabled a man to be more healthy:

> A man having due concoction and digestion as is expedient, shall in the morning, fasting, or with a little refection, not only have his invention quicker, his judgment perfecter, his tongue readier, but also his reason fresher, his ear more attentive, his remembrance more sure, and generally all his powers and wits more effectual and in better estate, than after he hath eaten abundantly.[6]

In other words, moderation in eating maintains both the body and the mind as beautiful and *useful* creations of God. *Inward* fasting, not external fasting, pleases God. External fasting is only a tool to achieve the "humbling and casting downe of ourselues, before the high maiestie of God, with sorrow for our sinnes,"[7] and such humility is the proper foundation for Christian living. The representations of fasting men in the drama essentially support this prescriptive advice, focusing on the inhibitions such extreme behavior has on the male character's ability to live the humanist "active life," both politically and socially.

In *Love's Labor's Lost* (ca. 1595), *Hamlet* (1600), and *Measure for Measure* (1604), fasting is associated with other unnatural behaviors. In *Love's Labor's Lost,* the king of Navarre persuades his attending lords to help him make his court "a little academe / Still and contemplative in living art" (1.1.13-14).[8] Fasting is part of this studious regimen, as described by Longaville:

> 'Tis but a three years' fast:
> The mind shall banquet, though the body pine;
> Fat paunches have lean pates; and dainty bits
> Make rich the ribs, but bankrout quite the wits. (1.1.24-27)

Longaville makes eating and intellectual activity totally incompatible, opposing the moderation advocated by the humanists. Berowne, another attending lord, immediately questions the usefulness of such self-restriction, for the academe will be denying itself access to life itself, the supposed goal of its study. And although Berowne gives in to the peer pressure of the king and the other lords to commit himself to the academe, another proscription of the academe, that which bars association with women, is immediately violated because the princess of France is scheduled to visit the court on state business. Thus the play undercuts the idea that self-denial in its broadest sense can be a kind of behavior that promotes intellectual endeavor.

A different perspective is offered in *Measure for Measure* in the character of Angelo, a man who is so much given in to ascetic practices that he is unaware of the emotional side of his being. "Lord Angelo," says Lucio to Isabella, is

> a man whose blood
> Is very snow-broth; one who never feels
> The wanton stings and motions of the sense;
> But doth rebate and blunt his natural edge
> With profits of the mind: study and fast. (1.4.57-61)[9]

This assessment is echoed by the Duke (1.3.50-53) and even by Angelo himself when he is confronted by the force of his passion for Isabella (2.4.7-17, 155). This imbalance in living, the ignoring of a vital part of being human, results in Angelo's becoming a danger to himself and the community, as the realization that he has passions causes his attempted seduction of Isabella, a sign of his loss of self-government and his abuse of Vienna's government. Although the tragicomic end of the play results in a restoration of Angelo's life and the health of the community, the dramatic representation of Angelo's ascetic practices is sufficiently threatening to demonstrate the undesirability of such extreme behavior.

While these two plays present fasting as a means of reducing worldly temptation as either impossible or self-destructive, *Hamlet* parodies the courtly lover's lack of appetite in its protagonist's self-imposed "antic disposition." When Hamlet was "repell'd" by Ophelia, says Polonius, he

> Fell into a sadness, then into a fast,
> Thence to a watch, thence into a weakness,
> Thence to [a] lightness, and by this declension.
> Into the madness wherein now he raves,
> And we all mourn for. (2.2.146–51)[10]

This lovesick behavior is corroborated by Ophelia's description of Hamlet's actions in her study: his clothing is disheveled, he gazes at her longingly, he walks out of her room with his head turned backward toward her so that "He seem'd to find his way without his eyes" (2.1.95). Hamlet, the Wittenberg-trained humanist, uses courtly love behavior as a weapon in his struggle to reconcile the humanist ideal with Denmark's political and psychological corruption.

In each of these examples, fasting is an extreme to be avoided, a perversion of human behavior, for it prevents the male characters from looking outside themselves. This kind of self-involvement directly violates basic humanist philosophy, which teaches that human beings are social animals who must use their talents in the world for social benefit. According to Thomas Elyot, humanity is "a general name to those virtues in whom seemeth to be a mutual concord and love in the nature of man"—that is, benevolence, beneficence, and liberality, all virtues of self-giving.[11] Fasting upsets the balance within an individual and thus the balance within the community, as the example of Angelo perhaps best demonstrates.[12]

While the moderation prescribed in religious and humanist texts thus holds true for the depiction of fasting men in the plays of the period, it is not at all true in the case of fasting women characters. This variance from the model suggests that women are a special case in the culture, a thesis that is supported by another kind of discourse focusing on the body of a fasting woman: the sensationalistic pamphlets that describe actual "fasting girls" or "miracle maidens" of the period, from both England and the continent. Before discussing the fasting women in the drama, I examine the rhetorical strategy of these popular accounts, for the conventions of this so-called "news" genre provide a window into the presentation of the fasting women on the stage.

Although the fasting female visionaries of the late Middle Ages are absent in Renaissance England, "fasting girls" who miraculously lived without food or drink became one of the age's more popular subjects for sensationalistic pamphlets.[13] Between 1589 and 1635 at least five pamphlets were written about these women, and popular allusions occur in diaries, ballads, and plays.[14] Most often these were young women, in their late teens or twenties, who had come to abhor food as a result of an illness and who believed they were healthy only *because* they had rejected food. This genre is character-ized by three conventions: first, the woman is presented as a miracle who proves God's goodness and might; second, the woman's story is validated by a thorough testing by the authorities; and third, a detailed description of the woman's body is provided, often supplemented with a woodcut. These three conventions outwardly seem to rationalize and contain the power of the female body, but they also subtly demonstrate the very real power of the female body in a male-dominated culture.

The first and second conventions outwardly affirm religious and state authority by eliminating the suspicion that the girl herself, or the girl in league with the devil, is exercising a subversive power. That the girl is a miracle explains the apparent violation of nature, so that her action actually becomes an affirmation of God's power rather than a disruption of the heavenly plan. For example, Catherine Cooper "yet miraculouslie liueth through the singular, pure, and incomprehensible grace of almighty God."[15] In the same vein the author of the pamphlet about Eve Fleigen asserts: "I haue translated [this] as to haue my Countreymen in *England* acquainted with so miraculous a power of Gods worke on so weake a creature, therby the more to magnifie his glory."[16] God is the active, powerful agent; the fasting woman is passive vessel.

The close inspection of the girl by government, religious, or medical officials also effectively strips the fasting girls of their power of self and transfers power to public authority, because it is only with this official validation that the girl's behavior is deemed real. In perhaps the most fully detailed account of such an examination, that of Jane Balan, the full title advertises that *"his Maiestie [the French King, Henry IV] in person had the view, and, (by his commaund) his best and chiefest Phisitians, haue tryed all meanes, to find, whether this fast & abstinence be by deceit or no."*[17] The examiners interrogated Balan's parents individually, and numerous townspeople, before questioning and examining Balan herself. The author asserts that the physicians "haue committed her from her Parents, diuers Noble and woorthie persons, some of which haue kept her close lockt vp, some foure, fiue, or sixe weekes, some for as many & more monethes together."[18] Likewise, in the examples he recounts, George Hakewill mentions the presence of medical or governmental exams. In one case, a Swiss woman named Margaret was

> by the speciall order from the Bishop of Spire delivered into the hands of the Pastor of the parish, and by him narrowly observed, and afterwards by the command of *Maximilian* King of the *Romans*, committed to the keeping of *Gerardus Bucoldianus* his Physitian, with whom hee joyned a Gentleman of his bed-chamber . . . [to watch her for twelve days]. . . . [19]

Thus, by taking control over this unnatural behavior, civil and church authorities co-opt any individual assertion of power that may have been intended by the woman or that might have been so interpreted by observers.

On the other hand, the public investigation shows evidence of a perverse voyeurism, as does the detailed physical description of the woman's body. The woman is watched closely, not only to see whether she eats or drinks, but also to see whether her body releases any waste, thus transforming a woman's personal body functions into public spectacle. This socially sanctioned intrusion by men into the most private areas of these women's lives recalls the court-ordered searches for the devil's mark on the bodies of women who were suspected of being witches, a practice that became more popular when James came to the English throne in 1603.[20] The information such an examination provides both emphasizes the girl's sexual attractiveness and attempts to minimize its threat, for the woman's primary sexual characteristics are described in great detail, but the emphasis is on the disappearance of these characteristics or on their transformation into asexual or unwomanly features.[21] For example, the head-to-toe description of Catherine Cooper includes the following comments:

> First her face is fair and sound, of good couller, ful of life and good disposition, her eyes cleere, quicke and well sighted as anie whole bodies, except that they be a little suncke into her heade, and that sometimes there arriseth a swelling vnder them which continueth not long. . . . Concerning her breast or stomach, her breath is sweet

and of good sauour, her pouls in both armes and feete naturall, in good order, proportionable and equall, but outwardly both before and behind her two shoulders, aboue and beneath shee is somewhat wearie and tired. Her brestes are more long, soft and hanging then Maidens vse to be. . . . As for her wombe, it is somewhat fallen as a voide & emptie bodie, and yet is outwardly reasonable plump, fleshy and fat, as also she is about the hips and the nether part of her chine. . . . Concerning her armes and legs, her armes are sounde and fleshy, especially the left which is very active, and in euery respect without default. . . . Her legs are meetly ful and fleshie, but so crooked that she can not stretch them foorth, yet can she somewhat moue her feet & her toes. . . . Throughout her whole body, she hath a temperat and kindly heate.[22]

The back-and-forth movement between scientific and prurient language in this passage, a typical wavering in this kind of discussion, demonstrates a real ambivalence in attitude toward the woman's sexuality on the part of her male examiners.

With very few exceptions, these miracle maidens are all virgins, or at least unmarried women. Such women are perhaps rendered more vulnerable to public authorities than are married women, whose husbands have uncontested control over the bodies of their wives. In any case, the fact that these women have never had sexual contact, that they are in some ways not yet "owned" by a particular man, allows an authority more powerful than the women's families access to their bodies. The virginal character of these women renders their bodies available for public erotic display.[23] Paradoxically, women's sexuality is revealed by the very lack of flesh their sexuality requires.

The ambivalence exhibited in these pamphlets between male power and female self-assertion, between an asexual woman's body and a normally sexually-enticing woman's body, is also an aspect of the depiction of fasting women in the drama, although the difference in literary form alters the way this ambivalence is represented.

At first glance, the fasting women in George Chapman's *Widow's Tears* (1605), John Webster's *Duchess of Malfi* (1614), Thomas Heywood's *Woman Killed with Kindness* (ca. 1603), and John Ford's *Broken Heart* (before 1632) might seem quite unlike the real-life fasting women, for their motivation is always that of affirming their roles as wives, rather than an apparent physical intoleration of food, and their intent is always death, whereas the fasting girls are famous because they have avoided this normal result of starvation. However, while the conventions of the news pamphlets are not explicitly part of the dramatic presentation, their ultimate effects are: first, the possibility of subversion in the fasting woman's act is recast as an affirmation of patriarchal order; second, the woman's physical sexuality becomes a vital presence on stage, not only because of the very absence of those female sexual characteristics but especially because the fasting female character is presented quite specifically in her role as possession and sexual object of her husband. Thus, as in the sensationalized pamphlets, the woman's sexuality becomes the center of attention. Because I am examining a culture's ongoing fascination with a particular concept, not tracing the development of an idea, I shall discuss these plays not in chronological order but in the order of ascending complexity in terms of presentation of the fasting women characters.

In George Chapman's *Widow's Tears*, the female protagonist denies herself food and drink to reflect a world that is already ordered—in other words, to show her fidelity and chastity to a husband she believes is dead. Her husband, Lysander, who is only pretending death, celebrates this proof of her love for himself:

> O Cynthia, heir of her bright purity
> Whose name thou dost inherit, thou disdain'st,
> Severed from all concretion, to feed
> Upon the base food of gross elements.
> Thou all art soul, all immortality.
> Thou fasts for nectar and ambrosia,
> Which, till thou find'st and eat'st above the stars,
> To all food here thou bidd'st celestial wars. (4.2.179–86)[24]

Clearly, Lysander recognizes that Cynthia's self-starvation is intended to lead to her death, and he approves of this suicide as a sign of her chastity. Furthermore, the self-starvation will essentially erase her body, leaving her nothing but "soul, all immortality." Other characters in the play view Cynthia's action in the same approving light (4.1.120–23; 4.2.23–33), indicating that what is valued in this patriarchal society is a woman's demonstrated loyalty to her husband—her sexual exclusivity to her husband—not her life. In this situation Cynthia's death verifies her fidelity: she is a possession, not an individual. The satiric nature of this city comedy ensures that Cynthia will fail in her intended self-starvation, but this irony only reinforces the gender-appropriateness of the intended action.

A complicating view is offered in John Webster's *Duchess of Malfi*. When the Duchess is apparently confronted with the bodies of her husband and children, she comes close to despair and threatens to take her own life: "The Church enjoins fasting; / I'll starve myself to death" (4.1.75–76).[25] With these words, the Duchess shows the thin line between controlled penance and suicide. Because her body has been the focus of attention for much of the play, both because of her pregnancies and because of Ferdinand's feverish images of her lovemaking, her threatened self-mutilation of her body is logical. Bosola reproves her and, when she verbally persists in her desperate intent, shows his horror: "Oh fearful! . . . O uncharitable!" (4.1.96, 105). Unlike Chapman, Webster explicitly shows the audience the equivocal nature of this particular church-sponsored penance, both in the Duchess's near despair and in Bosola's quick condemnation, but once again, female self-assertion is an issue, and the female body is foregrounded in the audience's mind.

The presentation of fasting women in *A Woman Killed with Kindness* and *The Broken Heart* is more problematic than in *The Widow's Tears* or *The Duchess of Malfi*, because the characters in the latter plays only threaten suicide but the women in the former actually do starve themselves to death. In both of these latter cases, the woman acts out of a sense of her sexual unfaithfulness to her husband, although only in *A Woman Killed* is adultery actually committed.

In *A Woman Killed with Kindness*, Anne Frankford, an adulterous wife discovered in bed with her lover by her husband, decides to starve herself to death when her husband merely banishes her from her home and family. Her words reveal that she sees her fasting as a penitential action that will provide absolution to her soul:

> [F]or from this sad hour
> I never will nor eat, nor drink, nor taste
> Of any cates that may preserve my life;
> I never will nor smile, nor sleep, nor rest,
> But when my tears have wash'd my black soul white,
> Sweet Saviour, to Thy hands I yield my sprite. (16.101–5)[26]

By denying herself food and drink, Anne follows the prescription of humanist educators who advocate fasting as a means for women to control their sexuality. "[M]oche fastynge shall be good," says Vives, "whiche dothe nat feble the bodye, but *brydell* it, and *presse* it downe, and *quenche* the heate of youthe" (emphasis added).[27] The verbs of control in this passage are pronounced; the clear inference is that a woman's body is a dangerous and potentially destructive thing that is not harmed by such rigorous restraint but, as Vives says, "shall kepe better theyr helthe."[28] While Vives is addressing virgins in particular in this passage, Anne's like response to her sin demonstrates her strong desire to reorient herself into this patriarchal mind-set. By starving herself to death, Anne returns order to the world she herself has disordered, for although her husband effectively divorces her when he discovers her sin, her self-starvation proves to him her repentance, and he "remarries" her at the end of the play, just before her death. The community in the play—servants, family, friends—affirms her self-denial as appropriate self-punishment and admires her "virtue."

What is interesting about this play is that Heywood, as much as he is able, makes Anne's physical body the centerpiece of his final scene. Anne's appearance on her deathbed can only be guessed at by the words she speaks and by the comments of the other characters, but it appears that she is to a certain extent experiencing some of the physiological effects of starvation, as detailed in the accounts of fasting girls. First, she apparently is suffering from diminished eyesight, because she explicitly calls attention to the fact that she recognizes Frankford by hearing the sound of his voice: "And is he come? Methinks that voice I know" (17.73). Second, she is greatly enfeebled, needing air when she first comes onto the stage (17.40) and lamenting that her faintness precludes her kneeling to Frankford (17.89). Finally, her paleness seems to indicate that she has physically wasted away from her earlier healthy self (17.55–60). In the final scene, Sir Charles Mountford remarks how Anne's "sickness hath not left [her] / Blood in [her] face enough to make [her] blush" (17.58–59), a picture of ill health that is in contrast to the rosy cheeks of the bride in scene 1. Such attributes signal the diminished capability of Anne's body.

The emaciation of Anne's body is in some ways an appropriate punishment for her sin of sexual indulgence. Margaret Bryan has argued that Anne's starvation is a culmination of the food imagery in the play, and specifically that Anne's rejection of food is a symbolic rejection of her sexual appetite.[29] Furthermore, by denying herself food she also neutralizes her female sexuality because her body loses its womanly attributes, always so threatening to men. In effect, Anne at the end of the play, destroys her body and becomes all spirit. That is why her action is so applauded by the play's community. Her virtue is restored, and the physical reminder of her earthliness no longer exists.

However, as in the pamphlets about fasting girls, the tension between patriarchal power and female self-assertion complicates this easy conclusion. Although Anne does not consciously challenge the patriarchal status quo, she nevertheless takes the initiative from Frankford in devising her own punishment—and she voices this initiative over and over again, paradoxically emphasizing her self-will even as she is denying it (16.57-64, 73, 80-82, 94). The apparent desexing of Anne's body is also problematic. When Anne comes on the stage in the final scene, she is carried in her bed—an ambiguous sign certainly, because it calls attention to the act of lovemaking even as it advertises Anne's physical revulsion from her sin. Also, the very signs of Anne's wasted body, noted above, call attention to her physical body, the same way the detailed descriptions of the fasting girls do in the news pamphlets. Consequently, the last scene in the play provides very mixed signals as to the real containment of woman's sexuality, for the ostensible message of patriarchal domination is undercut by the unconscious awareness of the female body on the part of the male playwright.

In John Ford's *Broken Heart* the character of Penthea starves herself to death when she is forced to marry a man she does not love. Although she is married against her will, Penthea feels that she has betrayed her true love: "For she that's wife to Orgilus and lives / In known adultery with Bassanes / Is at the best a whore" (3.3.41-43).[30] When she is on her deathbed, she links sexual appetite with appetite for food:

> To all memory
> Penthea's, poor Penthea's name is strumpeted;
> But since her blood was season'd by the forfeit
> Of noble shame with mixtures of pollution,
> Her blood—'tis just—be henceforth never heighten'd
> With taste of sustenance. Starve.... (4.2.147-52)

Unlike Anne Frankford, Penthea's "adultery" has been forced on her (Penthea herself calls her marriage a rape [2.3.79] and herself a "ravish'd wife" [4.2.146]). Therefore, although the Yorkshire community of *A Woman Killed with Kindness* affirms Anne's self-starvation as appropriate punishment, Sparta admires Penthea but finds her "A murd'ress to [her]self" (4.2.159).

In calling Penthea's death "self-slaughter" or suicide, the world of the play effectively admits that Penthea takes control of her fate and chooses her end by an act of her own will. Consequently, *The Broken Heart* more directly dramatizes the conflict of male authority versus female self-assertion than any of the three previous plays, and certainly more directly than the more sublimated conflict within *A Woman Killed.* However, this more explicit portrayal of a woman's self-initiating action that challenges patriarchal control is displaced in the play so that it is perceived as a tragic waste, not as a threat.[31]

Penthea's entrapment in an enforced marriage foregrounds her sexual nature. Other characters, in describing her position, refer to the act of physical consummation as the sign of Bassanes's ownership of her: Orgilus says Penthea was "Compell'd to yield her virgin freedom up" (1.1.51); Crotolon describes her as "buried in a bride-bed" (2.2.38); Penthea herself, as I mentioned earlier, calls her marriage a rape; and Bassanes himself, because of his jealousy, conjures images of adulterous lovemaking whenever he thinks of her (e.g., 2.1.3-7, 23-28, 30-40). Finally, Penthea's last appearance on stage is as a corpse, a silent but eloquent witness to Orgilus's murder of Ithocles. So once again the woman who fasts is presented as body, thus complicating the apparent desexing of her body through her own self-imposed starvation.

What conclusions can we come to in interpreting this "double standard" in the depiction of fasting men and women on the English Renaissance stage? One obvious point is that these differing depictions appear to be the result of different cultural perceptions about the human body—that a man's body is a symbol of God's beauty and authority, while a woman's body is a source of evil and disorder.[32] In other words, the Renaissance celebration of man does not extend to woman;[33] perception of woman remains locked in a dualistic mind-set, in which the body is not intrinsically an object of admiration but a source of evil. This double standard also affirms the cultural belief that a woman's body is not her own but the possession of her father or husband.

However, this dualistic world view is easily challenged. Within this repressive cultural understanding of woman's body both as evil and as male possession is also the double-edged threat that a woman and her body held for a patriarchal culture: first, that each woman character, in choosing to fast, demonstrates her strength of will and "power of self" even as she reinforces male authority; and second, that through the extremity of her action the woman draws attention to the very sexuality she transforms. Furthermore in refashioning their bodies these fasting female characters effectively subvert their husbands' control over their bodies by redefining femininity, thus suggesting that women's physiology and political authority are interconnected. These complications indicate that, while dramatic representations of women fasting contain and neutralize such threats as female sexuality and self-assertion, the fact of the representation itself nevertheless identifies the drama as a cultural locus for sexual politics.

Notes

1. Nicole Loraux, *Tragic Ways of Killing a Woman,* trans. Anthony Forster (Cambridge, Mass.: Harvard University Press, 1987).

2. This study focuses on male playwrights' descriptions and interpretations of fasting women in a fictional construct of their own making. Thus, its concerns are different from those of Rudolph Bell's *Holy Anorexia* (Chicago: University of Chicago Press, 1985) and Caroline Walker Bynum's *Holy Feast and Holy Fast: The Religious Significance of Food to Medieval Women* (Berkeley and Los Angeles: University of California Press, 1987), each of which examines how medieval women used fasting to define themselves.

3. The following discussion is indebted to the following sources: J. A. MacCullough, "Fasting," in *Encyclopedia of Religion and Ethics,* ed. James Hastings et al. (reprint; New York: Scribner's, 1960), 5:765–70; "Fasting," in *The Encyclopedia of Religion,* ed. Mircea Eliade et al. (New York: Macmillan, 1987), 5:288–89; "Fasting," in *A Catholic Dictionary of Theology* (Camden, N.J.: Thomas Nelson & Sons, 1967), 2:284–86; Patrick Collinson, *The Elizabethan Puritan Movement* (Berkeley and Los Angeles: University of California Press, 1967), 214–21; Bridget Ann Henisch, *Fast and Feast: Food in Medieval Society* (University Park: The Pennsylvania State University Press, 1976), 28–50; and Bynum, *Holy Feast and Holy Fast,* 31–47.

4. Bynum, *Holy Feast and Holy Fast,* 42–47, 237–44.

5. William Perkins, *The Whole Treatise of the Cases of Conscience,* 3 vols. (Cambridge, 1606), 2:424. See also *A very godly and learned treatise, of the exercise of fastyng* (London, 1580), 17.

6. Sir Thomas Elyot, *The Book Named the Governor,* ed. S. E. Lehmberg (New York: Dutton, 1975), 214–15.

7. *A very godly and learned treatise,* 26.

8. William Shakespeare, *Love's Labor's Lost,* in *The Riverside Shakespeare,* ed. G. Blakemore Evans (Boston: Houghton Mifflin Co., 1974), 179. All further citations are taken from this edition.

9. William Shakespeare, *Measure for Measure,* in *The Riverside Shakespeare,* ed. G. Blakemore Evans (Boston: Houghton Mifflin Co., 1974), 555–56. All further citations are taken from this edition.

10. William Shakespeare, *Hamlet,* in *The Riverside Shakespeare,* ed. G. Blakemore Evans (Boston: Houghton Mifflin Co., 1974), 1154. All further citations are taken from this edition.

11. Elyot, *The Book Named the Governor,* 120–21.

12. An exception to these portrayals of male fasting characters is Philologus in the late morality play *The Conflict of Conscience* (1581). In one of the two versions of the play, Philologus literally starves himself to death in repentance for his sin of apostasy. This depiction of fasting seems to be a product of an earlier age in which heroic asceticism, rather than moderation, was a Christian value.

13. Joan Jacobs Brumberg, *Fasting Girls: The Emergence of Anorexia Nervosa as a Modern Disease* (Cambridge, Mass.: Harvard University Press, 1988); Hyder E. Rollins, "Notes on Some English Accounts of Miraculous Fasts," *Journal of American Folklore* 34 (1929): 357-76; H. Schadewaldt, "Medizingeschichtliche Betrachtungen zum Anorexie-Problem," in *Anorexia Nervosa*, ed. J.-E. Meyer and H. Feldman (Stuttgart: Georg Thieme Verlag, 1965), 1-14.

14. The story of Catherine Cooper, a Dutch woman, was translated into English in 1589 in *A notable and prodigious Historie of a Mayden, who for sundry yeeres neither eateth, drinketh, nor sleepeth, neyther auoydeth any excrements, and yet liueth . . .* (STC 5678). The story of another Dutch girl, Veitken Iohans, was printed in Alexander Gurth's *Most Trve and More Admirable newes, Expressing the Miracvlous preseruation of a young Maiden of the towne of Glabbich in the Dukedome of Gulische . . .*, 1597 (STC 12531.5). The story of Jane Balan, a French woman, written by François Citois and translated by Anthony Munday, was published in 1603 as *A True and admirable Historie, of a Mayden of Confolens, in the Prouince of Poictiers: that for the space of three yeeres and more hath liued, and yet doth, vvithout receiuing either meate or drinke. . . .* (STC 5326). The story of Eve Fleigen took several printed forms: part of a pamphlet entitled *The Protestants and Iesuites vp in Armes in Gulickeland. Also, a true and wonderfull relation of a Dutch maiden (called Eue Fliegen of Meurs in the County of Meurs) who being now (this present yeare) 36 yeares of age, hath fasted for the space of 14 yeares . . .*, issued twice in 1611 (STC 20449 and 20449.5); a ballad in the Shirburn manuscript collection, entitled *Of a maide nowe dwelling at the towne of meurs in dutchland, that hath not taken any foode this 16 yeares, and is not yet neither hungry nor thirsty . . .*, in *Shirburn Ballads*, ed. Andrew Clark (Oxford: Clarendon Press, 1907), 55-59; a portrait, presumably of Fleigen when she was forty in 1615, called *The Pourtrayture of Eua Fliegen the Miraculous Mayd that liued at muers in cleueland with Food aetat. 40 . . .*, 1620? (STC 11088.3). George Hakewill's *Apologia; or, Declaration of the Power and Providence of God*, 1635 (STC 12613) lists several remarkable *Protestant* fasting women as examples "of wonderfull workes of God" (441). For contemporary references in popular literature, see Rollins, "Notes."

15. *A notable and prodigious Historie*, 12.

16. *The Protestants and Iesuites*, A2v. See also Gurth, *Most Trve and More Admirable newes*, A4r.

17. Citois, *True and admirable Historie*, title page; see n. 14.

18. Ibid., 2v.

19. Hakewill, *Apologia*, 1:439. See also Gurth, *Most Trve and More Admirable newes*, A3r-v, B2r-B3r; and *The Protestants and Iesuites*, A4r-v.

20. Joseph Klaits, in *Servants of Satan: The Age of the Witch Hunts* (Bloomington: University of Indiana Press, 1985), describes such a search as "rape-like humiliation [performed by] an urban, reformed patriciate" (56); see also 73-74 and 151-52.

21. That self-starvation desexes a woman's body is a well-known fact, due to the cultural fascination today with anorexia nervosa. The literature on this subject is voluminous. Studies I found particularly helpful include Hilde Bruch, *Eating Disorders* (New York: Basic Books, 1973), 211-305; Marlene Boskind-Lodahl, "Cinderella's Stepsisters: A Feminist Perspective on Anorexia Nervosa and Bulimia," *Signs* 2 (1976): 342-56; Marilyn Lawrence, "Anorexia Nervosa: The Control Paradox," *Women's Studies International Quarterly* 2 (1979): 93-101; and Noelle Caskey, "Interpreting Anorexia Nervosa," in *The Female Body in Western Culture*, ed. Susan Rubin Suleiman (Cambridge, Mass.: Harvard University Press, 1985), 175-89.

22. *A notable and prodigious Historie*, 6-7. See also Citois, *True and admirable Historie*, C4r-D3r; Gurth, *Most Trve and More Admirable newes*, B1r; and *The Protestants and Iesuites*, A4r.

23. For a fascinating discussion of "the semantics" of virginity from the viewpoint of a

social anthropologist, see Kirsten Hastrup, "The Semantics of Biology: Virginity," in *Defining Females: The Nature of Women in Society,* ed. Shirley Ardener (New York: John Wiley & Sons, 1978), 49–65.

24. George Chapman, *The Widow's Tears,* in *Drama of the English Renaissance: The Stuart Period,* ed. Russell A. Fraser and Norman Rabkin (New York: Macmillan, 1976), 323. All further citations are from this edition.

25. John Webster, *The Duchess of Malfi,* ed. Elizabeth M. Brennan (New York: W. W. Norton & Co., 1964), 65. All further citations are from this edition.

26. Thomas Heywood, *A Woman Killed with Kindness,* ed. R. W. Van Fossen (Cambridge, Mass.: Harvard University Press, 1961), 5. All further citations are taken from this edition.

27. Johannes Vives, *A Very Fruteful and Plaesant boke called the instructio[n] of a Christen woma[n],* trans. R. Hyrd (London, 1541), 18. Bynum notes that male writers since Jerome have associated food with lust, especially in manuals for virgins (214).

28. Ibid.

29. Margaret B. Bryan, "Food Symbolism in *A Woman Killed with Kindness,*" *Renaissance Papers, 1973* (1974), 9–17. See also Barbara J. Baines, *Thomas Heywood* (Boston: Twayne Publishers, 1984), 92. While she does not directly address the issue of self-starvation in the play, Laura G. Bromley notes the importance of the image of Anne's changed body in her act of repentance ("Domestic Conduct in *A Woman Killed with Kindness,*" *Studies in English Literature* 26 [1986]: 273). In general, however, scholars have not grappled with the meaning of self-starvation as the means of Anne's death; they simply see her end as a logical sign of her extreme repentance.

30. John Ford, *The Broken Heart,* in *John Ford: Three Plays,* ed. Keith Sturgess (1970; reprint, New York: Viking Penguin, 1985), 179. All further citations are from this edition.

31. While scholars generally have seen Penthea a victim of an enforced marriage, Sharon Hamilton has recently argued that Penthea is "a woman whose consolation for disappointed love is 'resolved martyrdom,' a carefully orchestrated suicide that will render her 'a deity' to future generations of 'wronged maids'" ("*The Broken Heart:* Language Suited to a Divided Mind," in "*Concord in Discord,*" ed. Donald K. Anderson Jr. [New York: AMS Press, 1986], 174).

32. See Ian Maclean, *The Renaissance Notion of Woman* (Cambridge: Cambridge University Press, 1980).

33. This study finds further evidence that women did not have a Renaissance, a debate initiated by Joan Kelly in her seminal article "Did Women Have a Renaissance?" in *Becoming Visible,* ed. Renate Bridenthal and Claudia Koonz (Boston: Houghton Mifflin Co., 1977), 139–64.

ANGEL'S FOOD:
A Case of Fasting
in Eighteenth-Century England

Joanna B. Gillespie

> My soul hath fed on angel's food and lives, on earth,
> the life of heaven.
> —Hester Ann Roe (1780)

A young woman in late eighteenth-century Midlands England living on little but "angel's food" is not a typical emblem of family warfare. But when Hester Ann Roe wrote "My soul hath fed on angel's food and lives, on earth, the life of heaven" in her private journal,[1] it signified an ongoing state of siege as well as a spiritual disposition. The metaphor implied that Hester had decided to live on religious rather than physical nourishment in order to purify her soul. Underneath the grace-filled image, however, was also the issue of control. She and her mother were locked in a conflict on which Hester Ann staked her own body.

Five years earlier, in 1775, as an unmarried nineteen-year-old daughter of a Church of England clergyman, she had become an embarrassment to her family. In the process of shedding the mores and culture into which she had been born in favor of the new Wesleyan regimen, she had offended the religious sensibilities of her family and her relatives. Hester Ann's attraction to the Wesleyans had evoked anger in people who viewed Methodists as "little better than common pickpockets," or evangelists who "filled some of their hearers with presumption and drove others to despair."[2] The religious practices of a budding Methodist were intense: daily or hourly self-examination (preserved in a diary for later soul-searching), immersion in the holy scriptures, prayerful analysis of personal behavior, and frequent attendance at worship were expected. And Hester Ann's special zeal made her seize on an even more singular discipline: fasting (living on "angel's food"), a physical act of spiritual conviction. She chose the ordinance of fasting, reclaimed from the early church and medieval ascetics by founding Methodist John Wesley, as the arena for the battle of wills between her and her mother.[3] Later, in 1792, writing as a mature woman, Hester Ann acknowledged that her early enthusiasm had led her to an extreme substitution of "the love of God shed abroad in my heart" for actual meat and drink (36).

That confession appeared in a retrospective *Account,* written fifteen years after Hester Ann's existence on "angel's food," the purpose of which was to tell the story of her religious journey up to her conversion to Methodism and after, since she knew she was terminally ill and must leave a spiritual legacy. Her *Account* followed the standard form for pious memoirs from its first locating sentence, "I was born in the village of Macclesfield, Cheshire, in 1756" (9). Her Church of England clergyman father had provided her early education, and she had demonstrated the requisite childish precocity in prayer. There were religiously significant memories of a five-year-old brother's corpse; of her father's dying commendation (when she was nine) to a life of virtue; and of an adolescent struggle with various worldly distractions, such as reading novels and histories, and fashionable clothes. There had been the inappropriate suitor who had to be relinquished *"fully,* or he would be the means of drawing me back . . . as he was yet unawakened[,] though outwardly moral" (21). And at the centerpiece was the prolonged fast that nearly killed her, the period of living on "angel's food" in 1775 when she was eighteen. Thanks to the soul-wrenching intervention detailed in the *Account,* she had recovered, and married the Rev. John Rogers in 1784 at age twenty-eight; they had five children. She died at age thirty-eight, in 1794, two years after commiting her memoirs to pen and paper. Her written heritage was the property of the entire Methodist "connexion" (as it was known before the formal break with the Church of England), not the property of her relatives. Composing such an account was seen as a final opportunity to influence and convert others, an exercise in posthumous usefulness. Hester Ann's self-starvation makes her narrative stands out from others in the genre and in the same era. Methodists rarely considered food a religious medium, even if manipulating one's physical nourishment had been sanctified by Wesley.[4]

Hester Ann had ample reason to believe that her "literary remains" would be valued among eighteenth-century English Methodists,[5] but she could not have known how long-lived they would be or that they would be reprinted many times for believers in nineteenth-century America. First published two years after her death, the *Account* consisted of only eighty 4-by-6-inch pages.[6] Later editions were supplemented with the sermon delivered at her funeral by a prominent Methodist, the Rev. Thomas Coke (originally published separately in 1795) and an appendix containing a tribute, by her husband. Twenty-seven of her letters were also added to the volume because several were addressed to John Wesley himself. Because both Coke and Rogers and Hester Ann herself (in the *Account*) quoted from her twenty-year manuscript diary (1774–94), that too was eventually edited by an unnamed Methodist minister and published as *The Journal of Mrs. Hester Ann Rogers.*[7] In this unusually extensive print record,[8] however, no one, not even the diarist herself in her *Journal,* mentioned her life-threatening fast. No one would have been aware of it even today if she had not made it the dramatic central feature of her *Account.*

Hester Ann's journal-keeping was a typical practice during the late eighteenth century (although more narratives by males survive).[9] The eighteenth century was "an age of diarists." Ordinary people carried notebooks with them as "footholds for the memory" in the recording of God's providence. Wesley's followers, especially, kept daily notes for personal edification, to monitor their "devotion of temper" and to share, in words, their experience of the perfected way of life. Spiritual ledgers were intended both for personal spiritual development and for corporate witness to the faith.[10] Wesley himself edited memoirs of Christians from earliest times— Saint Augustine, Saint Teresa of Avila, and others—in order to provide models of religious self-management for his fellow Methodists. Part of Wesley's strategy was to send correspondents a printed account of some exemplary spiritual pilgrimage to show that ordinary people could live extraordinary lives.[11] Hester Ann undoubtedly crafted her end-of-life *Account* with such purposes in mind.

Since writing the "self" into consciousness, religiously sanctioned, was the most basic legitimation for authorship, Methodist memoirs unwittingly created a vast subterranean stream of literary realism in the mid-eighteenth century. Numerous English women and men created documents, which later became memoirs, describing ordinary tasks such as sweeping the floor or visiting neighbors. No action was too small to have religious significance. Shoemakers, nursemaids, teachers, shopkeepers, and ministers all nourished their imagination on biblical language and saw God's providential hand in all their activities. Their intense religiosity demanded a diction that laced prosaic chronology with flights of scriptural imagery. But the *Account* by Mrs. Hester Ann Rogers is distinguished from the accounts of a few other first-generation women in English Methodism by what sounds to present-day readers like anorexia.[12] Self-created eating disorders are not just a contemporary phenomenon. Hester Ann reminds us that throughout history some women have used religious justification for restricting their food intake to crumbs—an exercise that has both physical and spiritual results.[13]

Hester Ann began her fast at the age of nineteen. By the time she recorded the "angel's food" metaphor five years later, she had, for a properly reared twenty-four-year-old Englishwoman, accomplished astonishing things. She practiced a "ministry" of visiting sick and dying neighbors, although no one in her era would have characterized her action by a word reserved for ordained males. She was fairly renowned in Methodist circles for her ability to testify, exhort, and pray. She had had theological conversations and corresponded with such leaders as John Wesley, Mary Fletcher, and the Rev. John Bosanquet.[14] And she had, by then, according to the *Account*, permanently damaged her health.

Thanks to the groundbreaking work of historian Carolyn Walker Bynum, the formerly opaque universe of food symbolism in the lives and writings of medieval women is now accessible to twentieth-century readers. Bynum's *Holy Feast and Holy Fast* reveals the spiritual motivation and imagination expressed through food imagery. Through Bynum's lens we can see young Hester Ann as one who chose food, "a particularly woman-controlled resource," to fight the devil and the constraining culture (so it seemed to her) into which she was born.[15] Fasting had served as a "tool of parental coercion" for Saint Catherine of Siena four centuries earlier. Although an Englishwoman of Hester Ann's background might have rejected conscious imitation of a medieval saint as too "Romish" (20), her mentor John Wesley drew no such line. Embracing a catholic range of early pious exemplars, he was the first Protestant in several centuries to commend the act of fasting as part of his prescription for religious self-management.[16] Whether or not Hester Ann was conscious of historical models for her stringent food limitation, she knew that Wesley justified fasting to "refrain one's soul." Fasting also suggested itself as a tool of impression-management vis-à-vis Hester Ann's family.[17] She was too young and single-minded to worry about any hazards to her health. She intended both to gain new heights of spiritual ascendancy and to establish a religious independence within her family. It is interesting to note that her daily diary did not mention her choice of means. Only in the reflective *Account* did it emerge, probably because at age thirty-six she felt obligated to explore its full theological significance.[18] The mature Hester Ann could admit that fasting had been a youthful folly, even in "the service of so good an end as religion." Writing her *Account* gave her a pulpit from which she could urge salvation on others, a standard pious-memoir stratagem. The vivid language confessing self-starvation would dramatize the audacity of pitting one's self against God.

Differences between the way the fourteenth-century Catherine and the eighteenth-century Hester Ann approached fasting are evident, but there are also similarities. Both women were highly intelligent and strong-willed; both were recognized among their peers as religiously gifted; both struggled for the right to embrace a mode of religious identity and self-expression that was different from that expected by their families. Bynum's study suggests that the fasting of medieval women was "allegorized," but for Hester Ann, a woman of the Enlightenment, fasting had to be literalized—shorn of any overtones of the miraculous. Catherine could view the bread of the Eucharist as the mystified and spiritualized experience of "eating Jesus," but an up-to-date English Methodist must view it more prosaically as a product, "communion bread," albeit hallowed in its symbolism. Hester Ann lived in an age that idealized rationality and conscious intention, even in the matter of grace. Wesley himself was anything but a mystic: "I am rarely led by impressions, but generally by *reason* and by scripture," he wrote Elizabeth Ritchie in 1786. "I *see* abundantly more than I feel."[19] The only "miracles" Methodists countenanced were those that might logically result from living an ordered, methodical life or doing business with double-entry bookkeeping— for example, financial success or new standing among one's fellows. Hester Ann's language of aspiration was practicality itself. She vowed "to use more self denial of all kinds; and whatever it cost me with respect to health or life[,] more fasting and prayer" (40). However, like Saint Catherine, Hester Ann studded her reflections with images of food. Hunger was the metaphor of spiritual quest, and spiritual nurture, for both women.

Today's reader, more comfortable with psychological than spiritual interpretation, is tempted to characterize Hester Ann's "inedia" as anorexia nervosa, but it is an anachronistic usage. The language of psychological illness was not yet in place, and her conscious motive for refusing food was a striving after sanctity. Only incidentally, and in retrospect, could Hester

Ann see it as also a stance against parental authority. Intrafamily dynamics were no part of any medical treatment for her, although by the late eighteenth century, British medical theory viewed the physical debility caused by fasting as "something to be cured"—that is, as an illness. Science, still primarily the handmaid of religion in the late eighteenth century, was not yet the overarching explanatory system it became in the nineteenth century, a measuring, categorizing mind-set.[20] One may even read John Wesley's glorification of "method"—a strenuous theology of disciplined sequential steps toward spiritual perfection—as its religious expression.[21] What made Hester Ann's severe fast alarming to her contemporaries, rather than admirable, was its irrationality in an era that gloried in rationality. However noble her intent, fasting was bound to seem retrogressive at that point in history. The forward movement of the time favored self-management and freedom from ancient bonds of mysticism or metaphysics. An intelligent young woman choosing to starve herself defied reason.[22]

The generational conflict that preoccupied the Roe household in 1774 was about future security, but it was security of an earthly rather than a heavenly kind. At age eighteen Hester Ann should have been headed into a marriage that would settle her (and her widowed mother) in a comfortable station in life. To that purpose, a wealthy lady of the gentry had been selected as her godmother, and a sum for her dowry was already pledged. Many late eighteenth-century Church of England clergy tried to tip the tenuous balance between respectability and poverty with a marriageable daughter. But Hester Ann, magnetized by the spiritual currents of Wesleyanism, was resisting her mother's plan. Her psychic rebellion began when she suddenly embraced an uncompromisingly literal view of the Words of Comfortable Assurance, from the Communion service: "If any man sin, we have an advocate with the Father." Well-brought-up English women were already confident about their spiritual location. Then, she remembered, she took an almost perverse pleasure in chastising herself on fine moral points—"tak[ing] the name of God in vain into my polluted lips" or "appearing before men engaged in devotion, while my heart was wandering to the ends of the earth" (27). How was an anxious mother to cope with this preoccupation in a marriageable daughter? Hester Ann's *Account* evokes a parent's helplessness against a daughter's intransigence—or willfulness—supported by a spiritual rationale.

Early one morning in April 1774, shortly before Easter, Hester Ann tripled her mother's concern, by ripping all her "finery, high dressed caps, etc.," into little pieces. She also "cut [her] hair short" to prevent its ever being "dressed" again and she made a "most solemn vow never to dance again" (refusing to be present at balls and assemblies ruled out the possibility of finding an appropriate husband). But her rebellion went beyond renunciations. Somehow, although neither her mother nor the family's friends knew anyone who was actually aligned with the Methodists, Hester Ann learned where and when they met. She rose quietly and slipped off to worship at a five-o'clock-in-the-morning service (28).

Free-form prayers and emotional paroxysms were reprehensible to the conventional Mrs. Roe, but her real fear was indoctrination. How could she forbid her daughter to read the Bible or engage in acts of charity when these were also prescribed by her own church? Eccentric dress and hairstyle were bad enough, but if Hester Ann became enmeshed in a group that exalted extremes of spiritual achievement, she would be lost forever to the aspirations of mother and godmother. The distraught Mrs. Roe invoked family disapproval as her major weapon against further Methodist entrapment. Hester Ann recalled: "If ever [Mother] knew me to hear them [the Methodists], she would disown me. Every friend and relation I had in the world, I had reason to believe, would do the same" (30).

The *Account* ardently chronicled the intensifying conflict step by step. An opened "floodgate of persecution" almost made Hester homeless. An uncle's intervention was the only thing that prevented the mother from locking her out, and then she was locked in. "For eight weeks I was kept closely confined," she recalled, a grown woman forbidden to leave the house. However, enforced separation from the Methodists, plus "tears and entreaties, and at other times, her [mother's] severities," were pitted against "divine strengthening of a feeble worm," as Hester Ann and her new friends styled themselves. High drama ensued. Relatives were imported to argue the foolishness of her new path: "My godmother came to talk with me, so did my mother's brother and my father's sister." Hester Ann recalled that her next strategy had been to "employ" a "discipline" of "retiring from company many times in a day" for private prayer. Such a powerful nonverbal statement, within the confines of her imprisonment, must have confounded the assembled kin. Her independence was a "refus[al] to conform in dress [or] in any thing my conscience disapproved," rather than a demonstration of their inability to control her. As an adult, the dying Hester Ann, describing these youthful tactics, could not eliminate overtones of gratification in recalling the struggle; the rhetoric of persecution for one's faith was an essential component of Methodist conversion narratives.[23] Although she was never inarticulate, Hester Ann credited divine assistance for "a mouth and the wisdom to plead my own cause" (31).

The visiting relatives, "finding all their efforts vain," gradually began to desist. An understanding that she "was to expect nothing from my god-mother as to temporal things" emerged—her mother being the disappointed one, not Hester Ann. "To me it was as nothing," she wrote (31). Their usual summer holiday at her godmother's residence—"quite contrary to my inclination, for I found it a great grief to be separated . . . from the dear people of God [her new Methodist friends]"—made no headway against her obduracy (31). Later that year, when she and her mother had settled back into the Macclesfield house, Hester Ann was ready to declare herself in unequivocal terms: "I must seek salvation to my soul, whatever its conse-quence." This time the daughter did the threatening. She was "determined . . . to leave . . . and go to be a servant, rather than be kept from the Methodists." Because that would have been deeply humiliating, Mrs. Roe softened enough to bargain, and Hester Ann agreed that she would greatly "prefer" to remain at home—though as a servant "willing to undertake all the work of the house"—if her mother would agree to let her attend Methodist services (32–33).

Poor Mrs. Roe, now clear that she was up against more than just genera-tional rebellion, again consulted kin. Their counsel to the beleaguered parent was unanimous and soothing. They assured her that Hester, who had been schooled for ladylike "employments," would soon "be weary and give it up" (32). Why not consent and keep her within the family circle, where her enthu-siasm could be monitored, possibly even subdued? The advisers must have known that a concession was a defeat rather than a truce, but they had little else to suggest. Hester Ann was no longer a child. In the long run, their Angli-can sensibility condoned a degree of freedom in exchange for the mainte-nance of surface unity—anything rather than force an irreparable breach.

What they could not then know was that Hester Ann had initiated two further disciplines that would strengthen her drive toward independence, while still under the maternal roof. In late 1774 she began keeping her journal. She also began systematically denying herself food. The burden of her unworthiness was what demanded a concrete physical act, she recalled fifteen years later. But at the time, joy in her new status and its implications of turned tables transformed "the most servile of all my employments": she was just never very hungry. Sweeping the hearth and changing bed linens was not odious because she could go to Methodist meeting as often as she liked. Excitement irradiated menial duties. "I could neither eat nor sleep much for many days and nights." The Bible itself, generally read in a kneeling posture, provided "light, strength and comfort to my hungry soul . . . sweeter than honey or the honey comb" (37).

To us it is remarkable that Hester Ann did not document her food-abstaining regimen in the diary. The period during which the fasting occurred was only hinted at in a two-sentence gloss; she alluded to being "hindered through various causes from writing my journal as usual . . . for some months confined with illness, many and severe trials to pass through."[24] Contrary to what we would expect in the way of self-disclosure in a private journal, she felt that writing "I am fasting" in her journal, even if visible only to herself, would corrupt the sanctity of her act. Any claim to extraordinary spiritual goals might indicate spiritual pride or suggest that she was calculating a reward from her "good works." "Be not as the hypocrites when thou fastest," Jesus warned, and Wesley endorsed that, saying, "Thy Father . . . seeth in secret, and rewardeth in secret."[25] That youthful asceticism, she later admitted, initiated the fragile health that plagued the rest of her life. "Indeed it was no wonder . . . that my body began to fail," she reflected in the *Account,* because of the "rigorous fasting" to which it was being subjected (37–38).

An eager Methodist like Hester Ann would have read and reread Wesley's thoughts on the Sermon on the Mount, especially his seventh sermon on the "much-neglected ordinance" of fasting. The most authoritative voice in Methodism viewed fasting as one of the "little instances of self-denial" that were God's means "chosen wherewith to bestow *great* salvation." So distinctive an austerity appealed to her vaunting ambition. The older Hester Ann who penned the *Account,* however, could see that her self-denial escalated into the danger zone because it justified her autonomy within the family. Intrigued with her own religious exaltation, she had totally disregarded Wesley's warnings against committing "a . . . holy revenge upon the self."[26]

Still, Hester Ann's disdain for "needful food" was genuine in that it was the result of intense passion; fasting was the natural by-product of her "deeply engaged" mind and spirit. For one as devout as Hester Ann, eating real food, would merely "divert [one's] thoughts from what they desire should engross their whole attention," her continuing deep unworthiness. She was determined to carve a spiritual profile—the "very ground, reason, and end of fasting"—out of "angel's food." She had chosen a means of grace that would directly mark the only canvass available to her: her physical body. Being young, new to this intense religiosity, and female, she could imagine no other spiritual gesture equal to her heroic aspiration.[27]

In the succeeding months her soul bloomed in what she fancied a military engagement with the forces of evil, while her body shriveled. She intended to "mortify and starve the evil tempers and propensities of my nature"—her own words (40). In Wesley's more temperate words, fasting should indeed "wean [one's human nature]... from all indulgence of inferior appetites which tend to chain it down to earth, to pollute as well as debase it."[28] Even as she watched the rapidly diminishing flesh on her bones, Hester Ann was adamant: "I could not be prevailed on to take anything which would tend to restore my health" (41). Enjoying her starring role in a cosmic drama, she interpreted dwindling flesh as "prophesying" a perfect conclusion to life and its warfare. The *Account* took pains to elaborate the younger Hester Ann's self-delusion, so that readers could receive the full impact of her awakening.

During the fast, her first cousin Robert Roe, headed toward Oxford and ordination in the Church of England, came for a visit. He was the first outside mirror by which Hester Ann could judge her impact.[29] Possibly the waxy emaciation of her starved countenance enhanced her sense of power; the journal recorded her gratification that "the great change in me was a matter of much grief to him." But "what most astonished him" was her spiritual ecstasy. "Instead of... melancholy and mopish," he found her "always happy, and resigned to suffering... which he well knew I could not [formerly] have submitted to" (37–38). In fact, she was triumphantly "the reverse of all I had been before." Even in the relationship with her mother, the daughter had become the caretaker. Her mother had come down with a serious illness, undoubtedly related to her frustration, and Hester Ann was the nurse during long night watches at the invalid's bedside. She intended to disarm her mother's opposition. By mid-July 1775 the combination of self-starvation and climbing stairs with chamberpots had taken its toll. "It was then nearly too late," an older, wiser Hester recalled. "My health had received such a wound, as it did not recover for many years" (39).

Fasting unto death. In the first flush of self-determination, that phrase was hypnotic. Hester Ann at the age of thirty-six remembered that she had held herself to a goal of transparent holiness; she would literally reshape her physical body into goodness. Each increasing debilitation was welcome: "I was impatient to be gone, that I might be freed from sin.... My body was reduced now to a very weak state... which I esteemed blessed tidings." Her iron will sustained her. With a body so frail she could no longer sit up unless propped by mounds of pillows, she was "so desirous... to quit the vale of sin, as I called it, here below, that I could not be prevailed on to take anything [that] would restore my health, and therefore continued to decline very swiftly" (41). Magnificent renunciation fed her spirit; seeing her bones protrude assured her that she was her own private altar, on which she could immolate her sinfulness. Her religious destiny was in *her* hands, though assigned to God's.

When the doctor attending her mother observed that she seemed to be "far gone in a consumption" and commanded her to stop "sacrificing her life" (39), Hester Ann stoutly refused. Perhaps by this time she was unable to assimilate nourishment. Certainly the immoderation of her fast upended the creed of moderation so revered in her birthright culture. From childhood her strong temperament had chafed for martyrish excess instead of gentility.[30] Early in the fast, on November 1, 1775, a day she wrote "very ill" in her journal, she copied poet Edward M. Young's effusions about the "Last Day."

> To smile at death! to long to be dissolved!
> From our decays a pleasure to receive!
> And kindle into transport at a grave!

After a much longer stanza she concluded smugly, "This will help pull down my earthly tabernacle!"[31]

Her journal also allowed her to retell, in the retrospective *Account,* an out-of-body experience. "I felt myself so weak that I believed I should rise no more till my soul took its light to the bosom of Jesus," her description began. "My joy on this occasion was inexpressible." The words strain toward "the beginning of endless glory, a taste of which I then felt. . . . A beam darted from the unclouded Sun of Righteousness . . . and left me in speechless rapture at his feet." She assured readers of her memoir that this indeed had been a foretaste, something "which those who are really dying in the Lord" experience "on leaving the body" (41). The older Hester Ann, who was really dying, rejoiced in that youthful vision, particularly in the midst of her present suffering.

At least some of Hester's infatuation with the rhetoric of death, dying, and angels arose from her striving to express the inexpressible. In the power of her spiritual obsession, only words of ultimacy could serve. Similar expressive limitation attaches to the word "ill" in her diary. Because there were fewer identifications for sicknesses in Hester Ann's day, the word "ill" covered everything from dizziness to tumors, postpartum psychosis, appendicitis, or a cold. (In contrast, some mid-eighteenth-century diaries, perhaps because the journal-keepers were more sophisticated, identify "head-ack," gout, or "a cancer.") She did cite "a dropsy" that killed a neighbor and the doctor's talk of "a consumption" when she was at her weakest. Such a label probably signified the general debility of self-starvation rather than the lung disease we know as tuberculosis. In 1794 the preacher at her funeral labeled her terminal disease "an obstinate windy complaint" (possibly colon cancer) that for three years "baffled all human skill, repelled the force of every medicine, and never left her till the day of her death" (216). The word "ill" had to cover vast physical and emotional territory for Hester Ann, as did the imagery of death.

Sometime toward the end of 1775 a breakthrough occurred. An older male cousin arrived with a "strengthening medicine," which of course Hester Ann was still "unwilling to use." But instead of backing away in awe, he attacked—with counterbalancing theology. Accusing her of the worst of all sins, that she "set up [her] own will" above God's, he said she only "*pretended* to submit to the will of God." Then he uttered the unthinkable: "By not taking proper medicines, you are a murderer" (42). Her fast was offensive, not ennobling, in the eyes of God and her fellow Methodists. Her own willfulness was making her "unfit for the works of [her] calling." She had ignored the caution that one should fast only "in proportion to our strength: for we may not offer God murder for sacrifice, or destroy our bodies to help our souls." A crude, unflattering light showed her renuncia- tion as self-blinding grandiosity. Retrospectively she credited the cousin's shocking indictment with saving her life. At the time, however, the realiza- tion that she must live for another "twenty, thirty or forty years" was bathed in regrets and tears. A person who would take the strengthening medicine and live, because "by suffering" her continued existence might "in any wise glorify [God]," would just have to find another channel for her religious expression.

Hester Ann was often confined to her bed during the recovery years (1776–80), although she did begin to eat. Her diary, later quoted in the *Account,* was littered with such observations as "This day I have much pain and weakness of body, but my peace hath flowed as a river" (57) or "Many are my symptoms of mortality" (61). Perhaps the confrontation with near death was too chastening for explicit diary analysis, though twentieth- century readers would welcome more revelatory detail. However, her letters from those years reveal an increasingly authoritative voice, the voice of one plucked from the jaws of death, with implicit reference to her dangerous fast. Food imagery undergirding her exhortations is as close as she comes to acknowledging self-starvation. "The scriptures I read are so impressed with divine unction on my heart as makes [them] lasting food and nourishment to my soul," she wrote in 1776 (59). In 1778, once again ill "to the point of death," she again quoted Wesley's sermon on fasting and urged a correspondent to "watch, fast, and pray"—the only disciplines powerful enough to transform the friend's "soul in drought" into "a watered garden." But the dimensions of her aim had been modified. She wrote her cousin Robert that though her body had once again been carried almost "to the borders of eternity," she now knew she "need not *drop the body* to enjoy the presence of my God" (emphasis added).[32]

One letter in 1780 contained a direct implication from her experience: "Let me advise you to take all the care you can of your body, for it is not your own but the Lord's," she advised a contemporary, Miss Salmon. Human beings have no right to "trifle with the precious talent of health, which is given us to improve to the glory of our God," was her painfully acquired wisdom. A journal entry about the unending struggle with her mother provides some context for her continuing need for "angel's food," however. Mrs. Roe still maintained that all Hester Ann's illnesses "were owing to my going among the Methodists," she noted wearily.[33] In the later *Account,* Hester Ann reminded readers (and perhaps herself) that "everything we can do for a parent, we ought . . . without killing ourselves; but this we have no right to do. Our lives are not at our own disposal" (59). She had learned that, at last.

Once fasting as the arena for spiritual achievement was relinquished, Hester Ann's drive turned outward, away from her own body. She had the exhilarating experience of meeting the venerable John Wesley face-to-face when he visited Macclesfield and of being asked to "take a class." It was a great honor to be tapped for public testimony in his presence. "I went forward and had such a time as I scarcely ever remember," she confided in her journal. "My heart was enlarged, my tongue set at liberty. I had words not my own; I was carried *out* of myself and let *into* God. All present felt his power, and four received pardon" (emphasis added).[34] She recorded a bold image comparing her "union with the Lord as a man with his friend" (220). Although a persistent general "bodily weakness" sometimes kept her from attending Sunday services, her influence in the local congregation increased, and her reputation spread even beyond Macclesfield. Her diary notes that, in 1782, a Mr. Willard said he would "walk seven miles at any time to converse with Miss Roe" (174).

Also in 1782 a special Methodist minister entered her life. This acquaintance led to wifehood and motherhood, though not in the economically advantageous terms once envisioned by her mother. Hester Ann, now an active lay evangelist who called on people with the Methodist pastors, naturally became a trusted co-worker of the new pastor, the Rev. John Rogers, and developed a deep and genuine friendship with his pregnant wife. The moving experience of that lady's holy dying in February 1784 was recorded at length in Hester Ann's journal (229–40), and in August of that year she married the newly widowed Pastor Rogers.

Together they embarked on a strenuous life of pastoral work, first in Dublin, Ireland, from 1784 to 1792, and then in Spitalfields, London, for the last two years of her life. Despite the residual weakness from her previous malnutrition, Hester Ann became pregnant five times and delivered five surviving infants. In his posthumous Appendix to the *Account,* her husband quoted a dream of Hester Ann's as proof of her special spiritual gifts. After four years as his wife, she was near the birth of their third child. Childbirth itself was an acute physical danger each time because of her ravaged physique, and she was apprehensive. But this dream addressed a more profound wifely concern. "I thought I was in an elegant house," Hester Ann wrote (her husband quoted from her diary), "and was desired [by an angel] to go into a room and see the late Mrs. Rogers." In the dream the "beautiful corpse" of the first Mrs. Rogers astonished Hester Ann by opening her eyes. She then smiled and "raised herself up," Hester wrote, and then she related: "Is it possible, I asked? Has the Lord permitted you to revive so as to speak to me?" With "unutterable sweetness" the former Mrs. Rogers assured the present Mrs. Rogers: "With God, all things are possible. He has permitted it for your comfort." Hester then exclaimed, "O what I would have given, to converse one hour with you since you were taken!" There had been no need for that, her predecessor lovingly reassured her. "God has been with you," to which Hester replied, breathing the deepest question of her heart, "O tell me: have I acted my part aright in your place? Does God *in this* approve of me?" At which the ghost again smiled and said: "He does, and in all things is well pleased, and will bless you to the end, especially in your approaching trial."[35] Hester Ann was so thrilled with that benediction that she had awakened her husband to share it, he recalled. He wrote, "This dream was made a great blessing to us both," and ended his memorial with these words: "The honor of being united to such a woman fills my soul with gratitude before God" (295).

As in many evangelical narratives, the diary focus of Hester Ann [Roe] Rogers became more mundane and more practical as she moved past the intense self-preoccupation of her early twenties. Her death-inviting plunge into what we would call anorexia, and her religiously inspired recovery, seemed to recede before more standard concerns. Hester Ann's diary entries after her marriage recorded the activities encountered by any eighteenth-century minister's wife. In the only quasi-public role women could then enjoy, she taught classes of women and girls, successfully winning them to Methodist salvation. On the domestic front she coped with sickly infants. Only in the crafting of her end-of-life narrative did her youthful self-starvation resurface, undoubtedly because it was useful as a symbol of destructive self-will. At the end of her *Account,* very ill (though she lingered two more years), she wrote the typical pious memoirs disclaimer to indicate that self-will had been largely conquered: "I feel no desire to prolong life." But Hester Ann could not forbear adding: "[Except] when I see my dear husband oppressed with trials, and my living seems as if it would be a comfort to him. Or when a silent resigned longing arises, to see my children grown, and partaking of regenerating grace" (80). She had become the ideal Good Wife who defined her earthly calling in terms of ministering to her own family. However, her eulogist wanted to elevate her influence by showing that she had contributed to a larger "family"—the entire people known as Methodists. He quoted her own poetic farewell, penned a few days before she died, in 1794, to show the generosity of her spirit and the inclusive view of "family" in her departing prayers. First she had addressed her nearest family.

> . . . Adieu! dear man!—O spare
> Thy flood of grief, and of thy health take care.
> My blessing to my babes: Thou wilt be kind
> To the dear infants whom I leave behind.

Then it carried her many mourners into the required (and in Hester Ann's case, unquestioned) note of anticipated relationship:

> Farewell to all who now on me attend,
> The faithful servant and the weeping friend;
> The time is short till we shall meet again
> With Christ to share the glories of his reign.[36]

In the Middle Ages, holy women were revered by their contemporaries as mirrors or lenses through which God's transforming grace was visible on earth; they were honored for the radiance of their lives as testimony.[37] But eighteenth-century Methodists like Hester Ann Rogers were celebrated more for their words.[38] Holy women in both the fourteenth and the eighteenth centuries probably did similar things, but later eyes perceived and valued their exemplarity differently. Eighteenth-century rationalists cherished action in everyday terms and did not look for extranormal interventions. It was too late for the miraculous gushing of blood from a near-saint's hands, although it was all right for saving rhetoric to flow from Hester Ann's pen. Her own *Account* closed by directing readers to a pamphlet she had written: "The Dying Bed of a Saint and Sinner Contrasted." Even as she expired, she continued to seek potential converts through her words.

Generations since have honored Hester Ann Rogers through republishing, but until now no one has commented on the life-endangering fast she herself dramatized. No one has raised the question about whether some responsiveness to her *Account* may be linked to its portrayal of an eating disorder.[39] Hester Ann herself supplied the clue to its significance in what she saw as salient to her autobiographical farewell. The fast was crucial to her spiritual growth, an emblem of her personal power for good or ill. She chose to build a cautionary *Account* around the dangers of self-willed inedia—a surprisingly contemporary ascetic legacy from an eighteenth-century "saint."

Notes

1. *Extracts from the Journal of Mrs. Hester Ann Rogers* (London [1818], 1839), 37 (April 3, 1780); hereafter cited parenthetically in the text.

2. *An Account of the Experience of Mrs. Hester Ann Rogers* (Bristol, England, 1796), 21. Most of the quotations in this chapter, noted hereafter by page number in the text, are from the first American edition, published in Baltimore (J. Kingston, 1811), which also contains her *Spiritual Letters* (Bristol, England, 1796) and the *Sermon on the Occasion of Her Death* by the Rev. Thomas Coke (Bristol, England, 1794), plus an *Appendix* by her husband with selections from her manuscript journals. See David Lyle Jeffrey, ed., *A Burning and a Shining Light: English Spirituality in the Age of Wesley* (Grand Rapids, Mich.: Eerdmans Publishing Co., 1987), 2, for the prevailing Established Church view that "unverifiable presumption of personal revelation or divine calling" was "delusory."

3. John Wesley first listed fasting as one of the rules of his societies in 1743: "The Nature, Design, and General Rules of the United Societies in London, Briston, Kingswood, and Newcastle-on-Tyne," in *The Works of John Wesley*, vol. 9, ed. Rupert E. Davies (Nashville, Tenn.: Abingdon Press, 1989), 73.

4. See contemporary discussions of the relationship between eating and self-will in familial conflict: Gail Corrington, "Anorexia, Asceticism, and Autonomy: Self-Control as Liberation and Transcendence," *Feminist Studies* 2 (Fall 1986): 53–61; and Hilde Bruch, "The Eating Disorders," in Danita Czyzewski and Melanie A. Suhr, eds., *Conversations with Anorexics*

(New York: Basic Books, 1988). A modern view of religious asceticism is "the pleasure of no pleasure" (Margaret Miles, *Practicing Christianity* [New York: Crossroads, 1990], 94).

5. The phrase "literary remains" by Sarah Jane Hennen, ed., *Sentiments and Experience and Other Remains of Lucy Cobham Hennen* (London, 1846), x, summarized autobiographical accounts such as Hester Ann's. Compiled or edited "memoirs" comprised a major genre of popular religious literature from the time of John Bunyan.

6. The *British Museum General Catalogue of Printed Books,* vol. 205, lists eight different editions, the latest in the mid-nineteenth century; the *National Union Catalogue of Early American Imprints,* vol. 501, pp. 180–82, lists forty-six different entries, the latest (n.d.) circa 1914.

7. *The Journal of Mrs. Hester Ann Rogers* (1818; reprint, London: John Mason, 1839). My experience with eighteenth-century pious memoirs indicates that while an editor may exercise selectivity he or she will not add to the author's words.

8. At the American Methodist Archives at Drew University, Madison, New Jersey, no other eighteenth-century woman has so much shelf space.

9. Leonore Davidoff and Catherine Hall, *Family Fortunes: Men and Women of the English Middle Class, 1780–1850* (Chicago: University of Chicago Press, 1987), trace the interaction between evangelical religion and the emerging middle class.

10. Richard P. Heitzenrater, ed., *Diary of an Oxford Methodist, Benjamin Inghan, 1733–1734* (Durham, N.C.: Duke University Press, 1985), 3, has most recently documented the importance of this practice for early Methodists' spiritual self-discipline.

11. I am grateful to Dr. Kenneth Rowe, Methodist Archivist at Drew University, United Methodist Archives, for explaining this practice and for his generous collegial assistance over the years.

12. Among the many memoirs of early English Methodist women I have studied, no others mention the discipline of fasting. I have not seen it in any of the men's memoirs I have read.

13. A contemporary study by Susie Orbach (*Hunger Strike: The Anorectic's Struggle as a Metaphor for Our Age* [New York: W. W. Norton & Co., 1986]) alludes to historical manifestations of what we today call anorexia: "Whenever woman's spirit has been threatened, she has taken the control of her body as an avenue of self-expression" (9).

14. Thomas Coke, *Funeral Sermon* (Birmingham, 1795), 43. In the published journal, Hester names at least a dozen important itinerant clergy with whom she collaborated; other women of various class backgrounds in early Methodism were similarly empowered. See my "Gasping for Larger Measures: Joanna Turner, Eighteenth-Century Activist," *Journal of Feminist Studies of Religion* 3 (Fall 1987): 31–55, and Paul Wesley Chilcote, "She Offered Them Christ: Legacy of Women Preachers in Early Methodism" (Master's thesis, Duke University, 1989).

15. Caroline Walker Bynum, *Holy Feast and Holy Fast: The Religious Significance of Food to Medieval Women* (Berkeley and Los Angeles: University of California Press, 1987), 190–92; *The Works of John Wesley,* vol. 1, sermons 1–33, ed. Albert C. Outler (Nashville, Tenn.: Abingdon Press, 1984), 592–611.

16. Letters between young John Wesley and Richard Morgan, father of one of Wesley's co-religionists in 1732, explain that the death-by-fasting of the son was unrelated to Wesley's prescription. See *The Works of John Wesley,* vol. 1: *Letters, 1721–1739,* ed. Frank Baker (Oxford: Clarendon Press, 1980), 335–44.

17. Erving Goffman, *The Presentation of Self in Everyday Life* (Garden City, N.Y.: Doubleday & Co., 1959), identifies the cultural process through which individuals "manage" the impressions others receive, at least semiconsciously.

18. Bynum, *Holy Feast,* 88; Wesley, Sermon 27, p. 600. Edited materials are by definition vulnerable. Because I have not examined the manuscript diary located at the Rylands Library in Manchester, England, I can only assume that the unnamed editors did not violate her journal by omitting any reference to a "means of grace" such as fasting.

19. *The Works of John Wesley,* 3rd ed. (Grand Rapids, Mich.: Baker Book House, 1979), 13:65, emphasizes his use of Enlightenment terms.

20. Davidson and Hall, *Family Fortunes,* 26.

21. William Mossner, *Bishop Butler and the Age of Reason* (New York: Macmillan, 1936), 236, describes the theology of that or any era as "a solvent of the intellectual and social climate of the times."

22. Jeffrey, *A Burning and a Shining Light,* 6. " 'Madness' was . . . the charge most often levied against any sort of serious and outspoken Christianity."

23. Heizenrater, *Diary of an Oxford Methodist,* 25, cites a letter from John Wesley to his brother valorizing opposition: "No one is a Christian until he is despised."

24. *Journal,* 1839, p. 30.

25. Outler, *Wesley Sermons,* 592.

26. Ibid., 605, 600.

27. Ibid., 598, 595; Bynum, *Holy Feast,* 83.

28. Outler, *Sermons,* 600.

29. Bynum, *Holy Feast,* 231, identified women who, even in medieval times, "claimed" a kind of priestly role.

30. Ibid., 241, 238.

31. *Journal,* 15.

32. *Spiritual Letters,* 12–13, 14. He died, in 1782, having also become a Methodist through her influence.

33. Ibid., 35–36; *Journal,* 67.

34. *Journal,* 212. Subsequent references to the *Journal* are again cited parenthetically in the text.

35. *Account,* 254–55.

36. Ibid., 139.

37. Bynum, *Holy Feast,* 7.

38. See, e.g., Thomas R. Albin, *Full Salvation: The Spirituality of Anna Reynalds of Truro, 1775-1840* (Cornwall, Eng.: J. Edyvean, 1981).

39. The only other scholarly treatment of Hester Ann Rogers' writings thus far is Paul Wesley Chilcote's "John Wesley as Revealed by the Journal of Hester Ann Rogers, July 1775-October 1784," *Methodist History* 20 (April 1982):111-23; he too ignores her fasting.

THE ORDER AND DISORDER
OF EATING IN BYRON'S *DON JUAN*

Peter W. Graham

W e are accustomed, these days, to think of eating orders and disorders as fairly particular matters—the habits of certain religions, cultures, or social classes, or the problems of specific individuals or demographic groups. Taking the particular approach to Lord Byron's involvement with eating yields a fascinating series of anecdotes. Byron, after all, was the man who professed an aversion to supper-swallowing women and who stated, only half-facetiously, "A woman should never be seen eating or drinking, unless it be *lobster sallad & Champagne,* the only truly feminine & becoming viands."[1] He was a Regency prototype of our present-day celebrities, a person turned to personage and trapped by his own personal myth and the expectations of admirers who took that myth for reality. As is often true today, the pressures of fame both caused and encouraged bad habits: Byron drank too much at some times and ate too little at other times. A naturally stout and sturdy man, he occasionally starved himself or resorted to strange diets that he might sustain the pale, slender, Byronic image he created in collaboration with his public.[2]

But all these "real" anecdotes and attitudes, fascinating as they have always been to Byron's public, and useful as they might prove to the psychoanalyst or biographer, are not the stories to be considered in this chapter. Besides the particular choices and pressures that determine what Lord Byron, or Ms. X, or the overachieving upper-middle-class American boarding-school girl, or the clay-eater, or the Brahmin, consumes, there is a universality to the orders and disorders of eating. My goal here is to explore some of the literary ways Byron presents this broad and basic topic in his comic epic *Don Juan,* a poem that is essentially about what it is to be human. One interesting and up-to-date feature of Byron's vision of humanity is his recognition of the close and intricate relationship between how one eats and how one feels. Throughout *Don Juan,* Byron intermittently considers different manifestations of this complicated business of cause and effect, effect and cause. But cantos 2, 3, and 4, where the protagonist experiences the low and high points of human existence, from shipwreck to idyllic love, contain many of Byron's most striking thoughts on eating orders and disorders, and the reading that follows will focus on that part of the poem. In the discussion of eating, drinking, and the various sorts of decisions attendant on these necessary acts, I use the words "order" and "disorder" to distinguish between patterns and choices that are beneficial or neutral in their effects and those that are harmful, whether their bad effects are physical, mental, or a combination of the two.

If all humankind is what Byron in another poem terms "half dust, half deity"[3] then one of the first things to acknowledge about eating and drinking is that they occur in an arena where soul and sense struggle for supremacy—or, perhaps more accurate, where the spirit fights to dominate the stubbornly resisting flesh. Within the human being, neither party can win. When the spirit ceases to press its claims, mere bestiality sets in; and while life remains, the body makes its needs and discomforts known. As a sharp-eyed realist and an idealist in spite of himself, Byron acknowledges the powers of both sides. In the cantos under consideration, his favorite rhetorical device for such acknowledgment is the witty antithetical pairing. While Don Juan's shipmates fight vainly to save their vessel, they take refuge in "rum and true religion,"[4] each a different kind of spiritual remedy with its own efficacy. After the ship and one of its boats are gone, the survivors are doubly sorrowful: "They grieved for those who perish'd with the cutter, / And also for the biscuit casks and butter" (2.61). As Juan, safely washed ashore on a Greek island, regains his strength under the care of the heiress of the isle, his days begin with a sea bath followed by a return to "coffee and Haidée" (2.171), breakfast being as important to his recovery as the maiden who provides it. Toward the end of the canto we find the famous alliterative lines pairing "wine and woman" and "sermons and soda water" (2.178)—one of literature's most frequently quoted appreciations of the pleasurable contrast between luxury and austerity. What all these antithetical pairings suggest is not so much that the higher social and transcendental feelings of Juan and all humanity are false (though they may be) as that lower, more visceral claims coexist with and often supersede such aspirations. In much the same way, the physical need for food overrides aesthetic, social, and even moral objections and drives the survivors of shipwreck to collective indulgence in what, to most of the world, must be considered a particularly extreme eating disorder—in a word, cannibalism.

Byron is deliberate and meticulous in representing the preliminaries to this act that his readers are likely to find disgusting. In stanza 47 of canto 2, he specifically lists the provisions stowed in the longboat before its thirty passengers embark: bread, water, wine, beef, pork, and rum. For two days the storm continues, each minute seems the last, and the food is not surprisingly untouched. But the third day brings a calm, and with it a return of appetite and hope, animal and spiritual qualities that, acting together, spur the improvident survivors to eat up all their provisions. A fourth day passes; the men fast. On the fifth day, "hunger's rage [grows] wild" (2.70). They kill and eat Don Juan's spaniel, an entrée he high-mindedly refuses. On the sixth day the dog's hide is consumed. Don Juan, "feeling all the vulture in his jaws" (2.71), can hold out no longer and "with some remorse" accepts one of the forepaws. As Byron's choice of words implies, Juan now eats not because his sentiments have changed but because hunger's increasing pangs have overbalanced this particular scruple, though not every one he cherishes. On the seventh day nothing edible remains. "Longings of the cannibal" arise (2.72), first unvoiced, then whispered, then spoken aloud as each sufferer realizes that his own suppressed and guilty thought is the common impulse. Before fulfilling their desires, though, the sailors endure another day of hunger, during which they chew "some leathern caps, and what remain'd of shoes" (2.74). This valiant but inadequate temporizing is easy to overlook, but it is nonetheless important in that it shows the sailors' lingering power of conscience or spirit (call it what you will) to fight in the face of physical agony and resist their acknowledged inclination for a more "disorderly" meal than that constituted by animal hides.

Byron's slow and detail-laden approach to the cannibalistic moment rises in part out of his having based this poetical shipwreck on published accounts of such real disasters—in part, perhaps, out of his desire to recreate something of the flow of events in the shape of his stanzas, but certainly out of thematic necessity. The narrator's view of the disagreeable facts he and the reader must face is objective. "None in particular had sought or plann'd it, / 'Twas Nature gnaw'd them to this resolution" (2.75), he observes, and in lines that come close to being extenuation he generalizes, "But man is a carnivorous production, / And must have meals, at least one meal a day" (2.67). If we readers are to be similarly nonjudgmental, we must have every assurance that these transgressors of our eating codes have done all they can to avoid what they end up doing. The narrative offers these assurances. Our notions of life and art may nonetheless insist that the cannibals in the poem should be punished for their disorderly conduct, and, as we shall shortly see, in his selection of narrative detail Byron teasingly holds out the possibility of such providential retribution only to force us to reject it.

When the horrid moment is at hand and lots are drawn, it falls on Don Juan's tutor, Pedrillo, to die that others may live. It is characteristic of Byron's sharp-eyed, now satirical, now compassionate view of humanity that Pedrillo, who has earlier shown himself to be both foolish and cowardly, summons up the inner resources to meet his fate with courage and dignity. Oddly and yet aptly, what permits Pedrillo to cope with the extraordinary situation of being butchered as mere meat is his conventional piety, though at this point it is not surprising that neither he nor anyone else on the boat is reflective enough to ponder the interesting potential connections between cannibalism and Catholic Christianity. Do Christ's example and the ritual of the Eucharist make it easier for Pedrillo to sacrifice his body and blood? Is the cosmopolitan narrator—who elsewhere shows himself interested in making cultural comparisons between insular British values and the ways of wider world—playing on his immediate audience's possible prejudices concerning transubstantiation, a Catholic doctrine that has sometimes been seen as cannibalistic when viewed from the less sacramental side of Protestantism? No explicit speculations on such matters delay or digress from the act itself now that the starving men have resolved to do it. As the narrator coolly comments, Pedrillo "but requested to be bled to death," a surgeon being at hand. Then

> He died as born, a Catholic in faith,
>   Like most in the belief in which they're bred,
> And first a little crucifix he kiss'd,
> And then held out his jugular and wrist. (2.76)

The surgeon happens to be especially thirsty, so his fee is "a draught from the fast-flowing veins" (2.77). Once life has ebbed with the lifeblood, poor Pedrillo is cut up in the conventionally wasteful way that prevails under ordinary circumstances of cattle-butchering on land. Here Byron's gruesome specificity demonstrates yet again the starving sailors' inability to think through their situation. These men are so frenzied for immediate sustenance, or so thoroughly the products of their culture, the "belief in which they're bred," that they fail to see that wasting part of Pedrillo now may result later in starvation, or another cannibalistic killing:

> Part was divided, part thrown in the sea,
>   And such things as the entrails and the brains
> Regaled the sharks, who follow'd o'er the billow—
> The sailors ate the rest of poor Pedrillo. (2.77)

The unhallowed and improvident meal is shared by all but Juan and three or four of the sailors, "who were not quite so fond of animal food" (2.78). What proves particularly relevant to a reading centered on eating disorders is the consequence of this meal: those who feed most heartily on poor Pedrillo go mad, blaspheme, drink salt water, laugh like hyenas, and die despairing.

As self-righteous noncannibals, we might be tempted to see this fate as the supernatural punishment of wrongdoing. But if we read things that way, we prove ourselves no more logical than the surviving sailors, who a few stanzas later will naively see omens of their personal deliverance in a rainbow, a "beautiful white bird" (which nonetheless they would gladly consume) and a hawk's-bill turtle that comes their way just as land is in sight. Despite any readerly wishes for an assertion of divine order, the cannibals who froth, rave, and die after their monstrous feast perish at the conclusion of a chain of natural events, one that requires no supernatural intervention. Immoderate consumption, in a starved state, of inappropriate food and drink proves traumatic to their physical systems. Their minds too play some part, whether direct, in imposing an unbearable burden of guilt for not respecting principles of bodily integrity, or indirect, as would be the case if violating one taboo (the chiefly moral injunction against eating human flesh) were to break down all others, including the purely practical one against drinking seawater. Thus, in the scene Byron presents, an eating disorder characterized by gluttonous cannibalism has a natural and harmful effect both on the bodies and on the minds of its practitioners, just as "orderly" eating of the sea turtle offers the surviving few, among them a handful of the more temperate cannibals, food "Which yielded a day's life, and to their mind / Proved even still a more nutritious matter, / Because it left encouragement behind" (2.99).

Despite this timely nourishment, Juan alone among the handful of survivors arrives living back on land, and his hold on life is tenuous. But two young women find him washed ashore, battered and unconscious. The mistress, Haidée, falls in love; her servant, Zoe, usefully prepares a breakfast: "eggs, fruit, coffee, bread, fish, honey, / With Scio wine" (2.145). As Juan partly regains consciousness, the beautiful, sweet-voiced lady tending him becomes part of his reverie. What finally and fully brings him back to his senses, significantly enough, is not the lovely Haidée but "the steam / Of Zoe's cookery," and when Juan wakes with "a most prodigious appetite" Byron again seizes an opportunity to contrast orders and disorders of eating (2.153). Although Juan regrets the absence of a "beefsteak," he is ready to fall with gorging intemperance on what's available. The infatuated Haidée would allow this feeding "past all bounds, because she smiled to see / Such appetite in one she had deem'd dead" (2.158). Zoe—older, more practical, less enslaved by her passions—realizes "That famish'd people must be slowly nurst, / And fed by spoonfuls, else they always burst" (2.158).

This is romance with a difference, not because the shipwrecked gentleman is fed by his lady rescuer (that convention stretches back to the *Odyssey*) but because Byron's presentation acknowledges the potential for disordered eating and the inability of either romantic principal adequately to manage the situation. Without Zoe, the prosaic member of the trio, the breakfast would not be prepared for or healthfully consumed by the malnourished man who needs it. Furthermore, Byron shows that this appropriately administered physical sustenance is an indispensable preliminary to love. We have already seen the relative importance of food and love in Juan's present circumstances accurately suggested by the fact that he was revived not by a kiss but by the aroma of breakfast, which will literally be a "break-fast" for him. The point becomes yet more obvious through a mythological generalization:

> . . . and some good lessons
> Are also learnt from Ceres and from Bacchus,
> Without whom Venus will not long attack us. (2.169)

Sufficiently encouraged by Ceres and Bacchus, Juan does become Haidée's lover in sense as well as in spirit, and this romantic situation is the poem's most sublime moment. But in *Don Juan* everything must change over time, even so perfect-seeming a relationship, and without spelling out the difference Byron signals it by altering the lovers' physical surroundings. In canto 3 the scene shifts from the rocky coast to the richly furnished house from which Haidée's father is absent. Juan's costume goes from rags to elaborate Eastern dress. The lovers' communion of a simple breakfast by the shore gives way to their return to society, as reflected in a sumptuous and elaborately served feast that is less natural nourishment than artificial ostentation:

> The dinner made about a hundred dishes;
>   Lamb and pistachio nuts—in short, all meats,
> And saffron soups, and sweetbreads; and the fishes
>   Were of the finest that e'er flounced in nets.
> Drest to a Sybarite's most pamper'd wishes;
>   The beverage was various sherbets
> Of raisin, orange, and pomegranate juice,
> Squeezed through the rind, which makes it best for use. (3.62)

It would be ridiculously puritanical to speak of this well-balanced menu, where the emphasis is on rarity and variety more than on profusion, as evidence of disordered eating. Instead, it is a public occasion for celebrating the good things of this world. But when we compare and contrast this tableau with what has come before—namely, the shipwrecked starvation that drives civilized men to cannibalism and the seaside breakfasts necessary to bring back the amorous side of Don Juan—we must recognize that Byron is yet again drawing on the choices that order eating to illuminate the human condition. The pleasures and orders of eating, however exquisite the dishes, prove our human connection to the earth, a connection that even the highest human love does sever.

What can break this connection is the disorder of *not eating,* and that is how Byron dispatches poor Haidée, who on losing Juan dies, though not of love—or not immediately of love, in any case. As was true in the presentation of cannibalism, Byron carefully lays out his heroine's progress toward death. Without being clinical about the physical consequences of emotional anguish or systematic about the stages of grief, the narrative shows us how mind and body collaborate in self-destruction as well as in self-preservation. When Haidée's father, the pirate Lambro, makes his presence known at the feast, stabs the combative Juan, and sends him in shackles to a slave ship,

Haidée's hot blood flows forth as if in sympathy. A "burst vein" in her head brings on a coma that lasts for days. She awakens without memory, and then a musician's love song recalls the past with power that "whirl[s] her brain to madness" (4.67). This derangement takes the form of a sleepless frenzy in which she refuses food until, twelve days later, she dies.

We would have to oversimplify on many counts to conclude that, in the death of Haidée, Byron is offering us an accurately described case of anorexia nervosa some sixty years before the syndrome had acquired a name. Even if we knew many more things about Haidée than the limits of fiction permit us to know, it would be difficult to establish a verdict of anorexia given that her last happy and unequivocally sane moments are passed at a banquet with her beloved. But Haidée does share a number of attributes linked to anorexia, or at least to how we perceive it.[5] As daughter of the piratical master of the isle, she has relatively high social and economic status; she is as *bourgeoise* as it is possible to be on one of the Cyclades at the end of the eighteenth century. She has grown up with the advantages and disadvantages of intense parental love, though the fact that only the father survives to provide this love distinguishes her from the classic anorexic, whose intense relationship with a living mother is often crucial. Like many a compliant anorexic, Haidée has taken on the role of mirroring her parents. In her case, such responsibilities are particularly intense: she reflects her father, Lambro, and at the same time she is obliged to be all that exists of her mother to that father. Byron presents her striking success in reflecting the one parent and embodying the other in such lines as the following:

> He gazed on her, and she on him; 'twas strange
>   How like they look'd! (4.44)

> Her father's blood before her father's face
> Boil'd up, and proved her truly of his race. (4.44)

> I said they were alike, their features and
>   Their stature differing but in sex and years;
> Even to the delicacy of their hand
>   There was resemblance, such as true blood wears. (4.45)

> She was not one to weep, and rave, and chafe,
>   And then give way, subdued because surrounded;
> Her mother was a Moorish maid, from Fez,
> Where all is Eden, or a wilderness. (4.54)

But in addition to the fact that Haidée's cool Grecian side (the paternal contribution to her psyche) is blended with her mother's hot African nature, Haidée is Lambro with yet another difference. During the days of Lambro's absence she has become a sexually experienced woman, and whether she knows it or not, she is carrying her lover's child. Thus Haidée's death by sensory deprivation shares some features of certain anorexics' fears of womanliness, sexuality, and childbirth. Starving herself and thereby minimizing the signs and substance of her female fertility, Haidée does what she can to remain the mirror of her father. The act can be seen yet more broadly as Haidée's denial of her own creatureliness now that the fellow creature she loves above all others has been torn from her by the father she has mirrored. Her denial takes the form of renouncing those physical pleasures — both feasting and accepting, even reveling in, her womanliness — that she formerly enjoyed with Don Juan. And most important, her abstinence from everything the body needs is, like the anorexic's fasting, an act of control carried out by a person who has felt herself controlled. Haidée's sensory deprivation is a potent piece of manipulation, punishing both the piratical father whose role of "enslaver" has been domestic as well as public, and the cherished daughter whose love for Don Juan has betrayed that father. Her self-starvation is a tangle of conscious resolve and mad impulse, of successive, mutually reinforced psychic and somatic pressures. Haidée's mode of death, like the other episodes we have examined, suggests that we humans are how and what we eat, but also that how and what we eat is not all we are.

Byron's method of bringing this truth home to his implied English reader is subtle and ingenious. Cantos 2, 3, and 4 range widely, as we have seen, through possible orders and disorders of eating, from starvation to sybaritic feasting. Byron "domesticates" these exotic experiences for the implied English reader, who is not likely to have experienced shipwreck or a Greek banquet, by making English tastes and values normative and thereby forging an intermittently visible link between the fictive situations and the reader's presumed experience. For instance, when offered Zoe's restorative breakfast, Juan falls "upon whate'er was offer'd, like / A priest, a shark, an alderman, or pike" (2.157). Among these exemplars of insatiability, only the shark is truly universal, the greedy alderman being a distinctively English stereotype, and the gluttony of priest and pike being associations respectively characteristic of though not unique to Protestant, northern nations such as Great Britain. Later, at the banquet already described, the British narrator evaluates the Turkish method of preparing coffee from his own cultural perspective: "Cloves, cinnamon, and saffron too were boil'd / Up with the coffee, which (I think) they spoil'd" (3.63). Most notable are the repeated references to the English indispensables beef and tea. Eight of *Don Juan's* eleven references to beef are in the shipwreck canto (see 2.13, 47, 67, 153, 154, 155, 156), and most of the references are more than mere matters of fact. They voice John Bull's characteristic prejudice in favor of beef as a sovereign remedy for seasickness and an ever-reliable source of health and strength. In the same vein the narrator notes, as if to regret, the absence of tea from Don Juan's first island breakfast, and this favorite English beverage is mentioned twice in canto 4. One allusion to tea is especially intriguing in that it broadens the relevance of Byron's speculations on eating orders and disorders to include not only the poem's characters, narrator, and implied audience but also even himself, the composing presence.

As Don Juan's adventures give way to the account of Haidée's death through self-deprivation in canto 4, the narrator, speaking in his most solidly authorial voice, suggests not only that Juan's story is what he chooses to make it but also that he, the maker of the fiction, is what his choice of beverages has for the moment made him:

> Here I must leave him, for I grow pathetic,
>   Moved by the Chinese nymph of tears, green tea!
> Than whom Cassandra was not more prophetic;
>   For if my pure libations exceed three,
> I feel my heart become so sympathetic,
>   That I must have recourse to black Bohea:
> 'Tis pity wine should be so deleterious,
> For tea and coffee leave us much more serious. (4.52)

A cup of tea (or, more precisely, an emptied cup containing tea leaves) has often been cast in the mythic role of sibyl. Here, however, Byron makes the beverage inspirational rather than merely prophetic and thereby exalts tea to the position of muse. Like many an outrageous-sounding assertion in *Don Juan,* this claim is at once false and true. The notion that an entire sentimental episode has been fostered by drinking China tea is absurd. Fond though Byron may have been of posing as an effortlessly spontaneous versifier, even he did not compose so rapidly. But a more general point is plausible: authors are human, and humans are to some extent shaped by their orderly and disorderly eating habits. Therefore cantos 2, 3, and 4 may be as they are in part because of what their author eats, drinks, or refrains from consuming. Speculating on the nature and extent of this possible relationship would be an engrossing and complex exercise that could evoke a series of equally fascinating psycho-bio-critical topics. DeQuincey's prose style as fluctuating response to pain and opiates? Anorexic qualities of Dickinson's verse? Relations between Shaw's didactic wit and his vegetarianism? In any case, what we have here and for the moment is Byron's acknowledgment that he is governed by the same rules and subject to the same constraints that operate in the world of his poem. The sovereign author, like his characters, his narrator, and his implied reader, is in fact a fiction shaped to some extent by orders and disorders of eating.

Notes

1. Lord Byron, *Letters and Journals,* ed. Leslie A. Marchand (Cambridge, Mass.: Harvard University Press, 1973-), 2:208, letter of September 25, 1812, to Lady Melbourne.

2. On Byron's concern with weight loss and dieting see his *Letters and Journals* 1:113–14, 115, 117, 119, 121-22, 122-23, 133, 144-45; 2:131; 3:212, 226, 235, 237, 257; 8:165; 9:180.

3. Lord Byron, *Manfred,* scene 2, line 40. Quoted in *The Oxford English Authors: Byron,* ed. Jerome J. McGann (New York: Oxford University Press, 1986), 283.

4. Lord Byron, *Don Juan,* canto 2, stanza 34. Subsequent citations to canto and stanza will come, as this one does, from the standard edition of the poem edited by Jerome J. McGann (Oxford: Clarendon, 1986) and will appear parenthetically in the text in this fashion: (2.34).

5. For the social and psychological traits characteristic of anorexia, three books are particularly useful. Hilde Bruch's *Eating Disorders: Obesity, Anorexia Nervosa, and the Person Within* (New York: Basic Books, 1973) is a well-grounded clinical study (see esp. pp. 227-84); Bruch's *Golden Cage: The Enigma of Anorexia Nervosa* (Cambridge, Mass.: Harvard University Press, 1978) is an account of the disease geared toward a more general audience. Joan Jacobs Brumberg's *Fasting Girls: The Emergence of Anorexia Nervosa as a Modern Disease* (Cambridge, Mass.: Harvard University Press, 1988) is a careful historical appraisal of the disease and of the various theoretical models that attempt to account for it. Both Bruch and Brumberg serve as useful correctives to the notion that anorexia nervosa is an easily characterized disorder with a single etiology: instead, anorexia rises out of varied and complex causes and follows diverse paths. My purpose here is to point out aspects of Haidée's situation that are comparable to those of some — but certainly not all — anorexics.

THE ANOREXIC SYNDROME
AND THE NINETEENTH-CENTURY
DOMESTIC NOVEL

Paula Marantz Cohen

Anorexia nervosa is an eating disorder that has been occurring in epidemic numbers among adolescent girls over the past twenty years. Girls with this disorder crave food obsessively but refuse to eat, displaying an equally obsessive concern for their weight and figure. Although anorexic behavior looks like a neurotic response to societal pressure to be thin, this is hardly a sufficient explanation for the psychodynamics behind the condition. Anorexics also imbue their relationship to food with intense moral associations. They see eating as sinful self-indulgence, and abstaining from food as heroic and virtuous. It is significant, moreover, that anorexic girls usually come from intact middle- and upper-middle-class nuclear families and prior to the onset of the disorder had the reputation for being "perfect" children.[1]

Some specialists studying the complex symptomatology of anorexia nervosa have begun to see the disorder as more than an individual psychological problem.[2] They contend that patterns of interaction in the "family system" may encourage the development and maintenance of anorexia in a daughter. In other words, their focus is not on the young girl struggling with the pressures of contemporary ideas about beauty and sexuality, but on the family struggling with the pressures that it, as a collective body, faces. This perspective has led me to "read" anorexia as a cultural symptom that can provide insights about the family as an institution. It has also prompted me to draw certain correspondences between the anorexic's case and that of the heroine in the nineteenth-century domestic novel, to perceive the novel system and the family system as analogous forms in which the heroine and the daughter perform analogous "regulating" roles.

The nineteenth-century Anglo-American domestic novel is part of a literary tradition that begins with Samuel Richardson (whose epistolary novel *Clarissa,* although written in the eighteenth century, effectively launches the tradition) and ends with Henry James, who remained attached to the formal and thematic concerns of his predecessors while ushering in the more individualistic themes and more open narrative form associated with modernism. The information about families provided by the novels within this tradition is not simply representational. If it were, there would be no reason to assume that a given novel, even a great and enduring one, is anything more than a reflection of a particular author's vision of reality. Instead, novels must be said to resemble families on the level of their form, for the genre of the novel evolved in tandem with the nuclear family and, inspired by and contributing to the same ideology, was subject to many of the same laws. The literary theorist M. M. Bakhtin has described the novel as "the only developing genre . . . the only genre that was born and nourished in a new era of world history and therefore . . . deeply akin to that era."[3] In other words, the novel is the only genre that corresponds structurally and dynamically to the experience in which it was written. Because the nuclear family is the generative site of experience in this "new era," its form becomes the logical focus for a correspondence to the form of the novel.

Although the germs of the modern family in western Europe have been traced to earlier periods, historians generally agree that a conspicuous transformation in family structure and function began to take place in the seventeenth and eighteenth centuries.[4] During this period, the family evolved from a relatively porous, extended network of relations, primarily concerned with the transmission of property, titles, and skills from generation to generation (i.e., in a temporal frame) to a more restricted, "nuclear" unit of relations concerned with the maintenance of affective interactions in a household (i.e., in a spatial frame). During roughly the same period, the novel underwent an analogous evolution. It moved away from its seventeenth- and eighteenth-century origins in the loosely stitched accounts of picaresque adventure to become the intricate, psychologically resonant narrative form—which I refer to as the *domestic novel*—that we associate with the genre's maturity in the nineteenth century. By the same token, just as modern literature has progressively defined itself through either a dramatic disregard for nineteenth-century literary conventions or a parodic attachment to them, the family in the twentieth century has exhibited escalating tendencies in these two directions as well: reactions against nuclearity are reflected in rising statistics on divorce and alternative life-style arrangements, and attempts to bolster nuclearity are reflected in the high incidence of such disorders as anorexia nervosa, which seem designed to maintain family closure at all costs.[5]

In the case of both the nuclear family and the domestic novel, then, we are dealing with systems that were characterized by stability and closure in the nineteenth century and that now appear to be experiencing instability and disruption. Of course, neither system was ever more than relatively closed. Just as families must depend on interactions with the world outside, so novels depend on readers and are subject to individual values, tastes, and interpretive approaches. Yet the ideology of closure in the nineteenth century was a driving force in the development and elaboration of the form that defined families and novels. Families were seen as retreats from a hostile external world; in the words of John Ruskin, intellectual spokesman of the nineteenth century, they were "the place of Peace; the shelter from all terror, doubt and division."[6] Hence, the definition of sex roles, the requirements of etiquette, the rearing of children, and so forth, evolved to enforce that isolation. Novels, for their part, were expected to tie up loose ends, both structural and thematic, and so the typical novel ended with a well-deserved marriage or with a death that either glorified or appropriately degraded its subject.[7] This ideological dominance of closure both in nineteenth-century domestic novels and in nuclear families suggests that these novels not only have families as their subject-matter but also operate *like* the families they represent: both are systems with boundaries seeking to maintain closure. It would follow that, if we can study the interactive patterns that govern the novels, we can apply those patterns to the families they represent and gain insight into the way these patterns may have evolved into the present.

The tools that make this analysis possible are the tools of family systems theory,[8] a relatively new branch of psychology, derived from general systems and communication theory, that views the family as a system of interactive parts struggling to achieve equilibrium. Family systems theorists are concerned with analyzing the patterns of interaction that govern families and particularly with identifying the repetitive patterns of interaction that can generate and support mental illness. Family systems concepts were originally developed for studying contemporary, pathogenic families and, as noted above, have encountered some success in the analysis and treatment of anorexia nervosa. But a systems approach to family operation can have even wider application. It can help lay bare the structure of the nuclear family in the context of its history. By studying the interactive patterns of characters in late eighteenth- and nineteenth-century domestic novels, we can learn how families operated during that period of greatest apparent stability and prestige for the nuclear family.

A decade ago, Sandra Gilbert and Susan Gubar called attention to the many female characters in nineteenth-century English literature who seemed to suffer from psychosomatic disorders, anorexia nervosa among them.[9] These critics concentrated on literature by women and connected the often muted or metaphorical symptoms of the characters to the oppressive conditions operating in the lives of their creators. But the representation of female illness in literature of the nineteenth century is not confined to the work of female authors. Heroines in Jane Austen, Charlotte and Emily Brontë, Elizabeth Gaskell, and George Eliot are often frail and at least temporarily sickly, but so are many of the heroines in Charles Dickens, Wilkie Collins, Anthony Trollope, Thomas Hardy, and other male authors of the period. Insofar as male authors also represented frail or sickly women as heroines, this representation of the heroine cannot be understood simply as a form of protest against constraint, as Gilbert and Gubar contended. It must also have performed a necessary role both in the novels and, by extension, in the culture. In other words, the heroines' symptoms must be seen as functional with respect to the effective resolution of the narrative, the stabilization of the family ideal which the novel generally depicted in its conclusion, and the facilitation of the heroine's own happiness. Indeed, we need to acknowledge that it is only our present perspective that labels these heroines as psychologically aberrant. In the context of the novels, their illnesses are represented as necessary, even exemplary methods of dealing with emotional stress. Thus, for example, Emily Lopez's illness following her husband's death in Trollope's *Prime Minister* serves as a form of expiation that makes it possible for her finally to accept the suitor she realizes she wants; Caroline Helstone's illness in Charlotte Brontë's *Shirley* serves to bring her into contact with her lost mother; Maggie Tulliver's self-starvation in Eliot's *Mill on the Floss* serves as rigorous practice for later, more subtle acts of self-abnegation that, while they lose her her reputation and culminate in her death, nonetheless help effect the reunion with her brother which she craves. Even when the heroine loses her life through her illness, as with Catherine Earnshaw in *Wuthering Heights* or little Eva in *Uncle Tom's Cabin,* the death is made functional by serving as the solution to an impossible dilemma or as an inspiration for the future. The quintessential example of such functionality, as I shall argue, is the death of Clarissa.

What these novels provide, therefore, is a perspective that coincides with the perspective of the modern-day anorexic who views herself as a heroine very much in the nineteenth-century mold. The anorexic sees herself as a veritable "angel in the house," superior to others in her self-restraint but at the same time in willing thrall to others. While today's culture "corrects for" the anorexic self-conception, the domestic novel, like the culture in which it was written, shared that conception and valorized such behavior. It did this largely because it was more invested in an ideology of closure for the family that depended on the daughter's regulating role. And indeed, despite a high incidence of female illness during the nineteenth century, the role as it fit into an overall family dynamic was temporarily successful in keeping the nuclear family in a state of relative stability, of maintaining it intact. Today, by contrast, the role has become destructive of the very stability and unity it seeks to preserve.

The epidemic of anorexia nervosa in today's society and the centrality of the heroine in the nineteenth-century novel can be correlated to produce a postulate about how the nuclear family was able to achieve relative stability during the nineteenth century and how that stability became increasingly difficult to maintain over the course of the twentieth century. The family has been maintained as a relatively closed system through the strategic use of the role of the daughter, who stereotypically occupies the position of least power in the family and is most likely to be assigned the role of carrying the family's emotional stress. Hence, she is most likely to exhibit psychosomatic symptoms. But how did the daughter's regulatory function get built into the workings of the modern family?

Basic to the conventions of nineteenth-century life and to the structure of nineteenth-century novels was the idea of sexual role-complementarity, of one sex providing the character traits and talents lacking in the other. Out of this role-complementarity within the nuclear family came a hierarchy: a system that aspires to closure must be governed; its boundaries must be maintained and, hence, it must rely on someone to define the structure and people who submit to it. This basic inequality was an accepted part of the concept of "separate spheres," which dictated that the woman was the emotional helpmate of the man (in John Ruskin's words, "Her function is praise"[10]) as well as his legal subordinate (in the words of Blackstone's *Commentaries on the Laws of England* [1765–69], husband and wife are "one person," the husband, with "the very being or legal existence of the woman . . . suspended during the marriage"[11]). Although the asymmetry of sexual roles cannot be said to originate with the nuclear family—it was probably present at the beginning of civilization, as Lévi-Strauss's work on elementary kinship structure suggests—hierarchical complementarity of the kind engendered by the relatively closed system of the nuclear family had to give rise to its own particular dynamic.[12]

Complementarity is a structural arrangement that is vulnerable to what communications theorist Gregory Bateson has termed "escalating positive feedback," a situation in which complementary positions escalate in opposing directions threatening the viability of the original, balanced system.[13] A systemic analysis of the nuclear family in a historical frame suggests that sexual complementarity as embodied in the companiate ("love") marriage (that began to replace the arranged marriage in the eighteenth century) would not function as the dynamic core of the family for long. This is because such complementarity, though initially checked by the counter-conventions of romantic love, would, once that love dissipated, quickly harden into conventional role-playing and escalate to the point where the system was no longer viable. (It is just such conventionalized, nonromanticized complementarity that fuels pornographic literature and gives it its escalating sadomasochistic quality.[14]) Because a stable complementarity is one in which the complementary elements also contain built-in checks that short-circuit or deescalate interactions when they surpass a certain level of intensity, the nuclear family needed to incorporate such checks early.

The couple that began to marry for love in the eighteenth century did indeed have the means to institute such checks through the strategic use of its children.[15] In other words, the problem of escalating complementarity could be solved by involving the child in the dynamic relationship of the couple so as to produce an alternative configuration able to contain and redistribute forces that would otherwise rupture the family. But this triangle of parents and child was, I contend, a stopgap measure, a temporary arrangement valuable principally in producing a new and more stable dyadic relationship consisting not of husband and wife but of father and daughter. This cross-sexual, cross-generational relationship of father and daughter functioned as the core of the nuclear family because, unlike the husband-wife relationship, where complementarity was purely a matter of convention (aided by the short-lived imaginative projection produced by romantic love), the father-daughter relationship was based on structural complementarity. While the basic hierarchy of sexual roles was preserved, the daughter, bred from infancy to complement the father, also tended to mold the father to her, creating something akin to the functional complementarity of parts in biological organisms. The result of this father-daughter complementarity was the arrested development of the daughter and the freezing of the father into a static relationship with her. Hence we can see how the daughter's continued emotional tie to her family of origin became the means by which the family, as embodied in the father, could be maintained in the wake of change. We can also understand why the feminine ideal became associated with a frail, sexually undeveloped female body, a girl's body.[16]

The disorder known as anorexia nervosa appears to dramatize the stabilizing role of the daughter in the nuclear family as this role has become increasingly strained and distorted in its passage from one generation to the next. The anorexic epidemic among intact nuclear families today thus seems to be the finally visible pathological result of a long-term series of short-term adjustments the family has made through the daughter since the eighteenth century.

Insight into the regulatory nature of the daughter's role in the family can be gained if we consider the plot of the novel that originates the genre of domestic novel and coincides with the emergence of the nuclear family as a cultural institution: Samuel Richardson's *Clarissa; or, The History of a Young Lady,* first published in 1748.

Clarissa Harlowe is the youngest child in her family. "From her infancy," Richardson tells us, she was "a matchless young creature . . . admired by all who knew her, as a very extraordinary child."[17] But this angelic daughter will suffer a mythic ordeal in the course of the novel. Courted by the aristocratic rake, Lovelace, her brother's enemy, and forced by her family to suffer the advances of the "squat," "very illiterate," but "Rich Solmes," she is driven to desperation. Through an elaborate stratagem that exploits her fear, Lovelace prevails on Clarissa to run away with him. He pretends to settle her in a reputable house, which in reality covers for a brothel, and attempts to seduce her. Suspecting his designs, Clarissa at last manages to escape, only to have Lovelace trick her back to the house and rape her.

Escaping again, she finds her own lodgings, where, refusing to eat and growing rapidly weaker and more wasted, she now occupies herself in an elaborate preparation for death. When she finally dies, her family and Lovelace are overwhelmed with remorse. Lovelace is killed in a duel with her cousin, expiring in the agonized consciousness of his crime, while the Harlowes spend what remains of their lives suffering the pangs of guilt and singing the praises of their daughter.

As this summary indicates, the novel contains many of the elements that crop up in anorexic case histories. The daughter, once seen as "perfect," suddenly becomes, in her family's opinion, recalcitrant and unreasonable. She experiences the physical and emotional changes of adolescence as at once seductive and threatening. She struggles with issues of merger and independence with respect to her family, and she uses self-starvation as a means of reconciling these contradictory desires. Like the modern anorexic, Clarissa's body becomes a canvas for independent expression and a means of self-effacement culminating in self-annihilation. (Clarissa goes so far as to have her coffin carved to her specifications and placed in her bedroom as she slowly wastes away.) The physical wasting turns Clarissa's body into something frail, childlike, and asexual, while it also allows her to exert extraordinary control over her family (albeit after her death) through the guilt and pity she ultimately engenders in those who have "done her wrong." In short, she becomes a kind of icon or fetish on which both she and her family can fix their attention. Moreover, for the novel to work, the reader must become equally obsessed with the self-denying trajectory of Clarissa's story. In this respect, Clarissa serves a regulatory function not only for the family depicted in the novel but also for the novel system itself, since it is through her story that we achieve the sense of satisfying closure that we come to expect from nineteenth-century novels.

Clarissa Harlowe can be called literature's original anorexic. The difference, however, between the eighteenth-century novel heroine and the modern anorexic daughter reflects the difference between the relation of self to family in the eighteenth century, when the family was experiencing a shift to nuclear structure, and that of the twentieth century, when the nuclear family is experiencing breakdown, or at least being reformulated according to terms that rely less on an ideology of closure. It is as if Richardson, writing at the advent of the industrial age, recognized that the family structure, which the new society was destined to embrace, needed an anorexic presence to support it in the absence of belief in more transcendent values (substituting what family theorists have referred to as a "family ledger" of credits and debits for the notion of divine love and retribution[18]). Clarissa's story serves to publicize the utility of scapegoating the daughter (since such scapegoating helps to define familial roles and draw the family together), while it also dramatizes the importance of enforcing limits on such scapegoating (by permitting its scapegoating to go unchecked, Clarissa is driven to her death and the family is completely subjugated to her memory). *Clarissa*, thus, can be read as an explicit warning against uncontrolled scapegoating of the daughter by the family and an implicit call for *controlled* scapegoating—that is, for the creation of daughter-heroines whose anorexic symptoms are mild or latent, kept from dangerous escalation.

The heroines of most nineteenth-century novels are indeed anorexic daughters controlled to a greater or lesser degree in the service of the family. Probably the best example of this type is the frail and morally scrupulous heroine of Jane Austen's novel, *Mansfield Park* (1814). Fanny Price is too bland to be likeable in the way that Austen's sparkling heroines, Elizabeth Bennet and Emma Woodhouse, are, but perhaps for this reason she succeeds in being Austen's most family-centered heroine. Adopted by her wealthy uncle and aunt Bertram when she is still a child, Fanny comes to live a life of sufferance with people who tend to neglect and slight her at every turn. At first, it is possible to imagine that the plot of *Mansfield Park* might follow the course of *Clarissa*, with Fanny scapegoated to death by her adopted family. But one soon realizes that Austen has built checks into the system. When the Bertram family takes its scapegoating of Fanny to unhealthy limits, she gets headaches and feels poorly, immediately arousing the family (and particularly her male cousin and her uncle) to adjust their behavior. (No such adjustment occurs in *Clarissa*, where Clarissa's faintness and feebleness tend only to inspire the family and Lovelace to escalate their abuse—at least until it's too late to make a difference.) Fanny's general frailty and sickliness thus function like a delicate homeostatic mechanism for the family. Any sign of breakdown in her signals the need for immediate compensatory action on the part of her male complements within the system. In the end, Fanny's delicate, long-suffering presence wins out. Her cousin, for whom she has been silently pining all along, finally recognizes that she is the girl for him, and they marry and settle next door to his father and mother (her adopted parents). As Fanny moves with her cousin (now an ordained clergyman) into the Mansfield parsonage, Austen tells us that this dwelling "which Fanny had [before] never been able to approach but with some painful sensation of restraint or alarm, soon grew as dear to her heart, and as thoroughly perfect in her eyes, as every thing else, within view and patronage of Mansfield Park, had long been."[19] All sites of pain have been dissolved, and the future, as Austen summarizes it, stretches before us as a static vision of perfect bliss for everyone concerned (with the exception, of course, of those who have been banished from the closed circle of Mansfield Park).

Insofar as Fanny is the *adopted* daughter of the Bertram family, the novel reflects its concern with the process of initiating the daughter into a new role as the basis for a new kind of family system. Clarissa was initiated into her new role through death, but in dying she also left the role open. Fanny, plucked from her workaday life in a traditional family (the Prices have all the hallmarks of an open-lineage, low-affect family), can be said to fill that gap.

My conception of scapegoating and guilt as a stabilizing dynamic for the nuclear family bears comparison to the functioning of the id and the superego as Freud conceived it with respect to the individual psyche. In *Totem and Taboo,* Freud postulated an originating story, a "primal myth," for his ideas. The sons of our earliest ancestors, overwhelmed by aggressive impulses, banded together and killed their father, he explained. The killing produced guilt in the sons, who though they had envied their father had also loved him. Forever after, Freud concluded, a collective sense of guilt about that original crime would keep the aggressive impulses in the human psyche in check and hence preserve the ego in a state of relative balance and health. Like Freud, Richardson's novel represents a kind of primal myth, but it is a myth describing the origin not of the modern psyche but of the modern nuclear family. The Harlowe family scapegoats Clarissa to death and generates an intense sense of familial guilt as a result. That story could now serve a cautionary function: it could warn others not to repeat the Harlowes' mistakes but to learn from them. In Austen's novel, the impulses that in Richardson are consecutive (the scapegoating "kills" Clarissa and leads to intense familial guilt) become simultaneous (the scapegoating of Fanny, used to create distinctions of role identity within the family, is continually *counteracted* and *kept* from dangerous escalation by a sense of familial guilt). If *Clarissa* is a primal myth, *Mansfield Park* is a paeon to the nuclear family. At the end of Austen's novel, the Bertrams, merged with Fanny, seem to become one undifferentiated mass—a family ideal that no longer conceives of individuals—the result of a perfectly balanced dynamic within a closed system.[20]

Mansfield Park stands as a kind of ideal type for the nuclear family. It demonstrates that if the "anorexic syndrome"[21] of scapegoating of and guilt toward the daughter were perfectly controlled, the self would become a conventionalized, flat part of the surface patterning and would not be separable from others in the family. If we were to try to imagine such a situation in clinical terms, it would be a case of such radical enmeshment that the notion of a symptomatic individual would cease to be meaningful. Indeed, the vision of perfect equilibrium achieved at the end of *Mansfield Park* would seem to describe a state that corresponds both to the most extreme health and to the most extreme pathology; it is the place where these two extremes meet. In the modern family, by contrast, the anorexic daughter represents the *disequilibrium* of the family system and as such reflects a tendency that, from one perspective, is toward sickness but, from another, is toward health. In other words, insofar as the anorexic is the by-product of a disequilibrated family system, she is also an indicator of the breakdown of that system and its tendency toward a new configuration for human interaction. This is the argument of the so-called "ecological systems thinkers" who say that all symptoms must be seen as therapeutic expressions of change.[22] The power of the female self in *Clarissa* and in her nineteenth-century progeny was associated with the power to bind together, to make the family whole. By contrast, the power of the female self in the contemporary family, as embodied most dramatically in the anorexic daughter, is associated with the power to rend apart and, in the process, create new relational patterns in which female self-sacrifice is no longer called for.

The courtship motif that dominates the nineteenth-century English novel expresses the equilibrium-based relationship of the daughter to her family. In courtship, the heroine is both inside her family of origin, when she is being courted, and outside of it in being singled out by her suitor. The novels that adopt this motif maintain their formal equilibrium by refusing to move beyond this limbo state: when the courtship period ends, the novel ends. Even in novels that portray bad marriages—one thinks of Dorothea's marriage to Casaubon in *Middlemarch,* or David Copperfield's marriage to Dora—the mistake is rectified in the final pages by the celebration of a new marriage. But the inner workings of these seemingly corrective marriages are not vouchsafed us. The conventions of the marriage plot in the nineteenth-century English novel condition us to expect that the marriage of the protagonists—the "good marriage"—will be left unexplored.

By failing to show us the actual workings of the good marriage, the novel thus reveals a contradiction in the ideology it espouses. It delineates the ground where pathological symptoms would be likely to arise and from which a reformulation of the family system might eventually take place. It is significant that by the end of the nineteenth century the courtship motif has become so inadequate to the reality of experience that it begins to be parodied or self-consciously subverted. Henry James's later novels offer good examples of this. Thus, Maisie Farange, Fleda Vetch, and Nanda Brookenham do not marry but form alternative kinds of relationships; Milly Theale, James's latter-day Clarissa, "turns her face to the wall" and dies when she sees how marriage is supposed to work; and Maggie Verver, James's final and perhaps greatest heroine, marries only to go about reconstructing her marriage from the inside. These heroines, in their unorthodox choices and strategies, are sometimes viewed as mad by the other characters. They anticipate the fiction and real lives of such modernist and postmodernist female writers as Virginia Woolf, Kate Chopin, Sylvia Plath, Doris Lessing, Margaret Atwood, and Margaret Drabble. For these female protagonists, both real and fictional (the line between the two becomes suggestively blurred at this point), madness is often self-consciously embraced as a response to marriage or as an alternative to it (madness and the creative life become closely allied).[23] In these authors' work, madness can be understood both as the extreme effort to regulate a disintegrating family and as the "voyage out" of a confining space and role into new and uncharted relational configurations. It would seem that if the daughter is the doomed regulator of a doomed family system, she is also the character most formed to be adaptive as a new context for experience emerges.

The idealized form in which symptoms like those suffered by Clarissa Harlowe and Fanny Price are presented in much nineteenth-century literature also tells us something about the blinding nature of ideology. Although a high incidence of so-called "female illnesses" were reported in the nineteenth century, anorexia nervosa among them,[24] the ideology supported the anorexic self-conception—so that instead of appearing pathological that self-conception tended to appear normal or even heroic, even when it was accompanied by physical symptoms that were degenerative. Only as a new ideology of interdependence and openness of relations began to emerge to replace the ideology of closure of the last century have we begun to "see" the daughter's disease of anorexia and identify it as a by-product of the structure and dynamics of the nuclear family. Yet we should restrain ourselves from pointing the finger at the Victorians and feeling too proud of our powers of diagnosis. We cannot know what aspects of our present behavior may some day spring into relief as pathological and serve as the clue to a more general cultural diagnosis.

Notes

1. See Hilde Bruch, *The Golden Cage: The Enigma of Anorexia Nervosa* (Cambridge, Mass.: Harvard University Press, 1978), for profile information on anorexics. See also Joan Jacobs Brumberg's comprehensive *Fasting Girls: The Emergence of Anorexia Nervosa as a Modern Disease* (Cambridge, Mass.: Harvard University Press, 1988), for historical and social background on the disorder.

2. This perspective was pioneered by Salvadore Minuchin, Bernice Rosman, and Lester Baker, *Psychosomatic Families: Anorexia Nervosa in Context* (Cambridge, Mass.: Harvard University Press, 1978), and by Maria Selvini-Palazzoli, *Self-Starvation* (New York: Jason Aronson, 1978).

3. M. M. Bakhtin, *The Dialogic Imagination: Four Essays*, trans. C. Emerson and M. Holquist (Austin: University of Texas, 1981), 4.

4. Surprisingly, the connection between the history of the family and of the novel has been made only obliquely by historians and literary critics. Ian Watt suggests it in passing in his chapters on Samuel Richardson in *The Rise of the Novel* (Berkeley and Los Angeles: University of California Press, 1957). Recently, Nancy Armstrong treated aspects of the subject in *Desire and Domestic Fiction: A Political History of the Novel* (New York: Oxford University Press, 1987), although she concentrates on the relationship of the novel to the definition of gender roles in society without linking these to the structure and dynamics of the nuclear family. George Lukacs, T. B. Tomlinson, and Michel Foucault have treated related issues, but without drawing an explicit connection between the form of the nineteenth-century family and that of the nineteenth-century novel.

5. The classic discussion of the novel's shift from a picaresque genre to a psychological one is Watt's. For discussion of the evolution of the genre into modernism, see Alan Friedman, *The Turn of the Novel* (New York: Oxford University Press, 1966). On privatization and related affective changes in the family, see Lawrence Stone, *The Family, Sex, and Marriage in England, 1500-1800* (London: Weidenfeld & Nicolson, 1977), and Randolph Trumbach, *The Rise of the Egalitarian Family: Aristocratic Kinship and Domestic Relations in Eighteenth-Century England* (New York: Academic Press, 1978). On the evolution of the bourgeois nuclear family into the twentieth century, see Mark Poster, *Critical Theory of the Family* (New York: Seabury Press, 1978), chap. 7.

6. John Ruskin, "Of Queen's Gardens," in *Sesame and Lilies* (New York: E. P. Dutton, 1960), 59.

7. On conventional thematic structure in nineteenth-century novels, see Evelyn Hinz, "Hierogamy Versus Wedlock: Types of Marriage Plots and Their Relationship to Genre of Prose Fiction," *PMLA* 91 (1976): 900–913, and Joseph Allen Boone, "Wedlock as Deadlock and Beyond: Closure and the Victorian Marriage Ideal," *Mosaic* 17 (Winter 1984): 65–81.

8. The field of family systems theory grows out of the work on biological systems done by Ludwig von Bertalanffy, *Organismic Psychology and Systems Theory* (Barre, Mass.: Clark University Press, 1968). Pioneering work in family systems theory was done in the 1950s. The groundbreaking paper of this period was "Toward a Theory of Schizophrenia" by Bateson, Don D. Jackson, Jay Haley, and John H. Weakland, reprinted in Bateson's *Steps to an Ecology of Mind* (New York: Ballantine Books, 1972).

9. Sandra Gilbert and Susan M. Gubar, *The Madwoman in the Attic: The Woman Writer and the Nineteenth-Century Literary Imagination* (New Haven, Conn.: Yale University Press, 1979).

10. Ruskin, "Of Queen's Gardens," 23.

11. William Blackstone, *Commentaries on the Laws of England*, (1765–69; reprint, Chicago: University of Chicago Press, 1979), 1:430.

12. See Claude Lévi-Strauss, *Elementary Structures of Kinship*, trans. J. Bell, J. von Sturmer, and R. Needham (Boston: Beacon Press, 1969). See also Virginia Goldner, "Generation and Gender: Normative and Covert Hierarchies," *Family Process* 27 (1988): 17–31, for a discussion of the way the inequality of the sexes may be built into the structure of nuclear family relations.

13. See Bateson's "Culture Contact and Schismogenesis," in *Steps*.

14. See Jessica Benjamin, "The Bonds of Love: Rational Violence and Erotic Domination," in *The Future of Difference*, ed. H. Eisenstein and A. Jardine (New Brunswick, N.J.: Rutgers University Press, 1985), for a brilliant feminist psychoanalytic treatment of gender complementarity and its relation to sadomasochism in *The Story of O*.

15. See Murray Bowen, *Family Therapy in Clinical Practice* (Northvale, N.J.: Jason Aronson, 1978), 373, on the concept of "triangulation": "A two-person system may be stable as long as it is calm, but when anxiety increases, it immediately involves the most vulnerable other person to become a triangle."

16. See Deborah Gorham, *The Victorian Girl and the Feminine Ideal* (Bloomington: Indiana University Press, 1982), 7, on the childlike qualities of the nineteenth-century feminine ideal. Sigmund Freud, "The Dissolution of the Oedipus Complex," *The Standard Edition of the Complete Psychological Works*, trans. J. Strachey, vol. 19 (London: Hogarth Press, 1953), noted the difficulty the daughter experienced in leaving home but attributed it not to an ongoing functional family dynamic but to a psychic structure built out of sexualized family relationships ossified in early life.

17. Samuel Richardson, *Clarissa; or, The History of a Young Lady*, 4 vols. (New York: Everyman's Library, 1962), vol. 1, preface, 21.

18. See Ivan Boszormenyi-Nagy and Geraldine M. Spark, *Invisible Loyalties: Reciprocity in Intergenerational Family Therapy* (New York: Harper & Row, 1973).

19. Jane Austen, *Mansfield Park* (New York: Penguin Books, 1966), 456.

20. See my more detailed family systems analysis of this novel in "Stabilizing the Family System at Mansfield Park," *ELH* 54 (Fall 1987): 669–93.

21. Minuchin et al. use the phrase "anorexic syndrome" to refer in general terms to the dynamic of the psychosomatic family in which one member is anorexic. I am attempting to postulate a more specific form for this dynamic in reference to the daughter, while also expanding its use by associating this dynamic with all nuclear families, even where anorexic symptoms have not (yet) become evident in the daughter.

22. See Lynn Hoffman, *Foundations of Family Therapy: A Conceptual Framework for Systems Change* (New York: Basic Books, 1981), chap. 17, for a discussion of this perspective among family systems theorists.

23. See Sandra Gilbert and Susan M. Gubar, *No Man's Land: The Place of the Woman Writer in the Twentieth Century*, vol. 1 (New Haven, Conn.: Yale University Press, 1988), for a discussion of related issues involving female creativity during the modernist period.

24. See Elaine Showalter, *The Female Malady: Women, Madness, and English Culture, 1830–1980* (New York: Pantheon Books, 1985), on how nineteenth-century female illnesses tended to present themselves and on cultural expectations as they affected diagnosis and treatment.

Note

Portions of this chapter appeared in my book *The Daughter's Dilemma: Family Process and the Nineteenth-Century Domestic Novel,* copyright © by The University of Michigan 1991. Published by the University of Michigan Press, Ann Arbor, Michigan.

WHAT SOME WOMEN CAN'T SWALLOW:

Hunger as Protest in Charlotte Brontë's *Shirley*

Deirdre Lashgari

> Does virtue lie in abnegation of self? I do not believe it. (10:190)
>
> You expected bread, and you have got a stone. (6:105)
>
> —*Shirley*

Individual eating disorders in Charlotte Brontë's novel *Shirley* (1849) are portrayed as part of a much larger picture, in which a dysfunctional society starves women, literally and metaphorically, and women internalize that dis/order as self-starvation. Contrary to some readings of the novel, Brontë is not selling the two heroines out to conventional female passivity, either when she has them stop eating or when she marries them off at the end of the story. Caroline and Shirley have both struggled against gender roles and relationships that are "killing them." When each in turn finds herself blocked from any effective overt protest and barred from speaking her pain, she asserts control over her life in the only arena available, inscribing her hunger on her own body in a desperate plea to be "read aright."

The novel's double-wedding closure seems to erase this emphasis on hunger by invoking the easy reassurance of romance. Then, on the last page, the narrator dares the "sagacious reader" to unravel the conventional surface and confront its darker, more dangerous subtext, where female hunger, as desire and as lack, persists beyond society's "happy endings."

A key passage early in the novel establishes the connection between literal and figurative hunger through the image of "stone." Immediately following the first scene in which Caroline encounters unexplained coldness from the man she loves, the narrator gives us an image of dis/ordered eating as a metaphorical protest against societal constraints that both starve women and silence their hunger:

> A lover masculine so disappointed can speak and urge explanation; a lover feminine can say nothing: if she did, the result would be shame and anguish, inward remorse for self-treachery. . . . Take the matter as you find it: ask no questions; utter no remonstrances: it is your best wisdom. You expected bread, and you have got a stone; break your teeth on it, and don't shriek because the nerves are martyrized: do not doubt that your mental stomach—if you have such a thing—is strong as an ostrich's—the stone will digest. (6:105)

It's no wonder that the women in the novel are eventually unable to eat, if what they are offered as sustenance is stone: the stony coldness and unresponsiveness of individual men; the stone wall of social taboo which blocks psychological or economic independence through work; the deadly "stones" of public hostility to serious ideas spoken or written.

The societal context for the story of female hunger is established from the first pages through a depiction of the larger world of the local male establishment. Issues of class and gender intersect in the curates' blustering arrogance toward the landlady who serves them their dinner, as they greedily polish off the food which the landlady's young son had hoped to get a share of. Subsequent chapters introduce us to other key male figures in the community (Mr. Helstone, the conservative rector; Robert Moore, the struggling young mill-owner; and Mr. Yorke, populist Yorkshire gentleman). The overarching structure of the narrative is shaped by the broad dynamics of class conflict between Moore and the starving weavers of the community, who have been put out of work by the mechanization of the mill.

The women are all but irrelevant to the public arena where these male concerns lie. Their story, the narrator suggests, as she opens the novel with a metaphor of food, will be scantier fare than that of the men: a dish fit for "Good Friday in Passion Week: . . . cold lentils without oil; . . . unleavened bread with bitter herbs, and no roast lamb" (1:39). It is almost one hundred pages into the novel before Caroline slips into the narrative without fanfare, and Shirley, the title character, appears only after two hundred pages, in the second third of the book.

This wider social frame closes the narrative as well, with a misleadingly positive return to the image of food: Robert's description of his brother as *bon pain,* as nourishing bread for the community, and his vision of a more compassionate relationship between owners and workers in which there will be work and bread for the "houseless, the starving, and the unemployed" (37:598).

Before reaching this highly problematic "happy ending," however, the text explores the interweaving hungers of the two principal women, the flamboyant title character, Shirley, and the more self-effacing Caroline, showing how their attempts to deal with unassuaged hunger lead them to starve themselves.

Their "plots" are deceptively simple. Caroline, the timid and unprepossessing young niece of the rector, loves the mill-owner, Robert Moore. Robert oscillates between tenderness (which he then fears will distract him from the important business of the mill) and a self-protecting coldness. Caroline realizes she is destroying herself by making Robert the center of her life, especially given his resistance to intimacy. She tries repeatedly to relinquish her longing for him and reclaim an independent reason for being, but she is blocked at every turn: by the impossibility of getting work, by the untrustworthiness of friendship, and by the emotional deprivation inherent in her envisioned role as old maid. Finally, facing a stone wall, she takes sick, stops eating, and is near death when a *dea ex machina* appears in the form of her long-lost mother. Robert, meanwhile, goes through his own experience of near-death, enforced powerlessness, and hunger, which awakens him to know and acknowledge his love for Caroline.

Shirley, a few years older than Caroline, seems as strong as Caroline seems weak. She is heiress of an estate, which she runs alone with confidence, courage, and flair. Playing on her masculine name, Shirley, she frequently takes a male role as "Captain Keeldar" and refers to herself in the third person with the masculine pronoun "he." At other times, she describes for Caroline her exuberant visions of female power and creativity, and her anger at the way women are shut off from effective power in the world. However, she frightens herself with the implications of her own visions, by what she sees as the irreconcilable dichotomy between being strong and being loved. At this point, I would argue, she abdicates her strength in a bad-faith redefinition of love. She both desires and struggles against a "pupil/teacher" relationship with Louis, the self-important and domineering man who had formerly been her tutor. In the surface text, she believes she is dying from the bite of a mad dog and, stoically unwilling to burden anyone else with that fear, she retreats into silence and lack of "appetite." Only when Louis takes the situation in hand by getting her to talk out her fears does she seem to emerge from her dangerous "decline."

The double wedding that ends the novel seems at first to be a conventional foreclosing of both women's lives. Once we accept the narrator's challenge to read beneath the surface, however, unexpected differences appear. Caroline emerges as the true protagonist, whose development is clarified by the parodic foil of Shirley's antiquest.

At this point, I want to look briefly at each of the women in turn, considering what she most hungers for, the context of that hunger, and the "stones" she confronts when she seeks food. Then I will focus more closely on the way each character, figuratively and literally, denies her hunger—in relinquishing her desires, in keeping silence, and in literally not eating. I will also examine the differing ways in which each woman emerges from self-starvation, and the implications of her emergence for our reading of the novel's ending.

Caroline's principal hunger is to be loved, but also to have meaningful scope for her energies outside of love. She wishes she had been born a boy so she could focus her attention on work. Lack of love and lack of work together constitute the void in her life, the emptiness she hungers to fill. Her longing to love and be loved, without fear of overstepping, has roots in her lack of love as a child. Her mother, desperate to flee an abusive marriage, had left Caroline first to the neglect of her father and then to the emotional stoniness of her uncle, Mr. Helstone. When Caroline says "I wish somebody in the world loved me" (21:362), she speaks not only from the present but also from the deep unfilled hunger of early childhood.

Robert at this point is the focus of her hunger for love. But he is even worse at providing emotional sustenance than Caroline's uncle has been. Mr. Helstone is at least consistently indifferent; Robert oscillates between tender affection and cold distancing, in a recurrent pattern that Shirley later calls "men's habit of soon petrifying." The verb works both ways: when Robert turns to stone he also "petrifies" Caroline into a stony immobilization.

Caroline is well aware how one-sided her relationship with Robert is, and she sees the dangerous power imbalance inherent in their disparate roles in the world. She tells Shirley, "Women have so few things to think about— men so many. . . . Robert used to be in the habit of going to London. . . . I found his absence a void: there was something wanting" (12:234). Caroline is dependent on Robert for meaning because she has no source of identity in productive work. More concretely, rejection by him means being shut out of the wife/mother role expected for a woman of her class, and facing a possible future with no way to feed herself.

Caroline is blocked in her attempt to seek work, first by societal taboos against any occupation besides that of governess, and then by the opposition of her uncle and Shirley, both of whom argue that "there really was no present pecuniary need" (13:246). They fail to see that it is not physical bread Caroline hungers for, but food for her spirit: "Many that want food and clothing have cheerier lives and brighter prospects than she had" (13:246). Mrs. Pryor, who does understand, convinces her that the demeaning role of governess will only exacerbate her desire to matter to someone.

Caroline muses to herself that "there is something wrong somewhere":

> [S]ingle women should have more to do—better chances of interesting and profitable occupation than they possess now.... People hate to be reminded of ills they are unable or unwilling to remedy.... Old maids, like the houseless and unemployed poor, should not ask for a place and an occupation in the world: the demand disturbs the happy and rich. (22:376–77)

She tries to reconcile herself to remaining single, but what she learns from the two old maids in the community is the hard, stone-cold isolation and emotional deprivation that seems inevitable in that role. Miss Mann is reputed to be so hard that her stare is like Medusa's, capable of turning men to stone (10:194), as patriarchal indifference has already "petrified" her. She is described as an "extenuated spectre," "ahungered and athirst to famine," to whom "a crumb is not thrown once a-year" (10:195). When Caroline tries to model herself after the other old maid, Miss Ainley, she feels herself starved; she "wasted, grew more joyless and more wan" (11:200).

Her friendship with Shirley sustains her for a time. The fact that each of them is the partner most ideally suited to the other, most capable of nourishing the other's spirits, is pointed out by Shirley's half-serious threat (in her "Captain Keeldar" persona) to challenge Robert to a duel for getting between her and Caroline. The social injunction that women not admit to unreciprocated love leads each of them to withhold important information about her feelings for Robert. As a result, Caroline believes that Shirley is the one Robert loves and means to marry. She thinks: "They will both be happy, and I do not grudge them their bliss; but I groan under my own misery. . . . Truly, I ought not to have been born: they should have smothered me at the first cry" (13:240).

Shirley at first appearances would seem as blessed as Caroline is unhappy. But she too finds her hungers unsatisfied. When we meet her initially, what strikes us is her passionate belief in her own energies and talents. In her exuberant depiction of woman as "Nature," or as a daring, primordial Eve who "could contend with Omnipotence" (18:314–16), she expresses her vision of unrestrained possibilities for herself as woman. At the same time, the prospect of living unmarried appalls her, as it does Caroline. Shirley yearns for a partner, someone her equal, for whom she would not have to "stoop" (12:226).

Despite all her privileges of class and independent wealth, Shirley too lives, as woman, in a male-dominated world. This may be why her sense of herself as confident, fearless, and powerful often takes on the cloak of a masculine persona: "They gave me a man's name; I hold a man's position: it is enough to inspire me with a touch of manhood" (11:213; see also 14:263). Shirley seems strong, but her hunger to live fully in the world is stonewalled. The men who pretend to respect her independence often treat her like a child-woman playing a role. They lie to her as well as to Caroline about "serious business," and her anger only amuses them (21:357). They, in Shirley's words, "fancy women's minds something like those of children" (20:343).

"Women read men more truly than men read women," Shirley tells Caroline. She thinks of writing what she perceives about gender relations, but immediately realizes the futility of trying to make herself heard: "I'll prove [my ideas] in a magazine paper some day when I've time; only it will never be inserted: it will be 'declined with thanks,' and left for me at the publisher's" (20:343). It is dangerous as well as futile for a woman to speak in public what can only safely be expressed in private, woman to woman[,] says Shirley: "The cleverest, the acutest men are often under an illusion about women: they do not read them in a true light. . . . If I spoke all I think on this point . . . , where should I be? Dead under a cairn of avenging stones in half an hour" (20:343). She is well aware of the weight and power of the institutions and ideology that men control, the danger in opposing them, and their ability to "stone" or silence any woman with the temerity to try. Shirley is also capable of sabotaging herself, as "when I've time" in the quotation above suggests. Later in the novel the narrator calls her "indolent," a person who would rather think of herself as a great writer than sit down and actually write.

Her desire for a worthy partner seems stymied by the absence of any men equal to her vision of woman. So she retreats to an earlier relationship in which the man was "above her" not because he was big but because she was small. Her love for her former tutor, Louis, is highly problematic, hardly satisfying food for her hunger, as recurring references to the silence and fixity of stone suggest.

Shirley compares Louis to a "great sand-buried stone head" (36:575), and he is impassive like stone—silent and unexpressive (36:583). She describes him as having the power to turn "life to stone," and his images of her, rhetorical and stereotypical, tend to fix her in unchanging form (36:584). He takes pride in making her "scared" and "silent," as unexpressive of feeling as himself (36:568, 571). And she is a good pupil, letting him shape her after his image.

Each woman finds her desires blocked by influences over which she has little control. And each, in different ways, responds by attempting to stifle her own hunger, at great cost. Shirley first denies her longing to write by refusing to risk acting on it. And she denies her mythic visions of woman, and her hunger to live to her fullest powers, by shifting the focus of her passion to a man who can appreciate her strengths only within boundaries that he himself defines. Moreover, having directed her desire toward Louis, she denies its satisfaction by refusing to reveal her feelings for him.

We experience Caroline's struggle more closely than we do Shirley's, not from outside but from within her consciousness, as she tries repeatedly to will herself free from her attraction to Robert: "I would be his wife, if I could; as I cannot, I must go where I shall never see him. . . . Sunder me then, Providence. Part us speedily" (14:262; see also 23:381). Each woman attempts to take control of a situation in which she is being starved by starving herself, killing hunger-as-desire and embracing hunger-as-lack.

The anguish involved in Caroline's denial of desire repeatedly deadens her physical appetite as well. With no acceptable way to speak her psychological starvation directly, she speaks it through her body. As her life is wasted, so too her body wastes away. Or, as the text explains her "decline," severe depression leaves her unable to eat and thus susceptible to disease and likely death. Her psychological distress is described in terms of deprivation of food:

> Life wastes fast in such vigils as Caroline had of late but too often kept; vigils during which the mind—having no pleasant food to nourish it—no manna of hope—no hived-honey of joyous memories—tries to live on the meagre diet of wishes, and failing to derive

thence either delight or support, and feeling itself ready to perish
with craving want, turns to philosophy, to resolution, to resignation;
calls on all these gods for aid, calls vainly, — is unheard, unhelped,
and languishes. (20:341)

Sheer youthful energy and lingering hope pull Caroline through early
bouts of wasting depression. Finally, however, she is "dead sure" that Robert
and Shirley are in love with each other. "At breakfast, at each meal of the
following day, she missed all sense of appetite: palatable food was as ashes
and sawdust to her" (24:399). She asks herself, "I look well; why can I not
eat?" (24:399). When she continues to get worse, Mrs. Pryor gets Mr.
Helstone's permission to stay with Caroline and nurse her. Despite this
devoted care, Caroline still "cannot eat" (24:400) and "fades like any flower
in drought" (24:401). When Mrs. Pryor asks Caroline, "Do you wish to
live?" she replies, "I have no object in life" (24:409). Her hungers, blocked
and denied, are killing her.

In Shirley's case as in Caroline's, though less obviously, the literal and
figurative aspects of malnourishment form a disruptive subtext to the novel.
The surface reason that Shirley stops eating is that she has been bitten by a
dog she believes to be mad and is afraid she is dying. Immediately after the
incident she excuses herself from lunch, claiming not to be hungry (28:465).
Over the next weeks people see her changed, as if a "shadow" has come
over her (28:466). When Louis, in his role as teacher, tries to get her to
reveal the cause, Shirley admits she hasn't been eating but denies being ill.
He pursues the issue, in his rather stiff manner: "Not only have you lost
sleep, appetite, and flesh . . . , but your spirits are always at ebb: I believe
confession, in your case, would be half-equivalent to cure" (28:475).

Shirley's admission that she fears she might be dying leads directly into
an oblique parrying exchange with Louis about her reasons for having kept
silent before. Here the content of her silence is clearly not just the "mad dog
bite" but also her (possibly mad and certainly self-diminishing) love for
Louis (28:476–83). There has always been a close affinity between Louis
and Shirley's big, ugly dog Tartar (26:430, 432). In fact, at one point Shirley
explicitly tells Louis he looks like Tartar: "You are my mastiff's cousin: I
think you as much like him as a man can be like a dog" (36:575). In
explanation of her cold silence toward Louis, even before the dog bite, she
says she has been unwilling to "compromise her self-respect: to seek where
she had been shunned" (28:483). More important, the love with which she
has been struggling is one that reduces her.

Earlier, talking with Caroline about the numerous examples of disastrous marriages in the community, Shirley had said, "If I were convinced that [men] are necessarily and universally different from us—fickle, soon petrifying, unsympathizing—I would never marry. . . . I could never be my own mistress more. A terrible thought!—it suffocates me!" (12:223). At the end of this conversation, Shirley gives us a clue to her later shift into a self-diminishing love: "Nothing ever charms me more than when I meet my superior—one who makes me sincerely feel that he is my superior. . . . The higher above me, so much the better: it degrades to stoop—it is glorious to look up" (12:226).

In Louis, Shirley finds not a man who is actually superior, but one whom she chooses to see as superior. It is significant that Brontë introduces him to us through his own first-person journal account, which we would expect to show him in the best light. In fact, it reveals him as pompous, arrogant, insufferably self-satisfied, and—worst of all—incapable of seeing Shirley except through trivializing stereotypes (31:520, 522; 36:584). By reverting to her old role as pupil, Shirley makes Louis, by definition, larger. With some subversive reading, given what we have seen of Louis so far and what we learn of him later, another possible interpretation of her "eating disorder" is that her warped love for him is the "bite of the dog" that's killing her, that in not eating she is em/bodying her own abdication of personal power.

By the final "winding up" of the novel, Shirley has shrunk, her voice grown smaller. Even in terms of the structure of the novel, she has wasted away, grown insubstantial. The last two chapters in which she makes much of an appearance at all are presented entirely through Louis's words in his journal, as if he has swallowed her up.

The "cure" for Shirley's eating disorder is in effect the highly problematic "kiss of the prince," which keeps her "fettered . . . , conquered . . . , and bound . . . " (37:592). Caroline's emergence from her deadly anorexic depression is significantly different. What saves her is not the magic kiss of romance but her discovery of her lost mother. When Mrs. Pryor reveals herself to Caroline, she gives her a crucial external source of unconditional love. With it, she gives her a reason to live and the ability, finally, to eat (24:416; 25:420). In being mothered, Caroline also gains for the first time an inner source of mothering—the ability to love and nourish herself. It is now possible for her to enter into a romantic relationship and marriage without the danger of letting herself be diminished.

There is, of course, another crucial element in this marriage equation. Robert, the defensive property-owner, has by now gone through his own ordeal by hunger. In Birmingham and London he had learned for the first time what it meant to be hungry. In both places, he made a point of going among the poor, "where there was want of food, of fuel, of clothing; where there was no occupation and no hope," where people "to whom lack of education left scarcely anything but animal wants" were "ahungered, athirst, and desperate as famished animals" (30:505).

On the way home from London by way of Stilbro', as he crosses the moor with his friend Yorke, Robert describes how he has shamed himself by trying to marry for money and how this shame and anguish have changed him. Using imagery that defines eating as potentially destructive, he suggests a possible restorative effect in the experience of lack, in purging oneself of food one should never have eaten:

> We err; we fall; we are humbled—then we walk more carefully. We greedily eat and drink poison out of the gilded cup of vice, or from the beggar's wallet of avarice; we are sickened, degraded; everything good in us rebels against us; our souls rise bitterly indignant against our bodies; there is a period of civil war; if the soul has strength, it conquers and rules thereafter. (30:505)

Suddenly, as he is speaking to Yorke, Robert is shot by a mad weaver, one of the poor who have suffered as a result of Robert's mill. Near death, he is in effect held captive at Yorke's house for more than two months by Mrs. Yorke and Robert's sister, Hortense. While there, Robert (according to Yorke's young son Martin) is mistreated and "starved" by the "Amazon nurse" Horsfall (34:551).

When Caroline finally manages to circumvent Robert's "wardens" and sneaks up to see him, she finds him noticeably changed. He tells her he has been in "sad pain, and danger, and misery" (33:540) and that he has longed for Caroline to come and despaired of ever seeing her again (33:541). Through his experience of suffering, of "hunger" in the broad sense of desire and lack, Robert has begun to unlearn the patriarchal hardness that determined his treatment of Caroline before. His "not eating" constitutes a dis/ordering of his masculinist assumptions, his taking for granted that he will be fed.

The fundamental changes in Robert as well as in Caroline allow us to give some credence to the "happy marriage" the text seems to bestow on them. But problems lurk still beneath the surface, and the text pulls against itself. For one thing, Robert quickly reverts to conceptualizations of Caroline and her relationship to him that reassert male dominance. He refers to his apparently transformative experience of hunger and powerlessness as a time in which he was "unmanned," and he speaks of himself in the proposal scene as "stone." Not good signs.

Things look even more disturbing for Shirley. In the final chapter the "tamed animal" image she now uses to describe her relationship with Louis is repeated by the narrator without ironic distance, as it was used several chapters earlier by Caroline (35:562):

> Thus vanquished and restricted, she pined, like any other chained denizen of deserts. Her captor alone could cheer her; his society only could make amends for the lost privilege of liberty: in his absence, she sat or wandered alone, spoke little, and ate less. (37:592)

She is still starving herself, physically and psychologically. Her abdication of power to Louis, however, turns out to have been by design:

> "Louis," she said, "would never have learned to rule, if she had not ceased to govern: the incapacity of the sovereign had developed the powers of the premier." (37:592)

This last sentence is peculiar in more ways than one. Shirley's "incapacity" is not inherent, but chosen. She removes herself from the picture, even as she disappears as "first person" from the sentence in which we are presumably hearing her own words.

Moreover, there is no implied judgment, no critical bite, in the narrator's description of Shirley and Louis. This unironic voice directs us to see their marriage as a straightforward happy ending. The imaging in these last pages, however, exerts an ominous subsurface force in a very different direction, as if in an everyday conversation we caught some terrible import beneath the tea-table proprieties.

Under the positive tone of these passages about Shirley what we actually find is fetters, chains, subordination, powerlessness, anorexia—a wasting away physically, as she has already faded from the novel. We also find an implicitly belittling view of the man. In effect, because Louis is small, Shirley must shrink herself down to make him appear larger. This is a far cry from her image of a man "so far above" her that she could only look up, suggesting a relationship in which she would be obliged to grow.

Shirley's response to getting stones instead of bread is a bad-faith abdication of responsibility. Finding her own hungers denied, and lacking the perseverance and courage to feed herself, she gives up her own autonomy. In contrast, Caroline never abandons her struggle to affirm herself. What happens is that her lack of any external source of emotional sustenance plays itself out as physical starvation. She learns what it means to "digest stone" in place of bread; she goes through the "Valley of the Shadow," where, forced to crush into silence the unreciprocated love she feels, she nearly crushes out the very life source in her as well.

Discovering her mother means a rebirth into self-affirmation. At this point, knowing herself loved, unconditionally, she can finally nourish herself. Moreover, she now has "something [she] can love well, and not be afraid of loving" (25:423). Consequently, she will never again be quite so dependent on Robert. She knows herself and has her eyes open. She chooses to accept Robert, with his limits.

Both Caroline and Shirley have faced a hard choice: accepting as nourishment the "stones" offered by the male-privileged society, or going hungry. The subtext of this narrative em/bodies a willed, and gendered, response to powerlessness on the part of the women, as each of them symbolically disrupts the dysfunctional society that has starved them by inscribing that hunger on their own bodies.

Shirley has abdicated her power deliberately, allowing marriage to immobilize her, like a "panther encaged." Caroline, however, will survive, in a relationship that promises—along with some real respect and affection— many more stones to chew.

Note

The chapter and page citations are to the Penguin English Library edition edited by Andrew and Judith Hook (New York: Penguin, 1974). According to the editors, "This edition follows the second and only other edition of the novel [besides the original 1849 edition] to appear during Charlotte Brontë's lifetime."

THE POWER OF THE POWERLESS:

A Trio of Nineteenth-Century French Disorderly Eaters

Lilian R. Furst

Eating and its corollary, noneating, are, as every infant quickly discovers, potent means to control one's life, to negotiate disagreeable situations, and to manipulate others. Eating may provide comfort and pleasure as well as satisfying or placating others, while noneating can be an assertion of will, an expression of one's own preferences in defiance of those imposed from outside. Such tactics are not confined to small children; the hunger strike too is familiar as the ultimate weapon of the disempowered victim. In less extreme though parallel instances, adults may resort to disorderly eating as a mode of self-expression, specifically as an affirmation of the power of the self in the face of coercion or constraint that cannot be countered in any other way.

This is the behavioral model I explore in three nineteenth-century French female fictive figures: Madame de Mortsauf in Balzac's *Le Lys dans la vallée* (1835), Emma in Flaubert's *Madame Bovary* (1857), and Gervaise in Zola's *L'Assommoir* (1877). These three could, at first glance, hardly seem more different in their social circumstances, their personal predicaments, and even in the nature of their symptomologies. Yet they all manifest their desires and frustrations indirectly in various disorderly patterns of eating, and in the last resort they all exhibit a similar psychic mechanism in venting their repressed rage in the abuse of food. Through their eating/noneating they reclaim a measure of power over themselves and over others that had been denied to them by the social configuration in which they live. Disorderly eating in one form or another is, for these women, the only way to deal with a stifling order — although, ironically, their protests prove self-destructive. However, the choice of eating style is the sole area where these women have the freedom to make an autonomous decision over their own fate.

Of the three, Madame de Mortsauf is the most comfortably placed in practical terms. An aristocrat by birth as well as by marriage, she leads a privileged life of ease with her husband and two small children on a luxurious estate in the luscious Loire Valley. In her late twenties when the action starts, she is in the flower of her youth, the "lily in the valley" of the novel's title. But as the observant visitor from Paris, the young law student Félix de Vandenesse, comes to realize, her existence is far from the idyll it appears to be. Indeed, it is only through the unremitting efforts of Madame de Mortsauf that her deeply troubled family manages to survive. The constant fear, tension, and intimidation to which she is subjected from various quarters amounts to a burden of stress that eventually breaks her morally and physically.

For years Madame de Mortsauf has accepted the role assigned to her by tradition: that of angel in the house. She has been the obedient daughter, the submissive wife, and the devoted mother, sacrificing herself in a saintly fashion to the needs of her family to the point where she has no awareness of any desires of her own, let alone any identity except as a relative creature. In every respect her psychological profile coincides with that typical of the anorexic, although the disorder remains latent and is activated into an acute and rapidly fatal phase much later in life than its common adolescent onset. That "abnormal eating is a late step in the development of the illness, a frantic effort to camouflage underlying problems, of a defense against complete disintegration, has only recently been formulated for anorexia nervosa," Hilde Bruch pointed out in 1973.[1]

Madame de Mortsauf, the only daughter of a family of the highest social class, fits this hypothesis well. Her problem originated in her adolescence in her damaging relationship with her mother, who was extremely domineering, keeping the young woman emotionally tied to herself. Her mother's pride in her has led her on the one hand to use her as a showpiece, an extension and projection of the older woman's self and ambitions, while on the other hand exercising an excessive control through icy order. When the young girl tries to win her mother's heart through obedience and sweetness, she is repaid only by greater tyranny. The bullying alternates with rejection when she is sent away to her aunt's care. This pattern of lack of warmth, lack of freedom to develop one's own tastes and personality and resultant submissive conformity to the wishes of others concurs with the normative silhouette of the anorexic. In these developmental distortions and misconceptions the foundations are laid for later aberrant behavior.

In her marriage to a man nearly twenty years her senior, Madame de Mortsauf experiences a "renewal" of her unhappiness.[2] Her relationship to her husband is a repetition of the earlier one to her mother. Again, her behavior is irreproachable in its docility. Determined as ever to please and to fulfill the nineteenth-century expectation of the self-effacing, compliant wife, she puts up with her husband's moods and outbursts without demur or complaint. Conditioned by her mother's authority over her, she is receptive ground for her husband's permanent discontent.

Monsieur de Mortsauf, a man of venerable lineage, is described as being forty-five years old but looking sixty: thin, monastic, angular, pale with a yellowish tinge to his skin, and restless, anxious eyes. Chronically nervous, suspicious, and withdrawn, he is given to fits of anger that verge on insanity and terrify his wife. The roots of his irritable temper and languid health are traced to his frightening and taxing adventures in the wake of the 1789 revolution. In the course of the narrative, he suffers from a serious acute gastrointestinal illness (perhaps some form of hepatitis?) from which he recovers only thanks to his wife's attentive nursing. But this episode intensifies his food consciousness and his conviction that he will succumb to a digestive disorder. Monsieur de Mortsauf appears to be a depressive with pronounced phobic tendencies.

His weakness is passed on to his two children, both of whom are dangerously fragile. They are so puny that Félix takes them to be fully three years younger than they actually are. Madeleine, at age nine, has hollow cheeks, cavernous eyes, skinny arms, and a concave chest. Jacques too fails to prosper, and is sickly with repeated bouts of alarming feebleness, although his frailty is less specifically designated than his sister's. She, at a later stage in the novel, manifests a lack of appetite as well as strange tastes in food that are disconcerting to her mother. It is the mother who bears the brunt of the worry and the responsibility for these children and who is locked into the incessant vigilance of the mortal struggle for their survival.

In this family, eating and noneating have become an analogue of the self for each of its members. There are violent, noisy scenes about eating and the refusal of food, particularly in the latter part of the novel as the hidden conflicts sharpen. These episodes are all the more conspicuous in a family that is otherwise so extremely proper and self-constrained. Constitutionally unable to express their feelings directly, the Mortsauf family finds a substitute outlet in eating disorders. This creates in effect a form of reciprocal coercion. The failure of communication between mother and daughter, husband and wife, parents and children surfaces in digestive terms: the father has stomach pains, the children are so picky as to be malnourished, and the wife dies of inanition. Eating, or rather noneating, becomes a manipulative device in this family, an oblique means of venting unconscious needs. The only character wholly exempt from this disorder is Félix, the outsider, who is said to have an excellent appetite (301).

The arrival of Félix is the catalyst that disturbs the precarious balance within the Mortsauf family, which has been maintained at the expense of Madame de Mortsauf. By offering her, at first silently and later more explicitly, the admiration, emotional warmth, and tenderness that she had never experienced, Félix disrupts her long established pattern of the denial and suppression of desires, never even recognized. It is Félix who realizes that she has remained a child in the realm of feeling, totally absorbed in the morbid circle of her family. Her emotional underdevelopment is indicated too in her frequent look of resignation and abnegation. Through her incessant self-restraint and self-sacrifice she has been cast as the victim in the family, always on the watch and on the defensive. A visit from her mother reactivates and exacerbates her acquired posture of acquiescence as she continues to submit to this old tyranny. Her husband's nearly fatal illness is the final precipitating factor in her breakdown, imposing the physical hardship of long, sleepless vigils in addition to the torment of anxiety.

In this context, Madame de Mortsauf is unable to handle the crisis posed by the presence of Félix. As a result of living for years under the duress of the imperatives from her mother, her husband, and her children, her personal emotional capacity has atrophied. She has so subjugated her wishes to those of others that she has no centrally sustaining sense of self. She has, almost literally, been devoured by her family, yet that has happened precisely in fulfillment of the nineteenth-century ideal of the daughter, wife, and mother. As that perfect daughter, wife, and mother, not to mention as a good Catholic, she cannot entertain the possibility of the totally other, emotionally and sexually more satisfying life held out to her by Félix.

His kind attentions have made her grasp for the first time both the extent of her victimization and the hopelessness of her situation. Such a pervasive feeling of self-despair and of personal ineffectiveness is frequently a factor in the etiology of anorexia, which is nowadays postulated as an affective equivalent of depression. To cite Bruch again: "Though anorexic patients may die from their condition, it is not death that they are after but the urgent need to be in control of their own lives and have a sense of identity."[3]

Her noneating is first noticed, significantly, by the loving Félix, who deems it "a childhood scene" (291). At the same time, in a character modification that is also a common concomitant of anorexia, she changes from the sweet, submissive creature she has been into an irascible crosspatch. She complains of stomach troubles, increasingly refuses food, and becomes emaciated and prematurely aged. In the end she dies of "inanition" (401). The wise old doctor tells Félix that it is "the incurable result of grief," "some unknown sorrow" (401), that is killing her. Indeed, he recognizes the psychosomatic origins of her disorder when he comments: "In order to cure the body, the mind would have had to be cured" (408). Young, rich, and beautiful, she dies by starvation as the only escape from an intolerable predicament. It is perhaps the one means at her disposal to assert the power of a self that had at last begun to attain consciousness of its powerlessness and its chronic exploitation by those whom she had served with such goodwill. The impact of her profound disappointment in herself as much as in her family is sufficient to drive her to a voluntary death that is both a final act of renunciation and the direst self-punishment.

The case of Emma Bovary is considerably more complicated than that of the innocent Madame de Mortsauf because she has such an unusually willful character. Bursting with longings, desires, ambitions, and curiosity, Emma is nonetheless as defined and confined as Madame de Mortsauf by her position as wife and mother. The fluctuations of her erratic eating can be directly related to her attempts to break out of the conventions prescribed for her. In Freudian terms she has been perceived as "a woman subject to the influence of an unresolved past, an adult in whose psyche still lives an infant, tyrannical and unreasonable, claiming repetition of frustrated love as the only emotional pattern familiar to her."[4]

Emma comes from an environment in which food is of crucial importance. She is the only daughter of a farmer in a part of Normandy where the production of comestibles is the staple of the economy. The high point of the year comes in the agricultural fair, at which prizes are awarded in such categories as general excellence in cultivation, the choicest pig and merino ram, the finest manure heap, the best drainage ditch, flax culture, fertilizer, and the use of oil cakes. In late summer a sweetish smell hangs over the town as every family busily makes preserves for the coming winter. In such a context it is natural that food should function as a channel for the expression of feelings. Emma's father, for instance, plants a plum tree to celebrate the birth of his granddaughter and rejoices in anticipation of the delicious compote she will one day enjoy from its crop. He conveys his esteem for his son-in-law through his annual tribute of a turkey; on the first occasion a mark of gratitude to the young doctor who has healed his broken leg, the turkey turns into a standing institution, which old Rouault tragicomically promises to honor even after Emma's death. Similarly, Homais brings his wife a special kind of bread as a gift from his trip to Rouen. The pervasiveness of this preoccupation with eating is suggested too by the recurrence of food-related imagery throughout *Madame Bovary.* Charles equates a kiss with a dessert[5] and savors conjugal love like a truffle (36). Rodolphe perceives Emma as gaping for love like a carp on a kitchen table gapes for water (138), while Léon envisages a promising future like a golden fruit from a fantastic tree (245). Happiness is in this world clearly conceived in terms of the gratification of the palate.[6]

Emma does not wholly subscribe to this ethos. She does not use eating as a source of solace—for example, when she loses her mother in early adolescence, she does not seek metaphoric sustenance orally. Her psychological processes are more complex and bizarre, but ultimately they do reveal themselves in her eating predilections as well as in her aversions. Her preferences are formed in the convent where she is brought up after her mother's death and where she absorbs not the pieties of religion but the cheap glitter of sentimental romance. She feeds her mind in its crucial formative years on an unremitting diet of junk ideas derived from popular romantic fiction, cloying music, and albums of high-flown pictures. From this fare she develops not merely a passing emotional indigestion that makes her resistant to the more wholesome spiritual nutrition of the convent; in fact, her taste becomes permanently perverted, as does her image of human existence. Throughout her adult life she will seek to capture experientially and gastronomically the *"bliss, passion,* and *ecstasy"* (37) that had seemed so beautiful to her in books.

Emma projects her feelings into eating, which becomes simultaneously the incarnation of both her desires and her frustrations. Her alternation of manic with depressive phases is clearly reflected in her eating behavior. Only the refined and the exotic attract her. Her thirst for excitement, as well as her sensuousness, is indicated by the avidity with which she drains her little glass of liqueur, tilting her head back, rounding her lips, and holding her neck taut as she extends her tongue to lick up the very last drop in the bottom of the glass (23–24). Her one tantalizing glimpse of high life at the ball at the castle of La Vaubyessard becomes imprinted on her mind in terms of the exquisite delicacies served there: lobsters, quail, oversize fruits, pomegranates, pineapple, shellfish bisque, milk of almond bisque, Trafalgar puddings, all sorts of cold meats trembling in aspic, maraschino sherbet, Rhine wines, and iced champagne (52–56). This is to her the gastronomic equivalent of the *"bliss, passion,* and *ecstasy"* for which she hankers. Only when she has ice cream at the theater in Rouen, and sorbets sent up to her hotel room for Léon and herself, does she achieve even the faintest approximation of her eating aspirations.

By contrast, the normal daily fare of her domestic sphere is repulsive to her. Her wedding breakfast, which she would have liked to hold at midnight by torchlight, is instead a gargantuan country beano of roast beef, legs of lamb, chicken fricassee, a suckling pig flanked by sausages, huge bowls of quivering custard, cider, brandy, and a grotesquely overdecorated cake (30–31). Her antipathy to Charles crystallizes at the dinner table[7] as she notices his boorish habits, his noisy slurping of his soup, and his practice of cleaning his teeth with his tongue (66). As Charles slowly and doggedly masticates his boiled beef, Emma feels a surge of disgust arising from the depths of her soul (70). Seated opposite him, witness to his stolid ingestion of plain peasant dishes (and his steady increase in girth), all she can manage is to nibble at a few nuts. Her appetite grows increasingly capricious: some days she drinks only fresh milk, on others cups of tea by the dozen, and occasionally she has the maid bring her dinner on a tray to her boudoir at a safe remove from Charles. Her refusal, or inability, to participate in the ritual of family meals is symptomatic and symbolic of her rejection of her marriage and her situation.

Although Emma's disorderly eating starts as an instinctive response, it does not take her long to learn the potential uses of food as a manipulative tool. Charles, in his naiveté, is the primary target of her stratagems. When she is out to please him, and incidentally to salve her bad conscience, she prepares him his favorite dessert, pistachio cream (286). She brings tears of joy to his eyes when she eats the slice of bread and jam he feeds her on her recovery from her collapse after Rodolphe has jilted her (222). At the news of her father-in-law's death, knowing what is proper, Emma feigns a disinclination for dinner (266). She even tries to ingratiate herself with her mother-in-law by requesting her recipe for pickled gherkins (205). But by far her most successful eating maneuver is to clinch the move from Tostes by fostering the appearance of ill-health:

> She grew pale and had palpitations. Charles prescribed valerian and camphor baths for her. Everything that was tried seemed to upset her even more.
>
> On certain days she would chatter on with feverish exuberance; then these bouts of exhilaration would suddenly be followed by a state of lethargy in which she neither spoke nor moved. What then revived her was to splash a bottle of eau de Cologne over her arms.
>
> Since she complained constantly about Tostes, it occurred to Charles that her ill-health might have something to do with the local climate, and, fixing on this idea, he thought seriously of moving his practice elsewhere.
>
> From then on she drank vinegar to lose weight, developed a little dry cough, and lost her appetite completely. (71–72)

Ultimately, however, Emma is as much the captive of a cultural stereotype as Madame de Mortsauf. Despite Emma's vehemence, her tempestuous mood swings, her lust for travel and adventure, and her energy, ingenuity, and inventiveness, she remains the prisoner of her station in life as the wife of a mediocre doctor in a dull little provincial town. Her lot, the common nineteenth-century middle-class woman's round of domesticity, children, religion, and charitable works, is the mocking antithesis of the chimerical mirages that animate her libido. The intensity of her acute pain and her constant consciousness of it distinguishes her from Madame de Mortsauf, whose docility long shields her from acknowledgment of the real state of affairs and makes her more inclined to accede to martyrdom. By contrast, Emma is impelled from the outset by strong desires that drive her away from the path assigned to her. Her revulsion at the customary food of her time and place signifies her repudiation of the life apportioned to her. Always extreme and uncompromising, if she cannot have what she wants, she would rather opt for the drama of suicide as her final flamboyant protest. She scoops up the arsenic rat poison with as much zest as the liqueur during her courtship. In effect, she dies through eating, and although her final meal is noxious and self-destructive, at least it is of her own choosing. That the poison is spewed back after her death as a liquid that oozes hideously out of her mouth leaves her thwarted even in her end, for she has not had the beautiful romantic death figured in her books and her imagination. Her determination to assert the power of her self is frustrated to the very last.

Unlike Emma, Gervaise in *L'Assommoir* does not even dream of autonomy. Her aim is simply survival in the most literal sense of employment, safe shelter, adequate nourishment, and the absence of pain. "My ideal," she tells her future husband during their courtship, "is to work in peace, always to have bread to eat, to have a nice, clean place to sleep, you know, a bed, a table, a couple of chairs, no more. Oh, and I'd like to bring my children up decently, if possible. I have one more ideal, and that is not to be beaten."[8] Even these modest goals prove unattainable to Gervaise. A working-class woman, a laundress by profession, she has had two children by Lantier, her good-for-nothing lover, before moving with him to Paris from the small Southern town where she was born. Lantier, after quickly squandering the little inheritance that had prompted his move, walks out on Gervaise, leaving her abandoned and destitute in a grim flophouse with two children to provide for and nothing but a stack of pawn tickets. It is sheer economic necessity that motivates most of her actions thenceforth, allowing her little freedom of choice or power of self-determination. She never has any sense of control over her life, merely reacting as best she can to the contingencies of fortune, and as the slings and arrows of misfortune hit her, gradually giving up on herself. Her progressive desolation becomes apparent in her increasingly disorderly eating and later also drinking.

Though at the opposite end of the social spectrum from Madame de Mortsauf, Gervaise is remarkably similar to her in both her character and her family relationships. She too was abused and neglected by her mother and her father, both alcoholics, who sent her out to work at age eight. Alcoholism runs in this family; her grandmother, a borderline personality, had succumbed to alcohol-induced insanity. Gervaise will in the long run follow this pattern in part, but at the outset she is sweet and amiable by disposition and wants even in the gruesome squalor of the Parisian slums to make life as agreeable as possible for all around her. She is not, however, very shrewd in judging how to spread the universal happiness she longs for. Her innate kindness and easygoing temperament make her liable to give in to others' wishes in a passive acquiescence that avoids immediate conflict but leads to situations that are harmful to her. The two cardinal instances of such misplaced softheartedness occur in her dealings with her husband. When he breaks a leg in a fall at work, she tends him with a devotion similar

to Madame de Mortsauf's devotion to her spouse and with a liberal expendi-
ture of funds she had carefully saved over the years to start up in business on
her own. As he recovers, Gervaise continues to coddle and infantilize him,
encouraging him to take more time off work, plying him with food and wine
to strengthen him, and sending him off to the bar for cheering company. She
thereby unwittingly initiates his decline into the chronic alcoholism that in
the end kills him and meanwhile ruins the family financially and as a
functioning human unit. Her inability to say "no," to take a firm stand and
assert herself, is even more disastrous when she lets her husband take her
former lover into their home, allegedly as a paying boarder. Lantier, the
accomplished parasite, ignores his monetary obligation and becomes an
added burden to Gervaise both financially and psychologically. So, tragically,
her own malleability contributes in no small measure to the stress under
which she is crushed. The quality that makes her so endearing and that,
incidentally, was so highly valued in a nineteenth-century woman, "com-
plaisance" (perhaps best translated as "obligingness"), is fundamentally
implicated in her destruction.

One of the foremost expressions of Gervaise's kindness is in her role as
nurturer. In the environment of the huge, menacing tenement house, where
she is constantly confronted by the misery of hunger, the regular provision of
sufficient food must be a central concern. To feed her family and on occasion
her neighbors is for Gervaise a means not only to please but also to validate
her sense of self and to achieve a certain respect. She insists on preparing
her husband's dinner even while she is in labor with their daughter. To offer
nourishment has symbolic connotations of giving love and support, particularly in this milieu. Her nurturing activities reach their peak at her birthday
feast, which fills the central chapter of the novel (221–63). It is interesting
that here the birthday celebrant throws the party for her family, employees,
and neighbors, not vice versa, as is surely more customary. Gervaise, usually
rather inarticulate and timid in social situations, is in her element as the
majordomo of the dinner. The preparations extend over several days as an
intricate series of courses is designed, the table is set up, and the seating is
worked out. This feast indicates her spontaneous pleasure in making others
happy by feeding them, but it is also a demonstration of her standing at that
point as the owner of a laundry business (even though that is built on a loan
and already in debt). As the smell of the goose cooking wafts over the
neighborhood, everyone is made aware of Gervaise's authority. The lavish
dispensation of food is a woman's one mode of socially approved active
self-assertion. Gervaise's generosity is also in striking contrast to the mean-

ness of her in-laws, the Lorilleux, who hang a blanket over their door whenever they cook a rabbit to prevent the smell from spreading; they want to avoid arousing envy or sharing their goodies with others less fortunate. That detail is a brilliant comic touch that serves at once to underscore the literal and metaphoric meanings of food to the struggling inhabitants of this area and Gervaise's inclination to an expansive benevolence that she can ill afford.

But Gervaise's birthday feast has sinister undersides, for it throws her far further into debt, and as an extravaganza of overeating and drinking it marks the beginning of her tendency to excess. Her sacrilegious worship of food is conveyed in her perception of the set table as "an altar" (228). Mostly it is the comic aspects of this grotesque gorging that are exploited in the enactment of the feast (with a realism that offended many of Zola's readers on account of its alleged vulgarity); nevertheless, the threatening potential of such behavior is legibly implicit. Even by then Gervaise has gained quite a lot of weight, which aggravates her limp. As her position worsens—with the addition of Lantier to the household, the exacerbation of her husband's alcoholism, the collapse of her business, her inability to meet their debts, and their ouster into dingy, cramped quarters—in the face of this avalanche of adversity Gervaise seeks solace in eating. "At each new distress, she plunged into her only pleasure, getting her three meals a day" (320). Food becomes for Gervaise not just a compensation for her misery and a brief escape from it; it also represents a fragile bulwark of security. Because she can never be sure where her next meal will come from, she habitually stuffs more than she needs as a safety measure. Physical appetite becomes distorted by psychological pressures; a treat for the palate is an anesthetic for the mind. Like many of the characters in *Madame Bovary*, but more engrossingly so, Gervaise locates happiness in certain kinds of food. For example, in thinking of her profligate daughter, Nana, who knows only too well how to look after herself, she fantasizes about her enjoying an endless supply of oysters (468).

Gervaise's gourmandism and subsequent gluttony is prompted and at least partially justified by the circumstances of her life, yet it is also fostered by her own temperament. The indulgence that she shows toward others has its parallel in her yielding to her own desires. Her hunger is a bodily manifestation of her deep and wholly warranted fears for her future. She tries to displace and assuage them through a kind of gustatory hedonism without realizing that all the little treats she allows herself amount, on the contrary, to self-injuries. To abdicate control of her eating is tantamount to writing herself off; her unwieldly corpulence is the visible sign of her psychological self-abandonment. The word *s'abandonner* ("abandoning herself") occurs frequently, especially in the latter part of *L'Assommoir* as Gervaise relinquishes her dignity and hope and gives in to her instinctual drives. This is an extension of her proclivity, apparent throughout, to take the path of least resistance. When the lenience she shows to others is applied to herself, it results in her surrender to overeating and later to drinking too.

Her drinking is an almost inevitable development, starting as a desperate attempt to banish the pangs of hunger with cheap liquor. Just as Emma's environment is dominated by food, so Gervaise's is overshadowed by alcohol. Old Colombe's bar, the meeting place of the neighborhood, is the site of the weird distilling machine whose pernicious product slowly but surely poisons its customers. Fumes of alcohol hang over the whole area. Gervaise is at first very opposed to drink, partly because of her oppressive memories of her parents' alcoholism and partly because of a bad early experience when she took horribly sick after drinking anisette with her mother.[9] But as her craving for oral satisfaction grows along with her despair and her hunger, she falls in with the brutal habits and appetites of her environment. The greater her insecurity and the dimmer her prospects, the more compulsively does she seek to stifle her misery by stuffing her mouth. She picks up scraps and rotting food from the garbage cans of restaurants, and she tries her hand at begging and at prostitution — unsuccessfully, however, for who would want such a ravaged hulk. When her old friend Goujet finally takes her in and offers her a meal, she grabs at the potatoes with her hands and wolfs them like an animal. Her death in a hole under the staircase is probably due, at least partially, to starvation. If this is the case, it is a final ironic reflection on her gorging as the instinctive thrust to self-preservation of a woman so devoid of the power of self-determination that she cannot even by hard work assure her own survival.

None of these three figures precisely fits current clinical pictures of eating disorders. Madame de Mortsauf comes closest as a late-onset anorexic. As the good girl, she has been submissive first to a domineering, ambitious mother and then to her overbearing, distant, and ill-tempered husband. Cheated out of her life, and made aware by Félix of what she has forfeited, she finally rebels, and punishes her family — and herself — by self-starvation. Emma Bovary is an unstable bipolar personality who goes through a series of highs and lows of increasing intensity. Her depressed phases correspond to anorexia, whereas her manic moments produce a lust for the foods that represent her desires. She is also highly manipulative, exploiting food to put pressure on others and get her own way whenever possible. For Gervaise too, food serves as a means to an end—initially as proof of her competence in caring for her family, later primarily as a quest for comfort. She has episodes of binge-eating within a long-term pattern of overeating. Because the aim of her eating is to nurture herself physically and morally, she never thinks of regurgitating what she has swallowed, as do many overeaters. To that extent, she exhibits anxiety-induced compulsive behavior and does not fit the diagnosis of bulimia.

No one in this trio has the persistent concern about body shape and weight that figures so prominently in eating disorders today. The nineteenth century, when thinness evoked the terrifying specter of tuberculosis, did not put the same premium on slenderness as the twentieth century.[10] Indeed, the current automatic association of eating disorders with a localized, contemporary ideal of an attractive physique masks some of the more fundamental issues central to the syndrome that become apparent in literary portrayals from earlier periods, which cherished models of beauty other than those of our time. The understanding of eating disorders through an analysis of their appearance in literary texts of other centuries thus backs recent medical opinion that these conditions may be "a form fruste of an affective disorder,"[11] an essentially psychosomatic disturbance, not curable simply by the appropriate adjustment of food intake, as once thought.

To eat in one's own style, whatever that may be, is a cogent and concrete way of asserting one's will within a social frame perceived as inimical. For nineteenth-century women, constrained by restrictive conventions of behavior, including the inappropriateness, indeed impropriety, of speaking out for themselves, disorderly eating was an expedient and effective means of self-expression. Barred from more direct outlets, they could precipitate strong and necessarily repressed emotions into their eating: anger, anxiety, frustration, fear, fantasies of aggression or of fulfillment, and longings for control and self-determination. For the disempowered, the choice of eating mode is perhaps the sole, and significantly silent, tool for enunciating their pain. Strikingly, the evidence suggests that this held for women of every social class. In a period when class gradations cut almost as deep as gender distinctions, this is an important unitary factor in the women's sphere.

Notes

1. Hilde Bruch, *Eating Disorders: Obesity, Anorexia, and the Person Within* (New York: Basic Books, 1973), 335. More recent medical opinion confirms this view. Late onset of anorexia nervosa has been recorded, including cases in women of seventy and of ninety-four, often with a previous history of mild, concealed, or undiagnosed episodes. Many of the adult instances have been found to occur in women between the ages of twenty-five and thirty-five — that is, of Madame de Mortsauf's age. See Walter Vandereycken, "Anorexia Nervosa in Adults," in *The Eating Disorders: Medical and Psychological Bases of Diagnosis and Treatment*, ed. Barton J. Blinder, Barry F. Chaitin, and Renée S. Goldstein (New York: PMA Publishing Corp., 1988), 295–304.

2. Honoré de Balzac, *Le Lys dans la vallée* (Paris: Librairie Générale Française, 1972). All subsequent references are to this edition, and all translations are mine.

3. Bruch, *Eating Disorders*, 269. See also Barry F. Chaitin, "The Relationship of the Eating and Affective Disorders," in *The Eating Disorders* (ed. Blinder et al.), 345–55.

4. Ion K. Collas, *"Madame Bovary": A Psychoanalytic Reading* (Geneva: Droz, 1985), 53; chap. 1, pp. 23–56, is devoted to "Food."

5. Gustave Flaubert, *Madame Bovary* (Paris: Garnier, 1947), 47. All subsequent references are to this edition, and all translations are mine.

6. See Lilian R. Furst, "The Role of Food in *Madame Bovary*," *Orbis Litterarum* 34 (1979): 53–64.

7. See Erich Auerbach's memorable analysis of this scene in *Mimesis*, trans. Willard Trask (Garden City, N.Y.: Doubleday, 1957), 426–34.

8. Emile Zola, *L'Assommoir* (reprint, Paris: Fasquelle, 1971), 49. All subsequent references are to this edition, and all translations are mine.

9. Chaitin, "Relationship," in *The Eating Disorders* (ed. Blinder et al.), 348, has found alcoholism in 83 percent of the families of overeaters, and often a family history of multigenerational impairment.

10. See Joan Jacobs Brumberg, *Fasting Girls: The Emergence of Anorexia Nervosa as a Modern Disease* (Cambridge, Mass.: Harvard University Press, 1988), chap. 9, "Modern Dieting," on the impact of the cultural mania for extreme slimness in recent years and its links to the epidemic increase in eating disorders.

11. Chaitin, "Relationship," in *The Eating Disorders* (ed. Blinder et al.), 352.

NEW ENGLAND INDIGESTION
AND ITS VICTIMS

Elsa Nettels

Prominent in American realistic fiction is the victim of what William Dean Howells called "New England indigestion,"[1] a morbid physical and psychological condition manifested in eating disorders such as dyspepsia, willed starvation, and secret gorging. In novels of New England life by Howells, Elizabeth Stoddard, Mary Wilkins Freeman, and Edith Wharton, among others, characters seek through the rejection or consumption of food to assert themselves and manipulate others in the face of perceived indifference or rejection. Victims of eating disorders were not confined to New England. In Howells's view, dyspepsia and loss of appetite afflicted so many Americans, particularly women, that American society in the 1870s seemed "little better than a hospital for invalid women."[2] But the majority of dyspeptics in American fiction are New Englanders, often lifelong inhabitants of isolated villages where Puritanism, bred in the bone, survives in stubborn will, guilt-ridden conscience, and repressed emotion—conditions that betray themselves in emaciation and physical pain.

With such characters, Puritanism acts like a lens magnifying symptoms and intensifying morbid impulses not confined to one time or place. Even when religious faith no longer animates the Puritans' descendants, their pathologies are aggravated, if not caused, by the heritage of Calvinism: a mistrust of sensual pleasure and fear of satiety; a conviction of personal sinfulness, often coupled with spiritual pride; and a compulsion to exercise one's will even as one felt powerless in the grip of one's predestined fate. "Inherited Puritanism," as Howells termed it,[3] so hospitable to morbidity, is preserved and strengthened by the entrapment of characters in remote villages where isolation fosters "diseased and abnormally exaggerated self-consciousness," as one analyst noted, and inbreeding results in the "exaggeration of personal characteristics" and "premature arrest" of physical and mental development.[4]

Howells observed that even a temporary affliction like a sprained ankle "intensifies [the] whole character" of the sufferer.[5] Deep-rooted physical and emotional disorders like chronic dyspepsia and anorexia reveal far more of the hidden life of the victim. When literary characters afflicted by such disorders are members of a particular national or racial or religious group, their maladies assume cultural significance that raises certain questions. We may ask which characteristics of the "New England indigestion" are traceable to the environment and the heritage of the characters. Are its manifestations determined by the sex, age, class, or marital status of the victim? Do its victims exemplify or subvert the traditional paradox that spiritual strength is achieved through physical weakness and suffering? What does the portrayal of their maladies reveal of their society—its values, beliefs, and assumptions about the roles appropriate to men and women?

To seek answers to these questions, we may examine works by four novelists—Howells, Stoddard, Freeman, and Wharton—who view New England characters from different perspectives. Two were born and raised in New England, in Massachusetts: Stoddard in Mattapoisett, on the coast; and Freeman in Randolph, south of Boston. The two outsiders lived for extended periods in New England: Howells in Cambridge and Boston; Wharton at the Mount near Lenox in the Berkshires. All four writers dramatize the importance of food in the lives of their characters, anatomize the kinds of power the invalid commands, and illuminate the legacy of Puritanism in the victories and defeats of its inheritors generations later.

Elizabeth Stoddard was the first American novelist to dramatize the link between Puritanism and eating disorders. In her first novel, *The Morgesons* (1862), set in pre–Civil War Massachusetts, she presented in Veronica

Morgeson the most detailed portrait of an anorectic to be found in nineteenth-century American fiction. By portraying Veronica from early childhood to her wedding day, the novelist shows the interplay of temperament and family relationships in the etiology of an illness rooted in the conditions of the victim's early life. Stoddard's novel, published in 1862, predates by eleven years the publication of case studies by the English physician William Withey Gull, who is credited with identifying anorexia nervosa and naming the disease.[6]

The protagonist of *The Morgesons* is not Veronica but her older sister, Cassandra, the narrator, whose moral and mental growth is the subject of the novel. But as the title suggests, characters are defined by their place in a family history, in which Veronica is second only to her sister in importance. As the most abnormal of the characters, Veronica functions like a Rorschach test to expose the attitudes of other characters. In turn, the sisters, belonging to the youngest of three generations of Morgesons portrayed in the novel, are shown to be shaped by their cultural heritage and the conditions of their time and place.

By the 1830s, the years of their childhood, the spirit of Puritanism is waning in Surry, the Massachusetts coastal town of their birth, although ministers from the Andover Theological Seminary continue to preach the Calvinist doctrines, and evangelical fervor periodically sweeps provincial congregations. For the sisters, the authoritarian repressive spirit of Puritanism is most powerfully embodied in their maternal grandfather, whose dark and silent house is the physical counterpart of a religion hardened to a "formal, petrifying, unyielding system."[7] The failure of his generation to imbue the young with the spirit of his faith is symbolized in a grotesque scene when Cassandra watches her grandfather try to read the family prayers, his teeth gone, unable to articulate the words. His death, coming early in the novel, marks the end of an era, but the effects of his harsh discipline survive. He has driven one of his daughters, the mother of Cassandra and Veronica, to reject the tenets of Calvinism altogether. Her sister, the children's Aunt Merce, who remained unmarried in her father's house totally submissive to his will, exemplifies for her nieces the fate of the woman unable to resist the authority of a patriarch and his church. Veronica, who refuses to visit her grandfather or attend his funeral, declares that he "nearly crushed" her mother and her aunt when they were girls and asks them: "Did you know that you had any wants then? or dare to dream anything beside that he laid down for you?" (64).

Cassandra escapes the confines of provincial Puritan culture by leaving her native village to live for extended periods with worldly relatives near Boston. Veronica rebels within the family circle, so uncontrollable as a child that 150 years earlier her parents might have thought her possessed by witches. She tears out her hair when angry, frightens the family by hiding, pulls an ugly bonnet off a servant's head, and burns herself: "A blazing fire was too strong a temptation to be resisted" (13). When commanded against her will, she becomes "so violent in her opposition" (87) that she is confined to her room. She suffers mysterious illnesses or "spells," when she lies paralyzed and speechless. Repeatedly she forces responses from her family by her refusals to eat. Obsessed with food, she commands the family cook to prepare elaborate meals, which she will not taste but which she insists the family must eat and describe to her.

The narrator offers no interpretation of her sister's behavior, but merely describes her as "strange," "baffling," and "mysterious." She could say of Veronica, as she says of her mother, "I make no attempt to analyze her character. I describe her as she appeared, and as my memory now holds her" (17).[8] By presenting Veronica through the view of a narrator who can say only that her sister has a "peculiar constitution" (238), Stoddard avoids a clinical diagnosis, but critics have classified Veronica as a sadomasochist (according to one),[9] an exalted hysteric (according to another).[10] Veronica also resembles the typical anorectic, although some of the distinguishing signs are missing. She is not the acquiescent child of innumerable case studies. She does not dwell on her appearance except to admit that she cares intensely about dress. But she exploits her peculiar eating habits to get attention, particularly when another member of the family threatens to eclipse her, and to assert her superiority, especially to Cassandra, who relishes food and eats heartily. The night Cassandra arrives home after a year's absence at her grandfather's, Veronica, aged thirteen, commands the scene in the dining room, where the family's life is centered, by announcing that she will henceforth "live entirely on toast" while her sister, she supposes, will "eat all sorts of food, as usual" (51). When Veronica diverts the family's attention from her newborn brother to herself by refusing food and falling ill, she is rewarded for her "mysterious disorder" by the solicitude of the maiden servant, Temperance, who assuages her own needs too as she weeps over Veronica and calls her "deary and her best child" (147). Even as Veronica is about to be married, she and Temperance still find their account in each other as Temperance prepares to "[turn] myself inside out to keep up her appetite" (237). When Cassandra asks wistfully, "Do you ever feel worried about *me?*" the servant squelches her appeal: "You great, strong thing, why should I?" (237).

Cassandra is strong, in part because she feels secure in her parents' love and knows that their mother "did not love [Veronica] as she loved me; but strove the harder to fulfill her duty" (13). Veronica's conviction that "mother was always against me" (23) drives Veronica to behavior that further alienates her parents and thus intensifies her need of their attention. In early childhood, she learns to associate food and adult concern when Temperance stayed with the children at mealtimes, as the narrator recalls, "to comment on our appetites, and encourage Veronica, who was never hungry, to eat" (13). In a family where both parents are remote from the children's daily lives—the father absorbed in his shipbuilding business, the mother uninterested in the management of her household—Veronica exploits what seems to be an inborn repugnance to food.

Also characteristic of the anorectic is Veronica's determination to cling to her childhood state, symbolized by her refusal to leave her parents' house even when she marries. "I never was a child," she tells Cassandra, "but I am always trying to find my childhood" (217). To others, however, she has never ceased being a child. A perceptive friend prophesies that Veronica "will be a child always. . . . She stopped in the process of maturity long ago" (150). When Veronica refuses to wear bombazine after her mother's death, Temperance indulges her: "She's a bigger child than ever . . . and must have her way" (210). Even Veronica's suitor, Ben Somers, who feels safer with a child bride than with a mature woman like Cassandra, wonders whether Veronica is "grown a human woman" (233). (Marriage seems inconsistent with her refusal to assume the duties and privileges of adulthood, unless she seeks in her husband another protector.)

No one in the novel connects Veronica to the saint whose name she bears. The narrator merely notes that their paternal grandfather insisted that the "Morgeson tombstones" not be consulted for the sisters' names (10). By early adolescence, however, Veronica is clearly imitating the life of a monastic. She pastes a picture of Saint Cecilia on the wall of her room, which she keeps in "orderly perfection" (136). In winter she refuses to have her bed warmed by heated bricks and endures the freezing cold rather than light a fire. She restricts her view of the world outside to the square of landscape visible from a single pane of glass, which she calls her "wicket," and at night she reads by the light of a single candle.

In certain ways her life even parallels that of the seventeenth-century saint, Veronica Guiliani, who in her autobiography recalled herself as a troublesome willful child, given to putting her hand in the fire and otherwise injuring herself in the presence of her family.[11] Her description of herself might have been written by Stoddard's Veronica: "I was stubborn and if I wanted something I would not quiet down until I won. I was the smallest, but I wanted to command everyone and I wanted everything done my way; and in effect everyone gave in to me."[12] Veronica in the novel undertakes no fasts such as chronicled by Sister Veronica, who in the convent repeatedly defied orders to eat and for years tried to exist on diets of bread and water. But Stoddard's Veronica welcomes suffering: "I need all the illnesses that come," she says, and she seeks to define herself in ascetic denials that set her apart from everyone else. As Sister Veronica eventually conquered her near fatal self-induced illness to recover her health and rule as abbess for eleven years, so her namesake, according to the narrator, wills "the darkness in her nature to break" and slowly gains health and serenity: "a spiritual dawn had risen in her soul" (60).

Whether or not Stoddard intended parallels between her Protestant character and the Catholic saint, her narrator insists that Veronica gains power through suffering. "Educated by sickness," Veronica acquires "the fortitude of an Indian" (59). Depriving herself of food, she "fed on pain . . . and at last mastered it" (60). The transports of suffering apparently fuel "the fires of her creative powers" (141), expressed in surreal paintings and performances on the piano of "wild, pathetic melodies" that move her listeners to tears while her own face remains "calm, white, and fixed" (62). She claims the advantages of her confined space, as Thoreau boasted of traveling widely in Concord. When Cassandra wonders that her sister can restrict her view to the "limited, monotonous" view from her wicket, Veronica answers as Emily Dickinson might have done: "If the landscape were wider I could never learn it" (135).

By romanticizing Veronica's illness as the fount of creative power or "genius" and spiritual beauty, Stoddard sought to present Veronica in a positive light. But that effort is continually compromised by the mere presence of Cassandra, whose contrast with Veronica informs the whole novel. Veronica's restricted life, "kept sacredly apart" (224), seems self-induced entrapment, her obsessive dread of the sea a life-denying fear, when compared with Cassandra's eagerness to move outward, journey to new places, ride, sail, and walk by the sea, where she utters her cry of longing for life: "Its roar, its beauty, its madness—we will have—*all*" (215). Beside Cassandra's healthy recognition of her sexual nature and its needs, Veronica's "delicate, pure, ignorant soul" (226), in which Ben Somers hopes to find "eternal repose," seems the morbid price of stunted growth. Her refusals of food appear regressive when compared with Cassandra's unfailingly hearty appetite, expressive of delight in the signs of her womanhood. "I had lost the meagerness of childhood and began to feel a new and delightful affluence. What an appetite I had, too!" (46-47). In Cassandra, Stoddard repudiated the convention that condemned a woman's appetite as a sign of licentiousness and moved writers to make their heroines "so indifferent to good eating . . . so impervious to all the creature comforts."[13] To her question "Is goodness, then, incompatible with the enjoyment of the senses?"[14] Cassandra gives the decisive answer.

In their childhood and adolescence, Cassandra and Veronica rebel against authority that would thwart their desires, but in the end Stoddard herself succumbed to the force of literary convention, forcing both sisters along the prescribed path, into improbable courtships and marriages to handsome degenerate brothers, fortunate chiefly in their family's wealth. Nothing in the novel suggests that the youthful self-assertion of either sister will flower in mature self-fulfillment. Veronica's musicianship may be genius, as several characters assert, but in her society a woman of genius is "an anomaly sphered between the sexes" (242) who has no orbit of her own except in solitude.[15] And yet, in the world of the novel, women surpass men in psychological strength and powers of survival. All the main male characters are casualties—bankrupts, libertines, alcoholics, and invalids, whose deaths outnumber female deaths by five to one. In the Morgesons' world, tradition and convention still empower men, but only women are strong in the power of the self.

Illness separates Veronica Morgeson from the vigorous active women that dominate the world of Stoddard's novel. In Howells's fiction, invalid women are so numerous that the completely healthy female character is the anomaly. Scarcely any of his thirty-seven novels lack a stricken woman suffering a physical or mental ailment. Bedridden women, attended by doctors and surrounded by family or friends, appear in more than half a dozen of the novels. Typical of the country place frequented in the summer by genteel city women is the New England farm in *Mrs. Farrell* (1875-76), more sanatorium than resort, where illness is the women's main topic of conversation and "two or three . . . were nearly always sick in bed."[16] The observer in *A Foregone Conclusion* (1875) who reflects that "all his countrywomen, past their girlhood, seemed to be sick" scarcely exaggerates.[17] Unlike Stoddard, whose female characters grow strong in resisting repressive authority, Howells portrayed women, members of a "sex which is born tired,"[18] as further debilitated by restrictive conventions ("our version of the Chinese foot-binding"[19]) that confined women to lives of idleness or vain social duties, deprived them of the physical and mental exercise enjoyed by men, and denied them the health-giving satisfactions men find in productive work and professional success.

From the beginning, Howells viewed the mental and physical sufferings of women as purely negative in their consequences, inducing unhealthy dependence, morbid egoism, and warped perceptions. That he should see no redemptive value in women's illness was inevitable once the deteriorating health of his eldest child, Winifred, stricken at the age of sixteen, became the source of the greatest anguish he would ever know. A classic case of the gifted and tenderly nurtured child who breaks down in adolescence, Winifred during her last nine years sank into total invalidism; her symptoms— vertigo, anorexia, melancholia, intense pain after eating—defied diagnosis and cure by any of the doctors Howells consulted. In the fall of 1888, when Winifred was twenty-five, Howells as a last resort placed her in the care of the Philadelphia neurologist S. Weir Mitchell, whose patients would later include Charlotte Perkins Gilman and Edith Wharton. At Mitchell's clinic, where Winifred engaged with the doctor in a prolonged "tussle of wills" (as Howells wrote to his father), force-feeding had by January 1889 raised her weight from fifty-eight to seventy-one pounds.[20] Two months later, in a sanatorium in Merchantville, New Jersey, where she seemed to be gaining strength, she died suddenly of heart failure. John Crowley, who has analyzed Winifred's case in the most detail, argues persuasively that she was trapped by the very conditions that seemed most to favor her.[21] Fearful of disappointing her own and her parents' dreams of literary success, she would escape through illness the demands of adulthood and remain in the protected world of her childhood.

Howells never made his daughter's illness the subject of his fiction, but in his later novels he gave the figure of the invalid woman even more prominence.[22] Eating disorders are but one sign of physical and mental illness in the invalid characters—they suffer from enervation, hypochondria, insomnia, anxiety, and depression as well—but of all their symptoms their abnormal eating habits have the most visible effect on their appearance and their behavior and thus function best as the symbolic expression of moral or psychological weakness.

The results of a "New England indigestion" are most apparent in the character described by the phrase: Adeline Northwick, the unmarried elder sister in *The Quality of Mercy* (1892). "Thin and tall," Adeline is starved to the point that "each rib" of her "bony waist . . . defined itself to [the] hand" (49). Her "weak frame" bespeaks psychological as well as physical deficiency: she is timorous, fearful, guilt-ridden, and given to fits of hysterical weeping. Her neurotic symptoms are aggravated by the collapse of her father, the treasurer of a New England milling company, who after years of embezzlement is exposed and flees to Canada, where he eventually dies. But Howells indicates that Adeline's physical and mental condition is rooted in inherited tendencies reflective of a degenerative Puritanism that helped turn her mother into a "timorous creature" ridden by "manifold anxieties," psychologically as well as financially dependent on her husband, and ruled by her "instinct for saving" even after he became a rich landowner (7). Adeline, a generation older than her sister, Suzette, seems a prolongation of her mother's meager life on a reduced scale. It is significant that she keeps her mother's watch, "that had never been wound up since her death" (155). The narrator's statement that in her behavior she adheres to "an earlier country fashion of self-repression" (19) implies the stifling of feelings and impulses that in her beautiful younger sister find expression in courtship and marriage. Adeline has never had a suitor, and her sister has always been their father's favorite daughter. In Adeline the "New England indigestion" that wastes the body signals emotional deprivation as well.

Within the novel, Adeline is also deprived through the attitude of the other characters, who habitually refer to her as "that poor old maid" and can see her in no other way. Although the narrator credits her with "the inborn New England love of justice" (49), he collaborates in the reduction of the woman to a stereotype, repeatedly designating her "the old maid" and characterizing her speech by such modifiers as "nervously," "feebly," "tremulously," "meekly," "submissively," "forlornly," and "guiltily." Unlike Veronica Morgeson, Adeline is virtually eclipsed by a spirited and self-confident sister whose beauty impresses others as "extraordinary," "superb," "magnificent," and "regal." When male characters inquire about the sisters, they unthinkingly speak only of Suzette, allowing Adeline to "[drop] from the question, as usual" (147). Adeline can command others' attention only by becoming so ill that the family doctor must be called repeatedly. Her feeble strength gives way entirely, and she dies soon after her sister becomes engaged to the most exemplary young man in the novel.

The Quality of Mercy also presents Howells's most important example of the male dyspeptic, an impoverished young journalist and aspiring playwright named Brice Maxwell, who brilliantly analyzes the social significance of Northwick's defalcation and later becomes engaged to a socially prominent Boston girl, the sister of the man who marries Suzette Northwick. The difference in Howells's depiction of dyspepsia in its male and female manifestations is noteworthy. Failing health increases rather than diminishes the romantic appeal of the "sick young man," who has a "thin, delicate face" and at first meeting impresses the girl he will marry as "very handsome, and interesting, and pale and sick" (145). His repugnance to food seems evidence of superior refinement and sensitivity when in a railroad station restaurant he nibbles a bit of toast "like a man of small appetite and invalid digestion" (90), while a fellow reporter, well-meaning but vulgar and crude, downs baked beans and mince pie. Maxwell's chronic indigestion, headaches, and fatigue result not from starved emotions but from overwork. He labors to support himself and his widowed mother as a journalist, all the while struggling to write his first play. A "ravenous reader of philosophy and sociology" (119), he draws his strength from ideas, compelling even his fiancée's class-conscious mother, who opposes the marriage, to admit: "He makes you feel his power more than any young man I've met" (293).

In Howells's fictional world, men are sustained in times of personal crisis by their work; women lacking such defense against depression and melancholia slide quickly into invalidism. The difference is dramatized in *April Hopes,* in which a New England couple—Alice Pasmer and Dan Mavering— suffer through misunderstandings, quarrels, and two broken engagements before they finally marry, at the end of the novel. Without Dan, Alice languishes, emerges from a long illness with "thin cheeks and lack-lustre eyes," and convalesces at a summer hotel called the Hygeia, where, unrefreshed by the sea air, "she grew more listless and languid."[23] When Dan is cast off, he suffers keenly, but work in his father's manufacturing business dispels even "the idea of being sick." Despite pangs of anguish, "he kept a good appetite" and found himself "hungry three times a day with perfect regularity" (153–54).

Gender differences are equally marked in the portrayal of the Landers in *Ragged Lady* (1899), Howells's twelfth novel set in New England. Husband and wife suffer contrasting metabolic disorders after he retires from his boys' clothing business, she gives up housekeeping, and they live a transitory life of "luxury and idleness" in expensive hotels.[24] "She had constantly grown in flesh, while he had dwindled away until he was not much more than half the weight of his prime" (15). The implication that she has fed on him is confirmed as Howells makes her gluttony the visible sign of her selfish craving for attention and sympathy. She secretly consumes candy "with childish greed" (19), and she feeds as voraciously on the energies of

Clementina, the young country girl she hires as her companion. Until her death from "cumulative over-eating" (194), she exploits her gastric attacks as her only means of compelling the girl's pity and obedience. Such power as she commands is short-lived, however, and she remains too repulsive and too helpless to inspire in the reader either pity or fear.

For most of Howells's characters, illness means unredeemed suffering, thwarted hopes, and often death. Their lives could illustrate the text of Henry James's letter to Grace Norton: "Try not to be ill . . . for in that there is a failure."[25] Only Howells himself offers in his own life testimony of the vitalizing power born of suffering. As his biographer, Edwin Cady, observes, the anguished years of Winifred's decline were the years of her father's greatest productivity, issuing in nine novels, including two of his best, *The Rise of Silas Lapham* and *Indian Summer.* In Cady's words, "it was as if the suffering he had once feared might destroy him instead unlocked new powers to create within him."[26] But Howells could not save his daughter, and he did not transfer his creative power to the characters of his imagination.

In the New England mill towns of Howells's fiction, vestiges of Puritanism have all but disappeared, surviving only in the "Puritanized consciences"[27] of superseded figures like Adeline Northwick. But in the fiction of Mary Wilkins Freeman, whose characters inhabit isolated villages untouched by industrial growth, Howells noted the survival of Puritanism "in the moral and mental make of the people almost in its early strength. . . . A people are not a chosen people for half a dozen generations without acquiring a spiritual pride that remains with them long after they cease to believe themselves chosen."[28]

No work of fiction better illustrates Howells's point than Freeman's novel of New England village life, *Pembroke* (1894), described by the author as "a study of the human will in different phases of disease and abnormal development."[29] Stiff-backed pride and unswerving resolve drive the members of three Pembroke families—Thayers, Berrys, and Barnards, who, in the absence of all outside influences and interests, allow petty grievances to possess their minds and consume their energies. The action of the novel begins when the tyrannical Cephas Barnard provokes his daughter's suitor, Barnabas Thayer, into a quarrel about politics and then drives him from the house. Barnabas vows never to return, and neither man relents until the final pages, after the quarrel has blasted the lives of young and old in all three families.

On the farms of Pembroke, where the kitchen is the center of family life and the raising of crops and the getting of meals are the primary occupations, food is the pivot on which almost all the action turns, the instrument through which characters seek to maintain their authority and control over others. Deborah Thayer punishes her son, Barnabas, for refusing to obey her command to return to Charlotte Barnard by forbidding him to "sit down to a meal in your father's and mother's house."[30] Cephas Barnard, who believes that salvation lies in diet, not in God's grace, forces his family to subsist on rye meal or garden greens, forbidding them food that "might strengthen the animal at the expense of the spiritual" (53). Passive victims of others' wills strike at themselves, as does an impoverished cousin, Sylvia Crane, who, when forced to beggar herself to serve her relatives a lavish tea, tells herself fiercely that "she did not care if she never ate supper again" (263), then bruises her hand on the chimney bricks as though to prove "her own freedom and power" (264).

The grimmest, most protracted struggle ensues between the implacable Deborah Thayer and her sickly son, Ephraim, a rare case of a male dyspeptic, who early in life recognizes in his sickness his one source of power—"power of a lugubrious sort, certainly, but still it was power, and so to be enjoyed" (107). When thwarted by his mother, he employs his most potent weapon, the ritual formula "I dunno as I want any supper, I've got a pain" (147), then writhes and moans "with attentive eyes upon his mother; he was like an executioner turning an emotional thumbscrew on her" (147). When he ate forbidden sweets on the sly, "his stomach oppressed him, his breath came harder," but in defiance "he had a sense of triumph in his soul" (100).

The contest of wills enters its final phase when Deborah loses control over her two older children and vows "to have one child obey me" (147). Convincing herself that she acts for the good of Ephraim's soul and not for the relief of her frustration, she deprives her son of all pleasure, including every food he likes, and forces his mouth to open to bitter medicine without sweetening, as if "[her] will were a veritable wedge between his teeth" (222). Like a warrior in battle, she thrusts the feeding spoon at him "as if it were a bayonet and there were death at the point" (222). Her harsh discipline, kept up in defiance of the doctor's warnings, eventually drives Ephraim to fatal rebellion. He steals from the house one night to coast in the moonlight, returns home to consume a mince pie in secret, and dies the next day. His mother's death, in an agony of remorse, follows soon after.

Whether Freeman's characters give food or withhold it, whether they deny themselves food or consume it in secret, they seek, like Sylvia Crane, to prove their own "freedom and power." Even characters so poor that they can scarcely provide for their next meal are moved by forces other than bare necessity. If nothing else, pride impels characters to go without food rather than accept charity from neighbors. But self-denial often springs from more complex feelings. In "A Taste of Honey," for instance, Inez Morse thinks she is motivated solely by her duty to her dead father when she asks her suitor to postpone their marriage and forces her mother to sell all the honey they raise until the mortgage on their farm is paid off. But postponing the pleasures of food and love affords Inez intense satisfaction. As the anorectic rejoices in each pound lost, so Inez feels a "keen delight" with each payment made.[31] She loses her suitor, who eventually marries another woman, but she seems resigned to the price she pays for three years of mastery, when she governed the lives of two people, succeeded where her father had failed, and was captive only to the force of her own will.

Characters in Freeman's stories deprive themselves to shield their egos as well as to assert their wills. In "A Solitary," Nicholas Gunn reasons that if he places no value on himself, nothing that happens to him can hurt him. To convince himself that he cares nothing for himself he becomes "a stern anchorite" who lives on uncooked cornmeal and water and in winter sleeps on the bare floor in a freezing cabin without a fire. In another culture, the narrator observes, Nicholas Gunn might "have been revered and worshipped as a saintly ascetic,"[32] but for Freeman's characters salvation comes through love, offered and received, often expressed in the giving and acceptance of food. Nicholas is freed from the prison of his ego when he participates in the saving economy of "need and supply" (235) by building a fire to warm a sick man and cooking a meal to nourish them both.

The lives of characters like the Thayers and the Barnards are far more limited and circumscribed than the lives of Howells's and Stoddard's well-to-do New Englanders. But Freeman's village characters have a kind of sturdy determination—*grit*, as Nicholas Gunn calls his power to endure— that ease and wealth have dissipated in the Morgesons and the Northwicks. Of Freeman's characters Van Wyck Brooks observed: "Those who prefer to starve rather than say they are hungry are living as the well-fed seldom live."[33] A perverted will can harden the heart, chain the mind, and warp the body. But the resolute will can empower the most submissive and sustain the meanest and poorest.

In her autobiography, *A Backward Glance,* Edith Wharton claimed that she wrote *Ethan Frome* (1911) "to draw life as it really was in the derelict villages of New England," a reality she believed was "utterly unlike that seen through the rose-coloured spectacles of my predecessors, Mary Wilkins and Sarah Orne Jewett."[34] One wonders which of their works she had in mind. Her description of the western Massachusetts villages as they were in Freeman's day—"grim places, morally and physically," where "insanity, incest and slow mental and moral starvation were hidden away behind the paintless wooden house-fronts of the long village street, or in the isolated farm-houses on the neighboring hills"—might be a description of Pembroke. But Wharton acknowledged Freeman only as a model to be dismissed, one of the "authoresses" who falsified life in their "rose-and-lavender pages."[35]

The reader may consider whether E. A. Robinson, who admired *Pembroke* for its "tragic background of subdued passion" and believed that "to one who knows anything about Puritanism the book will be interesting and impressive,"[36] is a fairer judge than Wharton of the verisimilitude of Freeman's work. The reader may decide whether the spectacle of Zenobia Frome driving her husband and her cousin to the suicide attempt that cripples them for life is more or less horrifying than Deborah Thayer's blind destruction of her invalid son. But whatever the relative merits of the two works as tragic realism, *Ethan Frome* remains, after *The Scarlet Letter*, the most famous novel of New England life.

The narrative is powerful in its intensity and simplicity. Where Stoddard, Howells, and Freeman expand and amplify, creating subplots and dozens of minor characters, shifting scenes and stretching time to months or years, Wharton concentrates on the three principal characters, the setting of the Fromes' isolated farmhouse and its environs, and the single action that builds to a climax within two days. Within this stripped-down world, nothing mitigates the effect of the paradox that gives *Ethan Frome* its peculiar horror: that energy resides only in the vengeful will of a sick woman, who alone of the characters conceives and executes a plan of action.

At first glance, Zenobia would seem to lack every advantage possessed by the invalid characters considered thus far. The Fromes are trapped in a kind of poverty never known by Stoddard's and Howells's characters. No family network like that portrayed in *Pembroke* supports Ethan and Zenobia or eases the pressure of poisoned relationships within their household. Without beauty or talent, Zenobia is not only the most physically repellent of all the characters—and Wharton spares nothing, not even the sight of her false teeth reposing in a glass of water at night; Zenobia alone of all the invalid characters is sexually repulsive, viewed as she is through the eyes of her husband, who never loved her and has come to love another woman. Zenobia alone so blights her world that others longingly fantasize her death.

Her one interest is her failing health, which creates her only contacts with the outside world: her patent medicines received through the mail and her visits to doctors in neighboring villages. But despite, or perhaps because of, her deprived state, she commands a power of will that nothing diverts from her purpose—to drive her attractive young cousin, Mattie Silver, from her house, when she perceives her husband's attraction to the younger woman.

The only invalid character seen thus far who determines the outcome of the action, Zenobia uses her illness as her most powerful weapon to control others and work her will. Her habitual complaint—"I don't feel as if I could touch a morsel"[37]—is, for her husband, "the consecrated formula" (116) that signals her determination to manipulate him through his sense of guilt and duty to an ailing wife. When he attempts to resist her on Mattie's behalf, her "shooting pains" send her to bed. When she returns from an overnight journey to a nearby town where she has hired a girl to arrive the next day to replace Mattie, her appetite returns, and at supper she "helped herself largely to pie and pickles" (134). The next noon, "she ate well," at what she thinks is Mattie's last meal with them, although her dyspepsia sends her to bed again when Ethan insists that he, not the hired man, will drive Mattie to the railroad station. Feeding or fasting, she exudes, to her husband's sense, "an evil energy secreted from the long years of silent brooding" (118).

Had Ethan simply hated his wife he might have defied her, but his power to resist her will is crippled not only by guilt but also by compassion. A true grotesque, she is at once hateful and pitiful in her exposure of Ethan and Mattie, as she tearfully confronts them with the fragments of the broken pickle dish, her prized wedding present that she never used. The barren marriage of the Fromes, symbolized by the empty pickle dish, is outwardly marked by a corresponding image: "a dead cucumber vine [that] dangled from the porch like the crape streamer tied to the door for a death" (51).

Ethan Frome magnifies the themes and images of the earlier novels: the isolation of the characters is more profound, the winter cold is more intense, the impoverished landscape is more bleak than in the other novels of rural New England. In starkest terms, *Ethan Frome* limns the situation of men and women represented in the fiction of Stoddard, Howells, and Freeman. The plight of Mattie Silver and Zenobia Frome, unable to support themselves and dependent on husband or relatives, could be the fate of all the women whose only hope of security and happiness appears to lie in marriage. The emasculation of Ethan Frome, who feels his wife's words "like a knife-cut across the sinews" (117), typifies the failure of male authority figures in other works: the bankruptcy of Locke Morgeson, the defalcation and exposure of Northwick, the fixations of the men in *Pembroke,* trapped by their blind wills. In the works of the three women, the vacuum created by the collapse of male authority is filled by the power of women determined to assert their needs and desires. In Howells's novels, men of integrity and strong purpose, like Eban Hilary in *The Quality of Mercy* and Elbridge Mavering in *April Hopes* (1888), sustain the power of masculine authority. But in the works of all four writers, female characters—denied entrance to the male worlds of business and the professions—discover in illness a way to define themselves and work their will. That illness should be their means to self-expression and power exposes dysfunction in the social order. That food should be their chief instrument of manipulation symbolizes the primacy of their need.

Notes

1. William Dean Howells, *The Quality of Mercy,* introduction and notes to the text by James P. Elliott (Bloomington: Indiana University Press, 1979), 19. Subsequent references to this text are given in parentheses.

2. William Dean Howells, *Suburban Sketches* (Boston: James R. Osgood & Co., 1872), 96.

3. William Dean Howells, "Puritanism in American Fiction," in *Literature and Life* (New York: Harper & Brothers, 1902), 282.

4. Rollin Lynde Hartt, "A New England Hill Town," *Atlantic Monthly* 83 (April 1899): 564, 468, 569.

5. William Dean Howells, *A Chance Acquaintance,* introduction and notes to the text by Jonathan Thomas and David J. Nordloh (Bloomington: Indiana University Press, 1971), 74.

6. For a detailed account of Gull's work in defining and treating anorexia nervosa, see Joan Jacobs Brumberg, *Fasting Girls: The Emergence of Anorexia as a Modern Disease* (Cambridge, Mass.: Harvard University Press, 1988), 115–25.

7. Elizabeth Stoddard, *The Morgesons and Other Writings, Published and Unpublished,* ed. with critical introduction by Lawrence Buell and Sandra A. Zagarell (Philadelphia: University of Pennsylvania Press, 1984), 28. Subsequent references to this text are given in parentheses.

8. What Howells said of Stoddard's second novel, *Two Men,* is true of *The Morgesons:* "The author seldom vouchsafes a word of comment or explanation on anything that her people do or say; and yet, from their brief speeches and dramatic action, you have the same knowledge of motive which you acquire from the philosophization of some such subjective romance as "The Scarlet Letter." "Two Men," *The Nation,* October 26, 1865, p. 537.

9. Sybil Weir, "*The Morgesons:* A Neglected Feminist Bildungsroman," *New England Quarterly* 49 (1976): 430.

10. Mary Moss, "The Novels of Elizabeth Stoddard," *The Bookman* 16 (1902): 260.

11. Rudolph M. Bell, *Holy Anorexia* (Chicago: University of Chicago Press, 1985), 59–61.

12. As quoted in ibid., 63.

13. Elizabeth Stoddard, *Daily Alta California,* October 7, 1855, as quoted by Sybil B. Weir, "Our Lady Correspondent: The Achievement of Elizabeth Drew Stoddard," *San Jose Studies* 10 (1984): 85.

14. Ibid.

15. The inferior status of women in *The Morgesons* is analyzed by Lawrence Buell and Sandra A. Zagarell in their introduction to *The Morgesons and Other Writings,* xvii–xix, and by Maurice Kramer, "Alone at Home with Elizabeth Stoddard," *American Transcendental Quarterly,* nos. 47–48 (Summer–Fall 1980): 159–70.

16. William Dean Howells, *Mrs. Farrell,* with an introduction by Mildred Howells (New York: Harper & Brothers, 1921), 13. The fullest treatment of Howells's portrayal of invalid women is Sidney H. Bremer's "Invalids and Actresses: Howells's Duplex Imagery for American Women," *American Literature* 47 (1976): 599–614.

17. William Dean Howells, *A Foregone Conclusion* (Boston: James R. Osgood & Co., 1875), 126.

18. Howells, *Suburban Sketches,* 96.

19. Ulrich Halfmann, "Interviews with William Dean Howells," *American Literary Realism* 6 (1973): 326–27.

20. *Selected Letters, Vol. 3, 1882–1891,* ed. and annotated by Robert C. Leitz III et al. (Boston: Twayne Publishers, 1980), 235 n. 1; 243 n. 4.

21. John W. Crowley, "Winifred Howells and the Economy of Pain," *Old Northwest* 10 (1984): 41–75.

22. Invalids in Howells's later fiction include Mrs. Mavering (*April Hopes*), Mrs. Dryfoos (*A Hazard of New Fortunes*), Mrs. Meredith (*An Imperative Duty*), Adeline Northwick (*The Quality of Mercy*), Mrs. Camp (*The Traveller from Altruria*), and Mrs. Lander (*Ragged Lady*).

23. William Dean Howells, *April Hopes,* introduction and notes to the text by Kermit Vanderbilt (Bloomington: Indiana University Press, 1974), 347. Subsequent references to this text are given in parentheses.

24. William Dean Howells, *Ragged Lady* (New York: Harper & Brothers, 1899), 14, 15. Subsequent references to this text are given in parentheses.

25. Letter of July 28, 1883, *Henry James Letters, Vol. 2, 1875–1883,* ed. Leon Edel (Cambridge, Mass.: Harvard University Press, 1975), 425.

26. Edwin H. Cady, *The Realist at War: The Mature Years, 1885–1920, of William Dean Howells* (Syracuse, N.Y.: Syracuse University Press, 1958), 58.

27. Howells's phrase in *Heroines of Fiction* (New York: Harper & Brothers, 1901), 2:253.

28. Howells, "Puritanism in American Fiction," 281.

29. Quoted by Edward Foster in *Mary E. Wilkins Freeman* (New York: Hendrick House, 1956), 128.

30. Mary E. Wilkins, *Pembroke* (New York: Harper & Brothers, 1894), 103. Subsequent references to this text are given in parentheses.

31. Mary E. Wilkins, *A Humble Romance and Other Stories* (New York: Harper & Brothers, 1887), 94.

32. *Selected Stories of Mary E. Wilkins Freeman,* edited with an introduction by Marjorie Pryse (New York: W. W. Norton & Co., 1983), 225, 235.

33. Van Wyck Brooks, *New England: Indian Summer, 1865–1915* (New York: E. P. Dutton & Co., 1940), 472. The power and strength of Freeman's characters are also emphasized by Susan Allen Toth, "Defiant Light: A Positive View of Mary Wilkins Freeman," *New England Quarterly* 46 (1973): 82–93.

34. Edith Wharton, *A Backward Glance* (New York: Appleton-Century, 1934), 293.

35. Ibid., 293–94.

36. Letter to Harry Smith, October 28, 1894, in *Untriangulated Stars: Letters of Edwin Arlington Robinson to Harry DeForest Smith, 1890-1905,* ed. Denham Sutcliffe (Cambridge, Mass.: Harvard University Press, 1947), 174.

37. Edith Wharton, *Ethan Frome* (New York: Charles Scribner's Sons, 1911), 116. Subsequent references to this text are given in parentheses.

CONSUMPTION TO THE LAST DROP:
Huysmans' Dyspeptic Tale of Eating *A Rebours*

Raymond Adolph Prier

> Lasciate ogne speranza, voi ch'intrate.
> (Forsake all hope, you who enter.)
> —Dante, *Inferno,* 3.9

> Master, have pity on the Christian who doubts, on
> the disbeliever who would believe, on the convict who
> embarks alone (*qui s'embarque seul*), at night, under
> a firmament that consoling beacons of ancient hope
> light no more!
> —J.-K. Huysmans, *A Rebours*

By the time the reader has arrived at the above last sentence of Huysmans' *A Rebours,* so reminiscent of the last line inscribed over the maw of Hell at the beginning of Dante's journey through the Devil's bowels, he or she is long familiar with the enervating undulations and aesthetically clogged reversals of the author's plot and his main character's dyspeptic life. Even the author's idiosyncratic style mirrors a process with which we are all-too-familiar, but over which our will usually disrupts any order. Thus, when as early as the second page of the novel we are told "The decline of this ancient house had, with no doubt, followed regularly its course" (80), or later informed that "These ideas twisted and precious, he knotted with an adhesive tongue, alone and hidden, pregnant with receding phrases, elliptic turns, and bold tropes" (327),[1] we sense much more than the historical facts of the hero's lineage in the first case or a philological description of Mallarmé's style in the second. What lies behind all this? A parataxis engulfed in a lexis of double entendre that floats on a fluid syntax. It rivets the reader's attention, and he or she becomes implicated in the involving, revolving, devolving, and reversing world of the intestine.

But does this intestine possess a locus? Is it within us or without? Huysmans never allows the reader the convenience of such a distinction. It would block the aesthetic, human point his narrator, in contradistinction to his hero, strives to make. It would also turn the intestine into a mere metaphor, a too easily manipulable image. What binds together this novel of decadence (Latin *decadere,* "to fall down from") is a human experience that governs the aesthetic metaphors caught within it. Huysmans' powerful explanation of events lies in the direct, human confrontation of the digestive experience itself. Unsure whether the mouth, alimentary tract, and anus are another's or one's own, the reader is thrown by the novel into a visceral nightmare of consumption and self-consumption, fecal waste in both a subjective and objective sense, food as nourishment and poison, life and death. When we eat, do we not somehow attempt to digest ourselves?

A Rebours (perhaps the most appropriate translation is "against nature")[2] appeared in 1884. It chronicles the decline in health, yet suggested salvation, of a certain Des Esseintes, whose story is gilded with catalogs of exquisitely described and experienced objects, cultural artifacts, and aesthetic moments. The author, Joris-Karl Huysmans, devotes considerable space to the sensual and sensuous description of corrupt and corrupting art, literature, and music, especially of the ecclesiastical genre and of the French nineteenth century. Sight, taste, smell, and touch become excuses for human self-destruction at its most rarified and exquisite levels. The sensibilities of the poet Baudelaire, author of *Les Fleurs du mal* (The Flowers of Sickness), are central to the perceptions of Huysmans' hero and to the descriptive language of his narrator. The symbolist poet Mallarmé's aesthetic sense of language and *l'objet d'art* is equally important for both, although it would be a mistake to identify Des Esseintes' aesthetic evaluation of both poets with that of Huysmans' narrator. By the end of the novel the two figures are clearly opposed.

Many of the most memorable descriptions in *A Rebours* deal directly or indirectly with food. The only full and direct aesthetic description of it occurs, however, very early on when the narrator speaks of the hero's re-creation of a notorious eighteenth-century funeral feast in black, bordered in the confines of a black-draped room, an ink-filled pond, charcoal-strewn paths, and black-rimmed plates. The necessarily all-black meal, thus so exquisitely framed and timed, consists of similarly forced, ultimately indi-

gestible foods: "They had eaten . . . turtle soup, Russian rye, Turkish ripe
olives, caviar, caviar of mullet, finely chopped, dried, salted, and seasoned,
black-smoked Frankfurt sausage . . . " (94). The alimentary riches grow ever
more saccharine and gagging in a welter of truffle cullises, amber-colored
chocolate creams, puddings, nectarines, pear jams, mulberries, sweet cherries,
wines of Limagne, of Roussillon, of Tenedos, and port, all diarrhetically
embellished with coffee, a "digestive" of distilled walnut husks, kvass,
porter, and stout. This is hardly a mother's home-cooked delight, and as the
reader forces down the obvious and very successful parataxis of all this
indigestible fare, the overwhelming temptation is to vomit.

Yet, Des Esseintes, Huysmans' consuming and self-consuming hero, who
swears "he who dreams of the ideal demands illusions" (97), early in the
novel rejects the public grandeur of such ghastly-ghostly feasts in order to
starve himself on a lean and simple daily menu: two boiled eggs, toast, tea,
coffee, and, at five in the morning before retiring, a *petite dinette* (a
minuscule doll's dinner) at which he would merely pick (*picorait*) (102).
Secluded in the small village of Fontenay, he chooses to live his death-
directed life at night enclosed within the body of a house within a house, the
intestinally orange, indigo-vesseled walls and rounded ceiling of which
"often transforms itself into a nasturtium red, a red fire" (98). These walls
"in reality" consist of a fine, crushed garment of Moroccan leather, "with the
skin from the Cape, made rough by strong steel plates under a powerful
press" (98). Nothing could resemble more the texture of the intestinal wall
or a fine dish of tripe. Then too in Des Esseintes' decision "to have his walls
bound (*à faire relier* ['hooped' in the case of casks]) as books" (98), how
could he better approximate the texture of undigested and poisonous fecal
waste into which his library, his art, his music, his aesthetic objects must
ultimately be reduced? The narrator compares Des Esseintes' dining room
to a ship's cabin, constructed like a box within a box that was originally "the
real (*véritable*) dining room" (103). This sea-borne and hence free-floating
intestine expectedly possesses two windows to the outside world, one into
which air might enter, the other blocked by a small round porthole, itself
constipated by an aquarium in which Des Esseintes from time to time plays
with colored essences, mechanical fish, and artificial seaweed. The experience calls to mind little else except the poisonous effects perpetrated by
unpassed fecal waste.

Herein Huysmans' hero will transubstantiate food into art, but the transformation is more than metaphorical because, although slight on food, Des
Esseintes' diet becomes rich in alcohol. Long before the sensible doctor in

the novel's penultimate chapter discovers albumin in his patient's urine, the reader senses that the man is destroying his kidneys and his health with unaccompanied strong drink. Drunk as sound from discrete stops of a musical instrument, specifically an organ, and dispensed from behind the dining room's intestinal walls through spigots with an effect little different from the squirt of digestive juices into the stomach, curaçao sec, kümmel, crème de menthe, anisette, kirsch, gin, scotch, brandy from the residue of grapes, arak, mastic, Benedictine, Chartreuse, rum, and Irish whiskey (138–40) exhale in the hero's brain strange and soon terrifying fantasies that drive him mad. Thus amid the bevy of languages, books, art, music, cultivated artifacts of all kinds, in short those aesthetic objects with which *A Rebours* is clogged and so fashionably turned, Huysmans constructs an underlying and progressive self-poisoning that brings the hero ever nearer death and the reader ever nearer an aesthetic enervation that creates a novel one can take only in small doses.

"Real" food, as opposed to that of a more or less metaphorical variety, however, does not recur in the narrative until five chapters before its end when in a crazed, starved, and nauseated state Des Esseintes forsakes the intermediation of his gastric-juicing apparatus to lay hold of the whole bottle of Benedictine. First, by now a slave to the irrelevant, fecal decadence of his own thought processes, he ruminates on the hypocrisy signified by the discrepancy between the container and its contents, "between the liturgical contour of the bottle and its soul, completely feminine, completely modern" (290), then ranges in his imagination step-by-step through the making of the liquor itself, and at last takes a sip: "but soon this fire which the teardrop of wine had lit in his bowels was roused" (290). Enervation spreads to his brain. But at this moment nothing other than the unmasterable will to live overtakes the man, and "for the first time" since his arrival in his eccentric abode he breaks out into the real world of his garden.

Blear-eyed and sick, he cannot see through "a greenish fog" (*un brouillard verdâtre*) that blocks his view as if he were "on the bottom below the water (*au fond de l'eau*) where were only doubtful images, the aspect and tone [or 'quality'] of which would continually change" (291). We realize that Des Esseintes' body has become the unsatisfactory digestive apparatus he has built simultaneously within his house and mind. But in his ever-reversible world, prefigured by the glass bubble lodged before the window to the world without, his anus has become his eyes, his aesthetic metaphor, at base, a metonymic confrontation with indigestion and death.

What, however, does he see once he emerges from his sickly fog? Onions, cabbages, lettuce, and beyond "a row of white lilies, still in the heavy air" (291). At last the hero confronts plain, good food, bordered, it is true, by a symbol of the spiritual nourishment the *narrator* is going to acknowledge as Des Esseintes' proper aesthetic goal all along.

The hero's perception of the flowers, however, is not immediately catholic, but Baudelairian, as is much in the novel. Both the earlier poet's and his desire "for flowers in nature that imitated fakes" (191) prevails, and, with the aid of Nicander and Albertus Magnus, he shrouds the lilies in perverse sexual connotations that reverse their religious symbolism and make them indeed *les fleurs du mal*. Nonetheless, his next confrontation in the world outside once again is with plain food, although framed in a common and repulsive guise: a boy described with "two green bubbles beneath the nose, disgusting lips encircled with a white filth from the sandwich made of cheese smeared on bread and sprinkled with green onion" (291). The reader, by this time familiar with the fastidious nature of Des Esseintes' palate and nose, once again might well be inclined to vomit but is surprised by yet another alimentary reversal: Des Esseintes' mouth waters, and he is sure "that his stomach, which had refused all nourishment, would digest this horrid mess and that his palate would take joy in it as a treat" (292). His stomach, to be sure, led him to the desire for this food in the first place, and the reader, if he or she were to discard the poisoning gastronomic pretensions of the hero, should be able to discover little unhealthy in the three items the hero asks his servants to fetch: "a round loaf of bread, some white cheese, some onion" (292). At last, in spite of the hero's aesthetics, his stomach calls for *la nourriture terrestre:* bread.

Des Esseintes, his system by this time near septic and overcome by an aesthetic revulsion toward children, ultimately gags at the sight of his snack and dips a biscuit in a bit of J.-P. Cloete Constantia, only later to drink some Nalifka, itself described by the narrator as "this unctuous, raspberried syrup" (296). It is the narrator also who at last declares what anyone with a normal digestive tract could have told the reader after chapter four: "These remedies unfortunately were no longer effective, since his ills were real (*réels*)" (297). Chapter thirteen ends with a cramp in the hero's stomach.

In chapter fourteen, the hero buys a *cuisinière* (musher) into which a concoction, boiled four hours, of roast beef, a little leek, and a carrot is poured and squeezed:

> One pressed the stringy meat and drank a mash (*cuillerée*) of muddy, salted juice, deposited at the bottom of the digester

(*marmite*). Then one felt (*on sentait*) [something?] on the order of tepid marrow (*tiède moelle*), a velvet caress, descend (*descendre*). (303–4)

What repulsive stuff and diarrhetic to its core, both in consistency and color. Stylistically intestinal, two similes, one in parataxis to the other, clog the objectless narrative path that descends. (*Sentir* is not usually an intransitive verb.) One might note also the effective seduction of the reader in the use of the indefinite pronoun *on,* but most interesting is Des Esseintes' uncontrollable desire for nourishment. This predigested slop ceases "the abdominal pains and the nausea caused by an empty stomach" (304). It is not generally encouraging, however, that the remainder of chapter fourteen is devoted to a lengthy discussion of literature. The hero, as usual, consumes aesthetic objects, not food.

The penultimate chapter finds the hero divested of any enthusiasm for his *cuisinère,* plagued again with dyspepsia, hallucinations, eye troubles, a hacking cough, throbbing arteries, illusive ringings in the ear, a burning fever—in short "the last stage of his sickness" (335): starvation. At last Des Esseintes looks at himself in a mirror: "the image was earthen in color, lips swollen and dry (*boursouflées et sèches*), tongue corrugated (*ridée*), skin wrinkled (*rugueuse*)...eyes gaping and watery in their own liquor, that burned with a feverish glitter from this skeleton's head, bristling with hair" (342). The hero's misdirected aesthetic journey has turned, once again, in reverse, and transformed him into a monster whose symptoms, listed so medically by the narrator, add up to a nasty state of affairs indeed: starvation, dehydration, kidney failure, and, perhaps, a touch of hepatitis compounded by the signs of tuberculosis, commonly consumption.

Clearly this situation cries for a higher authority. Life, under no voluntary choice of the hero, calls, and Des Esseintes sends for a specialist renowned for curing "illnesses of the nerves" (343). The doctor, after quizzing the staff about the patient's style of life and examining his urine, attacks the seat of the problem, not the nerves but the intestine, and, with an act both curative and quintessential in this upside-down novel of reversals, perversions, and fecal waste, prescribes the beginning of a cure: "an enema [*lavement,* literally a 'washing out'] of partially hydrolysized protein" (345). The reader must still deal with the "last drops," whether they be poisonous or nutritious.

Des Esseintes is delighted: "nourishment thus absorbed was, without a doubt, the last committable deviate act" (345). With one aperture substituted for the other, the hero re-turns to health. Expectedly, however, enemas assume for him the position of all other gastronomic-aesthetic delights. A few days later, faced with an enema of quite a different smell and color, he reads aloud the doctor's prescription-recipe (346), a text printed for the reader in its proper style, with one expectedly French ingredient:

Cod-liver oil . . . . 20 grams
Beef tea . . . . 200 grams
Burgundy . . . . 200 grams
Yolk of Egg . . . . . . one

Immersed in his decadence to the end, the hero begins conceiving recipes much more perverse in nature, ones, for instance, that might allow for the Church's Friday demands.

The prescribing physician, however, soon has his patient swallowing "by ordinary routes (*les voies ordinaires*), a syrup in the form of a toddy from powdered meat with the vague aroma of cocoa, pleasing to his real (*réele*) mouth" (347). Once, moreover, the physician's outside authority rights his patient's wrong-turned intestine, he is able to declare "that he had tackled the most critical concern in reestablishing the digestive functions (*les fonctions digestives*) and that he had now to attack the neurosis which had in no way been cured" (349). Des Esseintes, fated still to succumb to the order of a watery flow, is informed that, in order "to embark on the whole hydrotherapeutic treatment" (349), he must leave his intestinal abode and return to life, that is to Paris. Dramatically, but nonetheless insightfully, the hero cries: "So it's either death or the penal colony!" (349). The chapter closes with the doctor's wordless but worldly smile, at last the narrator's full admission of the comic irony with which he has treated his hero and his tale all along.

Yet, once Des Esseintes' intestine has been turned right-end up, he too must deal with the neurotic aesthetics of indigestion with which he has consumed himself in the preceding pages. In an expectedly unexpected narrative turn, Huysmans closes his novel musing on the most privileged feast of all—at least for Christian kind: the Transubstantiation of bread and wine into the body and blood of Christ. What better metaphor to express the vain aspirations for goodness the hero at last experiences in the empty dyspeptic growling of his bowels?

The last chapter opens with Des Esseintes sunk in an armchair ruminating "over this precisely expressed rule" (352) that was so soon to remove him from Fontenay. He reflects on the deprivation and decadence of society as a whole: his onetime friends, the aristocracy, their mansions, their pomp and crooked financial dealings. It is on this last commercial note, graphically described as an "itch for cash" (*prurit de lucre* [354]), that he arrives at the clergy, their foot cures, their sale of chocolate, Trappistine, pasta flour, liniments of macerated arnica, stomach soothers of biphosphated chalk, arquebus water, antistroke elixirs, Benedictine, and Chartreuse (354). Yet, in spite of all, the hero admits that he has always been drawn to the ecclesiastical type. (This is no news to the reader who has been privy in chapters three and twelve to his longish disquisitions on liturgical Latin style and Catholic authors.) But where in the past Des Esseintes was able to savor "the distinctive character of this literature: the constant immutability of ideas and language" (264), that is its constipating and poisonous lack of nourishment, now he has to assume a different tack. Intestinally he realizes "that he in no way [could] float (*flottât*) between skeptical ideas and leaps of conviction, buoyed up on (*sur l'eau, soutenus*) a life-saver of memories from infancy" (355).

So his love of the Catholicism "salted (*salé*) with a little magic" under Henry III would have to go, as would that spiced "with a little sadism" (355) one found at the end of the eighteenth century. To the contrary, the hero would have to force himself to possess the faith,

> to encrust (*incruster*) it [intestinally within] as soon as he contained it, screw it down for himself, to cramp it down (*visser par des crampons*) in his mind, to make an end to the defense offered by all his reflections [his metaphors], that shake it (*l'ébranlent*) and root it out (*la déracinent*). (355)

In short, Des Esseintes must face the involuntary gnawing of "his religious craving, his starvation" (*sa faim religieuse* [356]).

The intestinal hero, however, so willing "to let himself be carried by this [watery] current" (*se laisser emporter par ce courant* [356]) can find only one all-too-human fault: men have tampered with the ecclesiastic recipes. The food offered up for transubstantiation is not the real thing.[3]

Not only had holy oils been adulterated with poultry fat, the candles with bones burnt to ash, and the incense with vulgar resin, specifically that of old Javanese spice bushes, but the wine and bread had been denatured (*dénaturées* [357]) by multiple dilutions of Pernambuco bark, danewort, alcohol, alum, ester of salicylic acid, bean flour, potash, and pipe mud. The principle of decadence, always a restatable issue in the novel, applies to all things:

> But God refused to descend (*descendre*) in starch . . . it was impossible to consecrate bread made of oats, buckwheat, or barley, and even if one might demur ever so slightly in the case of rye bread, it was impossible to sustain (*soutenir*) any discussion, to countenance any litigation whatsoever, when it came to starch, which . . . held no title to the approved and legal matter [or substance] (*matière compétente*) of the Sacrament. (357)

All is outrageous deceit. "The mystery of the Transubstantiation has almost ceased to exist" (358). In this hunger for the one humanly nourishing aesthetic moment, the novel ends with a welter of doubt, the image of the Fauboug Saint-Germain that as a dried fecal waste "was pealing off in the dust of disuse" (358), the sorry state of intelligence, honesty, art, and society, for example the penal colony of America that had found its way to Europe. Even the words of Schopenhauer and of Pascal are deprived of "all signification, all sedative force, all effective and gentle vigor" (360). No clearer statement of Huysmans' intestinal agenda is ever advanced: what words and hence life *mean* in his novel deals with food, its assimilation, and its fated journey down, through, and out of the alimentary canal.

The result of such a metonymic, unreflected identity between digestion, culture, and its poisonous or, for that matter, positively efficacious aesthetic moments can lead to only one, fundamental end. Hence Des Esseintes' final attack on the bourgeois assumes the form of a question, the force of which makes its claim as fecal waste:

> Was this filth (*fange*) [both actual and moral] going to keep flowing and overspreading (*continuer à couler et à couvrir*) the old world with corruptive pestilence (*pestilence*) where nothing other grew than the sowings (*semailles*) of sin and the harvests (*moissons*) of shame? (361)

The reader may choose either or both of the related cloacal images: both the intestine and the sewer open wide their respective mouths in final homage to a novel so faithful to its construction. What flows diarrhetically in both tubes requires no direct expression. Its stench lies in its metaphors.

Des Esseintes can only anticipate "a tidal wave" of human mediocrity that must "swallow (*engloutir*) the refuge, the sluices (*digues*) of which I open involuntarily (*malgré moi*)" (361). Unaccustomed fare must enter the hero's metonymically physical, immediately experienced, and aesthetic-religious mouth, filling the involuntarily muscled sack of his intestine. This leap of faith, however, neither rationally nor culturally willed, admits a food that in no way takes its force from the poisonous metaphors of his reversible, involuted, and perverted imagination. At best he can open his mouth and perceive himself in horror before the Devil's maw: a doubly objective and subjective megacosmos that is made real only in his own microcosmic experience with food that churns in his bowels. Who eats whom? "Lasciate ogne speranza, voi ch'intrate."

An alimentary reading of *A Rebours* cannot be complete without some concluding emphasis on the bizarre and highly ironic nature Huysmans ascribes to the humanly cultural nature of food and its digestion. Although metaphorical, and in that sense ornamental, the long descriptive catalogs of Western cultural artifacts and their effects that fill the novel would otherwise be unjustly ignored. After all, the view, shared in the end by the narrator and the hero, that our life in the West has fallen to a nadir of indigestible fecal waste cannot be easily swept aside, and the paratactical piling up of the related objects within the catalogs that fill the novel speak primarily of aesthetic moments that purposely clog and poison its narration and its style. Thus, from the funeral feast through the silver and early medieval Latin canon, the painting, prose, and poetry of the latter part of the nineteenth century, horticulture, and the languages and presences of scents and tastes, the reader is faced with metaphors that are strewn down-scale and relished for their exquisite, jewel-like core, the reverse of any primacy and robust worth.

One memorable episode in the novel involves a begemmed tortoise, burdened and eventually killed under artificially produced *fleurs du mal.* Described from the beginning of chapter four as "an immense shield of gold" (131), the animal has been dipped in gold and ornamented with a spray of flowers and border of elaborately chosen gems. Des Esseintes refuses most of the traditional gems for this *objet d'art:* diamonds, oriental emeralds and rubies, topazes, amethysts, blue sapphires, oriental turquoises, pearls, coral, and opals (133–36). His choice, expectedly to the contrary, consists of gems that are, for the most part, described as much for their artificial resemblance to food and drink or water as for their color: the bouquet's leaves were set with stones of an accentuated and fixed (*accentué et précis*) green: asparagus-green chrysoberyls, leek-green peridots, olive-green olivines. These stood out in relief from branches of almandine and uvarovites of violaceous red,[4] throwing their gem flaws (*paillettes*) in a dry peal (*éclat sec*), the same as the darkling residue (*micas de tartre*) that shines in the inside of casks. (134)

For the artificial flowers themselves, the hero selects colors and effects even more consonant with his intestinal journey: Western turquoises, "in which their pastel-green blue is engorged [or obstructed, *engorgé*], opaque and sulfurous, as if bile-yellow" (135). Petals in bloom assume an even more diarrhetic function and appearance:

> He composed them solely of Ceylonese cat's-eyes, opalescent chrysoberyls, and blue chalcedony.
>
> These three stones emitted, in effect, mysterious and perverse sparkles, achingly extracted (*douloureusement arrachés*) from the frozen fundament (*du fond glacé*) of their troubled water.
>
> The cat's-eye of greenish-gray (*verdâtre*) [see Des Esseintes' "greenish fog," above], stretched with concentric veins which seemed to fidget (*remuer*). . . .
>
> The opalescent chrysoberyls with [their] sky-blue watered silks (*moires*) running on a lacteal tinge (*la teinte laiteuse*) that floats (*flotte*) in the interior.
>
> The blue chalcedony that ignites the bluish flares of phosphorus on a fundament of chocolate, brown and deaf. (135)

Rhetorically, Huysmans piles one short paragraph atop another to suggest the movement and colors of the fecal waste that flows through his hero's intestinal world. Des Esseintes completes his masterpiece with an oval border of "hyacinth of Compostella, mahogany-red; aquamarine, glaucous green; balas-ruby, vinegar-pink; Sudermanian ruby, palish slate" (136).

As is the vomitous funeral feast that occurs near the novel's beginning, the tortoise is described in terms that can only make the reader at best uneasy. But in Des Esseintes, perversely enough, it arouses an appetite (*il avait appétit*), and soon the reader finds him moistening toast coated in butter of the highest quality (*extraordinaire*) in a tea composed of "an impeccable (*impeccable*) blend of Si-a-Fayoune, Mo-you-tann, and Khansky, yellow teas brought to Russia from China in very special (*exceptionnelles*) caravans" (136). The hero's intestinal feast moves on to the spirited digestive juices examined above, and chapter four closes with Des Esseintes' visit to a dentist for the purpose of extracting a tooth and with the death of the tortoise. What, might ask the reader, could possibly be the connection between the decayed "blue tooth hung with blood" (143) and the tortoise? The aesthetic similarity lies in their appearance that foretells an enervated, putrid, and exquisitely refined death.

Des Esseintes, in short, is much too involved with essences that should nourish but ironically do not. In his critique of nineteenth-century French literature, for example, the hero makes a preferential claim for the *poème en prose* (prose-poem) with an expected, suckingly intestinal, and extracted diarrhetic flair:

> In a word, the prose-poem represented for Des Esseintes the concrete juice, the sublime essence (*le suc concret, l'ormazôme*) of literature, the essential (*essentielle*) oil of art.
>
> The progressively refined succulence (*succulence développée*), reduced to one drop (*réduite en une goutte*), already existed in the work of Baudelaire and also in those poems of Mallarmé that he sucked in (*humait*) with such deeply fundamental (*profonde*) joy. (331)

The narrator and the upright reader know that Des Esseintes' search for essences is logically flawed from the beginning: the hero "had long been an expert in sincere and fleeting tones [in the sense both of color and sound]" (91). Anyone who privileges external qualities over essences soon falls into the error of attributing to superficial likenesses the real core his mind and body seeks. What might be attributable offhandedly to a logical error, however, can, in the end, only be resolved, revolved, and involved for the better in the dyspeptic upheaval that engulfs the novel's narration, its hero, and its world. It is food, not artifact, that sustains life in the novel. It cannot, therefore, surprise the reader that it ends with talk of the Transubstantiation of the Host over any praise of *Les fleurs du mal*. The narrator knows well that only in a consumption and subsequent assimilation of the former does the inevitable fecal waste of life vacate a nourished rather than poisoned past and self. Good taste, good food, and trust in the Catholic Self give a positive valence to an experience best stated in French. *Qui mange se mange:* He who consumes, consumes himself.

Notes

1. "La décadence de cette ancienne maison avait, *sans nul doute,* suivi régulièrement son cours" (80; emphasis added). "Ces idées nattées et précieuses, il les nouait avec un langue adhésive, solitaire et secrète, pleine de rétractions de phrases, de tournures elliptiques, d'audacieux tropes" (327). The style in both cases is clogged.

Hereafter, the numbers in parentheses in the notes and text refer to Huysmans' *A Rebours* (Paris: Gallimard, 1977).

2. "A rebours" is not an easy phrase to set into English for this novel. Both "against the grain" and "in reverse" are possible translations of the phrase itself, but "against nature," used in the double sense of a human being's physical constitution and of an Universal Nature, best approximates the double entendre that links, but at the same time separates, the novel's microcosmic and macrocosmic worlds.

3. Such, as both hero and author note, has been established by R. P. Fr. Pie Marie Rouard de Card in his *De la falsification des substances sacramentelles* (Paris: Poussielgue-Rusand, 1856).

4. A most unusual uvarovite indeed. The stone, named after the Count Sergei S. Uvarov, is "an emerald green calcium-chromium garnet $Ca_3Cr_2(SiO_4)_3$." (See "Uvarovite" in *Webster's New Collegiate Dictionary* [Springfield, Mass.: G. C. Merriam, 1974]; a less exact definition, *Oxford English Dictionary,* 2nd ed. [Oxford: Clarendon Press, 1989].)

THE DEATH OF
THE BUDDENBROOKS:
Four Rich Meals a Day

Martha Satz

Near the end of "A Hunger Artist," Franz Kafka's sparse, grotesque tale of a circus performer who fasts for a living, the title figure explains that his lengthy fasts are not extraordinary because, in fact, he has never found a food he liked.[1] Of the characters in Thomas Mann's more robust but equally terrible story, *Buddenbrooks*, one might say it is impossible to find a food to like. In Mann's grim depiction of the decay and destruction of a family, its way of life, and the surrounding culture, the characters can find no healthy or satisfactory relationship to food — or to existence. Life in Mann's portrayal of the disintegration of the bourgeois family Buddenbrooks is an inexorable march toward a grotesquely portrayed death with the small successes and failures of family members mere epiphenomena of the process of dying. Food, because its most primary function is life-sustaining and life-nurturing, becomes a compelling expression of the characters' uneasy metaphysical relation to life. As Hilde Bruch, eminent authority on eating disorders has said, "Food is endowed with complex values and elaborate ideologies."[2] In the case of the *Buddenbrooks*, the serving and consumption of food becomes a symbolic language echoing, undercutting, and enhancing the language of the text of *Buddenbrooks*.[3]

Thomas Mann, a supreme ironist, mocks this symbolic discourse even as he uses it. As Frau Consul, the mother of the novel's focal generation, becomes increasingly and bizarrely religious, she invites a clergyman, who sings a hymn solemnly and devoutly:

> I am a reprobate,
> A warped and hardened sinner;
> I gobble evil down
> Just like the joint for dinner.
>
> Lord, fling thy cur a bone
> Of righteousness to chew
> And take my carcass home
> To Heaven and to you.[4]

Upon hearing the song, her daughter leaves the room "bursting with suppressed giggles" (230), yet the hymn's apparently absurd connection between food and value in life interlaces the text, variously transformed and permuted, but omnipresent.

Food indeed becomes an underlying metaphysical trope in a variety of characters' lives. The generational drama of *Buddenbrooks* foregrounds the grandchildren of Johann Buddenbrook, a strong patriarchal figure who has founded a very successful business, an apparently happy family, and a prosperous way of life. Thomas, his grandson, who in his own time becomes head of the business, the family patriarch, and, in the political sphere, even a successful senator, is, as we learn late in his life, a tortured figure. Not long before his death, he comments: "I always think . . . of what Grandfather used to say about a dish that had no particular taste or consistency: it tastes as if you were hanging your tongue out of the window. One, two, three, and you've finished with the whole stupid thing" (497). As his philosophical ruminations will reveal, Thomas regards his life in very much the same way.

To remind the reader of the significant symbolic value of food, Thomas Mann shadows the family drama with the poor relation Clothilde, linked by her name to a controlling fate, who desperately tries to enter the warmth of the family and experience the joys of life by eating and eating and eating:

> She had two large helpings both of fish and ham, with piles of vegetables; and she bent short-sightedly over her plate, completely absorbed in the food, which she chewed ruminantly, in large mouthfuls. . . . She ate; whether it tasted good or not, whether they teased her or not, she smiled and kept on, heaping her plate with good things, with the instinctive, insensitive voracity of a poor relation — patient, persevering, hungry, and lean. (22)

But her attempts to take in the life of the family by consuming the food of its table are futile. As Thomas observes later in life, "It was a mystery how much good and nourishing food that poor Clothilde could absorb daily without any result whatever! She grew thinner and thinner. . . . (200).

Yet the overconsumption of food is not confined to poor relations. The whole society overindulges; people ritually stuff themselves at family meals to demonstrate to others, as well as to themselves, their well-being, their contentment. This signification of food apparently continues into contemporary German culture. Bruch notes, "It seems that under the special conditions of German culture, obesity in men has an entirely different sociological significance from that in women; in men it seems to add to their sense of power and prestige."[5] Indeed, as we are first introduced to the Buddenbrooks, they are engaged in a family celebration, a housewarming. Mann lavishes detailed description of the food they eat, communicating their sensual pleasure as they consume hams, turkeys, puddings, cakes:

> The plates were being changed again. An enormous brick-red boiled ham appeared, strewn with crumbs and served with a sour brown onion sauce, and so many vegetables that the company could have satisfied their appetites from that one vegetable dish. . . .
>
> And now came, in two great cut-glass dishes, the "Plettenpudding." It was made of layers of macaroons, raspberries, lady-fingers, and custard. At the same time, at the other end of the table, appeared the blazing plum-pudding which was the children's favorite sweet. (19, 23)

The overflowing family meals are emblematic of their sense of security, well-being, and ease. Yet the meals never quite manage to mask the subterranean family disruptions. After the very meal described, when one family member wants to broach the subject of a rift with another, the narrator observes: "The sour smell of the onion sauce still hung on the air" (33).

Indeed, the societal dietary habits are symptoms diagnosed by the local physician. When a young man ill with indigestion says he will never eat again, the doctor thinks the contrary to himself:

> He would soon eat again, this young man. He would do as the rest of the world did—his father, and all their relatives and friends: he would lead a sedentary life and eat four good rich, satisfying meals a day.... He had held the head of many an honest burgher who had eaten his last joint of smoked meat, his last stuffed turkey, and, whether overtaken unaware in his counting-house or after a brief illness in his solid old four-poster, had commended his soul to God. Then it was called paralysis, a "stroke," a sudden death. (27)

The doctor, in effect, declares that the whole society is eating itself to death. Bruch identifies the crux of the problem of eating disorders victims as not knowing when they are hungry and either consuming food or refusing to do so as a result of other needs or functions.[6] As we follow the course of Mann's narration, we discover that, certainly within the family he chronicles, very few needs are gratified while nutritional requirements are overwhelmed.[7]

Perhaps the preeminent example of this syndrome is Thomas, the third-generation patriarch, whose suitability for material success conjoined with the odd physical trait of defective teeth ("His teeth were not very good, being small and yellowish" [10]) is underscored from his earliest introduction. His guiding moral principles are those of rationality, control, equilibrium, and the consequent suppression of emotion, desire, and introspection. He continually rebukes his younger brother Christian for his emotional self-indulgence, seeing the propensity in himself as a fault overcome. As he discusses Christian's character with his sister Tony, he remarks:

> I have thought a great deal about this curious and useless self-preoccupation, because I had once an inclination to it myself. But I observed that it made me unsteady, hare-brained, and incapable— and control, equilibrium, is, at least for me, the important thing. There will always be men who are justified in this interest in themselves ... poets who can express with clarity and beauty their privileged inner life.... But the likes of us are simple merchants, my child; our self-observations are decidedly inconsiderable.... It would be much better, deuce take it, if we sat down and accomplished something as our fathers did before us. (218–19)

And Thomas does indeed deny his emotion and his pleasure. He loves a girl who works in a flower store, but he ends the relationship because of its unsuitability and demands that his sister do the same in similar circumstances. Regardless of the circumstances, he behaves with the utmost propriety, revealing his reasons in a rare open eruption of fury at his brother. Christian makes a telling accusation against him:

> You have made a position for yourself in life; and there you stand, and push everything away which might possibly disturb your equilibrium for a moment—for your equilibrium is the most precious thing in the world to you. But it isn't the most precious thing in life. Thomas. . . . Yes, you are without pity, without love, without humility. . . . Oh, how sick I am of all this tact and propriety, this poise and refinement —sick to death of it. (468)

And Thomas responds to him with a "ring of feeling, 'I have become what I am because I did not want to become what you are. If I have inwardly shrunk from you, it has been because I needed to guard myself—your being, and your existence, are a danger to me—that is the truth'" (468). Emotion, love, feeling, and introspection are threats to Thomas and the preservation of his way of life, including his overflowing dinner table. And later in his life, poignant indeed are the supper table scenes in which he quizzes his artistically inclined beloved son Hanno, his sole heir, on the workings of granaries and the names of ships, a process that fills the boy with anxiety and nausea. But Thomas continues to officiate at the dinner table as if all were right, as if this exchange were or could be an expression of love.

When his business fails, when his wife turns out to be in love with another, when his son proves a disappointment to him, when much that he values in life turns out to be illusion and disappointment—in short, when he feels "hopeless and thwarted" (499), he by chance picks up a volume of Schopenhauer, and then, for the first time, Thomas is happy, indeed "breathless and enthralled" (525). He experiences novel feelings, "heavy lethargy and intoxication, overpowered by the heady draught he had drunk, incapable of thought" (525). And what does Thomas read in Schopenhauer that causes this revolution in his life? The narration, not very specific here, does give some clues, eavesdropping on Thomas' thoughts:

> Was not every human being a mistake and a blunder? Was not he in painful arrest from the hour of his birth? Prison, prison, bonds and

> limitations everywhere! The human being stares hopelessly through
> the barred window of his personality at the high walls of outward
> circumstance, till Death comes and calls him home to freedom!
> (526)

Apparently Thomas learns from Schopenhauer that this life and the quest
for achievement contained within it is an illusory sham of no consequence.
He finds inspiration in this message because it promises succor from death:
" 'I shall live!' said Thomas Buddenbrook, almost aloud, and felt his breast
shaken with inward sobs. 'This is the revelation: that I shall live!' " Ironically,
however, the message that inspires him with hope also abnegates his life.
The text recognizing this fact, Thomas soon puts Schopenhauer down in
favor of the faith of his fathers:

> He never succeeded in looking again into the precious volume—to
> say nothing of buying its other parts. His days were consumed by
> nervous pedantry: harassed by a thousand details, all of them
> unimportant, he was too weak-willed to arrive at a reasonable and
> fruitful arrangement of his time. Nearly two weeks after that memo-
> rable afternoon he gave it up—and ordered the maidservant to
> fetch the book from the drawer in the garden table and replace it in
> the bookcase.
>   And thus Thomas Buddenbrook, who had held his hands stretched
> imploringly upward toward the high ultimate truth, sank now
> weakly back to the images and conceptions of his childhood. (528)

With this passage, the narrative elevates Schopenhauer's text to metaphysical reality.
    It is worthwhile, then, briefly to explore Schopenhauer's thought. Schopen-
hauer has a dismal view of nature, whose hallmark he sees as contest and
struggle. According to Schopenhauer, nature is governed by the will, that
blind, greedy, immoral force which in human beings blurs pure perception.
For him, the phrase that encapsulates the workings of nature is *Homo,
homini lupus,* Man is the wolf for man.[8] According to Schopenhauer, only
when man ceases to be governed by the will within him—namely, the desire
for self-preservation and gain—only when he frees his perception from a
narrow, individual perspective can he conceive that ideal order of the
universe: "For, at the moment, when torn from the will, we have given
ourselves up to pure, will-less knowing. We have stepped into another

world, so to speak, where everything that moves our will, and thus violently agitates us, no longer exists."[9]

Although at points in his life Thomas apparently enjoys success, by the end of the narration we realize his complete unsuitability for life. He cannot function on the level of nature as Schopenhauer characterizes it. If we picture Schopenhauer's watchword, "Homo, homini lupus," we see creatures tearing each other limb from limb with their sharp fangs. Thomas, as his defective teeth signal, is incapable of that type of aggression. In fact, on the only occasion he attempts an unsavory business deal, it ends disastrously. As revealed in his disputes with Christian, he has a sensitivity, a consciousness, that prevents him from unselfconsciously participating in life—but these aspects of his personality he believes he must "choke down." The narrator says of Tony, clearly differentiating her from Thomas: "This child of fortune so long as she walked upon this earth, had never once needed to suppress an emotion, to choke down or swallow anything she felt" (537). In contrast, Thomas chokes down and swallows all his emotions as he does his food. And he denies himself everything—his humanity and his spirituality. In the end, Thomas dies ignominiously of a toothache, lying in the gutter, spattered by mud. It is fateful that Thomas' vulnerability expresses itself in dental deficiency, for with teeth we grasp food, and hence within the symbolic structure of the narrative, life. Thomas' defective teeth express his incompatibility with life, and the flawed link between him and experience is the source of his demise. The doctor has said that the burghers of the society eat themselves to death. This is true of Thomas, for he swallows his feelings, as smiling and facile, he presides over his overflowing dinner table as if nothing were wrong.

Christian is the nemesis of Thomas. Whereas Thomas embraces his position in the family, suppressing all the feelings that might undermine it, Christian exercises all his power in negation, rejecting the values of his family and the culture in which it is ensconced. He signals his resolve to deviate from the familial and cultural path by resisting the household ritual of gorging at the dinner table.[10] It is he who, at the housewarming initially presented in the narrative, calls out in despair, "I don't want to eat anything, ever any more. I'm ill, I tell you, damned ill!" (26). And it is Christian who equates food with death:

> The family are at table eating dessert and conversing pleasantly the while. Suddenly Christian turns pale and puts back on his plate the peach into which he has just bitten. . . .

"I will never eat another peach," he says.

"Why not, Christian? What nonsense! What's the matter?"

"Suppose I accidentally—suppose I swallowed the stone, and it stuck in my throat, so I couldn't breathe, and I jumped up, strangling horribly—and all of you jump up— Ugh . . . !" and he suddenly gives "a short groan, full of horror and affright, starts up in his chair, and acts as if he were trying to escape. . . . "Heavens, Christian! —you haven't swallowed it, have you?" For his whole appearance suggests that he has.

"No," says Christian slowly. "No"—he is gradually quieting down—"I only mean, suppose I actually *had* swallowed it?"

The Consul has been pale with fright, but he recovers and begins to scold. . . . But Christian, for a long, long time, eats no more peaches. (55)

Remarkably, in this passage, Christian imagines his own death—a death that is in fact very similar to the account of his mother's long, anguishing gasps for breath. However, narrative accounts of death, like Christian's sudden nightmarish fantasy, are unanticipated intrusions, for the characters suppress a knowledge of death, and each time death narratively appears it is at once portrayed as a surprise and the only reality of life worth recording. But Christian disrupts this repression by graphically and realistically imagining his own death. As he does so, he battles death by refusing to eat, for to eat is to participate in life, thereby rendering death inevitable. As Mervyn Nicholson expresses it, "if you don't need food, you are not quite human as others are: you are superhuman, not dependent on the world of eater-eaten. You cease to be a contingent being."[11] But in the incident of the peach, Christian, by anticipating his death, must come to terms with the finitude of life and correlatively the need to seek what he considers significant.

It is no surprise, then, that Christian does not participate in the false structure of suppressed feelings of which family meals are emblematic. And indeed Christian concertedly does not uphold the family order. As a youth of fourteen, he becomes infatuated with an actress and presents her with flowers, much to the horrified embarrassment of his family. He is a miserable failure at every business venture he undertakes. When he briefly joins the family firm, his association proves a disaster when, at the club, he intimates that all business people are cheats and rascals. His intermittent bouts of anorexia and other neurasthenic complaints plague both him and the family. In middle age he explains to his family:

Strange—sometimes I can't swallow. . . . It enters my head that perhaps I can't swallow, and then all of a sudden I can't. The food is already swallowed, but the muscles—right here—they simply refuse. It isn't a question of will-power. Or rather, the thing is, I don't dare really will it. (217)

His whole being, apparently, concentrates on refusal. Later in his life, his complaints are summarized this way: "He often suffered from that long-standing dread of paralysis of the tongue, throat, and oesophagus, even of the extremities and of the brain—of which there were no actual symptoms but the fear in itself was almost worse" (531). Indeed, paralysis and nega-tion characterize Christian. He succeeds at nothing. At the end of his life he marries a prostitute, and she has him committed to a mental institution.

Yet Christian, from the first, is identified as talented. The town poet says of him as a boy: "Christian is a devil of a fellow—a young *incroyable*, hey? I will not conceal my *engouement*. He must study, I think—he is witty and brilliant" (9). He has gifts for mimicry, drama, and poetry, but apparently no qualities that will bring him satisfaction in life. His talent, sensitivity, engagement with emotion, and sincerity have no better consequences than Thomas' prudence, practicality, and repression.

It is important to note that Thomas and Christian are always seen in tandem. Just prior to the poet's comment about Christian's brilliance quoted above, he comments that "Tom is a very solid chap. He'll have to go into business no doubt about that" (9). In an early chapter, they are character-ized as schoolboys thus:

Thomas had been marked from the cradle as a merchant and future member of the firm . . . an able, quick witted, intelligent lad, always ready to laugh when his brother Christian mimicked the masters, which he did with uncanny facility. Christian . . . was not less gifted than Tom, but he was less serious. His special and particular joy in life was the imitation in speech and manner of a certain worthy Marcellus Stengel who taught drawing, singing and some other of the lighter branches. (53)

The chapter that describes Thomas' entry into the firm is followed by a chapter that describes Christian's misadventures with an actress. The brothers' characters, it seems, form in reaction to each other. Each, as explicitly stated in arguments and encounters, constitutes a threat for the other. Nevertheless, in spite of their apparent antipodal differences (Thomas exerts great power to repress all feelings that might undermine his bourgeois success or disgrace his family, and Christian exerts great power to resist succumbing to the presiding repressive values of his family and culture), each lives a terrible life. Thus, in its portrayal, the text undermines the oppositional binary system represented by Thomas and Christian, stuffing oneself or refraining from eating, tenaciously affirming the values of the bourgeois society, or uncompromisingly negating them. Each term of the opposition, the text seems to claim, yields devastation. Life, at least on the terms in which it is presented to Thomas and Christian, is incongruous with human beings. Bourgeois society presents no liberating alternatives. Hence, there is a problem with food.

The sister, Tony, because she is female, must construct her life on terms different from those of her brothers, Thomas and Christian. Her choice is not whether she will enter the family business and by her behavior uphold its values and traditions or choose another path in life. Her value to her family and to the culture is constituted by her choice of marriage partners. In the crudest of terms, she is part of her family's and family firm's capital to be advantageously converted. Her worth lies not in her deeds, talents, or character, but in her femininity, her body, her sexuality, for these will determine her exchange rate. As a young girl she understands this, at least in abstract terms, as she confidently asserts: "Of course . . . I shall marry a business man. He must have a lot of money, so we can furnish elegantly. I owe that to my family and the firm . . . you'll see, that's what I shall do" (72). However, there is a gap between her theoretical understanding of the situation and her actual encounters with it. When she meets the actual males who want her in exchange, she is disgusted.

Tony, throughout the text, is associated with sweet food. A narrative detail such as "she dipped her fourth piece of currant bread into her coffee" (99) is common in conjunction with her description. As a child, she is attracted to a brother of a classmate "because of the luncheon he took to school: not bread but a soft sort of lemon bun with currants in it, and sausage or smoked goose between. It seemed to be his favorite luncheon. Tony had never seen anything like it before. Lemon bun, with smoked goose—it must be wonderful!" (50). When she requests some, Hermann, her schoolmate's brother, offers to bring it if she'll give him something in return. Much to her shocked chagrin, what he demands in return is a kiss. Thus she learns that what she has to offer in payment are her sexual favors, her body. The sweetness of the lemon bun with currants is meant to be bartered for a sexual demand, and the surprising lesson of the lemon tart resounds for Tony throughout the text, for when over and over she recounts her sadnesses and disappointments she always begins with the lemon tart. Her desire for sweetness, for indulgence, for sensuality perhaps, is met with the demand that she herself be a commodity, that she be consumed.

When she first encounters Bendix Grünlich—her family's choice as both a suitable, financially well-endowed husband and the means of a promising economic merger for their firm—he is described in terms of his consumption:

> He ate a ragout of shell-fish, julienne soup, fried soles, roast veal with creamed potatoes and cauliflower, maraschino pudding, and pumpernickel with roquefort; and he found a fresh and delicate compliment for each fresh course. Over the sweet he lifted his dessert-spoon ... and spoke aloud to himself, thus: "God forgive me, I have eaten far too well already. But this pudding—! It is *too* wonderful! I must beg my good hostess for another slice." (83)

Thus, Bendix, from the very beginning, is portrayed as a consumer, an indiscriminate gorger of food. He readily identifies with the family's values by participating in their overflowing table.

And Tony identifies Bendix himself as a distasteful item of food. As she begins her seaside vacation, she comments to Tom: "I wish I could leave a certain pair of yellow mutton-chops even further behind!" (95). The reference to Bendix's facial hair, and by extension Bendix himself, as mutton-chops (*Koteletten* in the original German) renders him repugnant. Tony also characterizes Bendix this way: "All I know is, he has a yellow beard, like a goat's and a flourishing business—" (85). The reference to the goat's beard further underscores Bendix's identity as an indiscriminate consumer of food. These descriptions contrast with the appealing references to honey associated with her seaside stay in Travemünde and her relationship to the young and idealistic but impecunious Morten there.

Indeed, honey becomes associated with Tony's happiness, her sensual and unadulterated desires. When her parents inform her of Bendix's proposal, she chokes down her eggs, bread, and cheese, but says "thank you" for her honey (85). In response to news of Bendix's proposal, she berates and insults him, concluding, "I can't understand how he can possibly endure me. The man must have some sort of pride in his bones!" And the narrator adds, "She began to drip honey on her bread" (87).

On her vacation she falls in love with Morten, an outspoken young man who is passionate about politics and his chosen profession, medicine. Morten, in contrast to her brother Thomas, "display[s] unusually regular teeth, glistening in close ranks of polished ivory" (99). Her time in Travemünde is characterized by health and honey, and it becomes the touchstone for her of happiness, a time she will later sensually recall by eating honey. Her family naturally forbids a match with Morten and insists on her marriage to Bendix.

And it would seem that as a result Tony develops indigestion. She cannot eat the food she desires. In remembrance of her sorrow, she will frequently remark, "Honey is a natural product—one always knows what one is getting." Even as a business deal, the transaction that her family makes—exchanging her for Bendix's capital—proves to be a bad one. Bendix turns out to be dishonest, misrepresenting the state of his business and his finances. Later, Tony tries to reconstitute her value to her family the only way she can. She marries again, her new husband Herr Permaneder, but she is unhappy in that marriage chiefly because she must reside in southern Germany, far from her family and in an unfamiliar environment where a different dialect is spoken. She expresses her alienation in recounting a conversation with her maid about food:

> And when I say "croquettes," she doesn't understand me, because here they are called "meaties"; and when she says "broccoli," how could any Christian know she means cauliflower? When I say "baked potatoes," she screams "How?" at me, until I remember to say "roast potatoes," which is what they call them here. (299)

It seems that if one cannot communicate about food, one cannot communicate about anything. And Tony expresses her alienation from her husband also in terms of food: "Yesterday, we had sorrel and currants, but I wish I hadn't, for Permaneder objected so much to the sorrel—he picked the currants out with a fork—that he would not speak to me the whole afternoon, but just growled; and I can tell you, Mother, that life is not so easy" (299).

Tony's marriage to Herr Permaneder ends when, in the course of an argument resulting from her discovery of her husband's flirtation with the maid, Permaneder insults Tony. For Tony the insult decisively ends the relationship. Even though her family urges her again and again to return to her husband, saying that the affair with the maid is inconsequential, she replies she cannot because of the terrible insult. However, she refuses to repeat the insult because it is so unspeakably terrible, and so the insult gains narrative power by being anticipated and imagined but withheld. But finally it is revealed. Herr Permaneder says, speaking in the characteristic dialect of southern Germany, that she is a "Saulud'r dreckats," a shit-eating sow. The remark insults and shocks Tony to the degree that it does apparently because, like all insults that are very hurtful, it contains a measure of truth. Instead of the honey Tony craves, she is forced not only by her family but also by the values that she herself affirms to partake of what is least desirable to her. Indeed, she eats shit in her two marriages because she participates in a vulgar transaction with men who are repellent to her. The text marks her tragedy, named by Permaneder's telling metaphorical insult, by giving her the characteristic attribute of indigestion. Narratively, she is contrasted to Thomas, for she always speaks about all the bad things that have happened to her; she has never been asked to "choke down or swallow anything she had felt" (537), but in the same passage in which this attribute is noted, she bears the marks of her trouble, for the narrator comments: "Her digestion was not perfect" (537). Mann gives Tony the typical features of the portrayed nineteenth-century female. She bears nothing stoically; she "chokes down" nothing. However, she takes in life secondarily, through her romantic relationships. She desires honey, "a natural product," but instead she ends the way Permaneder characterizes her, and so throughout her life she suffers from indigestion.

The last hope for the family is Hanno, Thomas' son. Hanno differs from his father, for he is gifted and artistic. And yet he differs from his Uncle Christian as well, for he has some outlet for his gift in music, the piano. It does seem his only outlet. Like the other members of his family, he can be characterized by mouth and teeth. His music teacher, Herr Pfühl, explains why he is using the theoretical method in his teaching: " 'He has enough gift,' Herr Pfühl said, and nodded. 'Sometimes I look into his eyes, and see so much lying there — but he holds his mouth tight shut. In later life, when his mouth will probably be shut even tighter, he must have some kind of outlet — a way of speaking —' " (410). Yet Hanno is linked to his father by his deficient teeth:

> His teeth had been particularly bad, and had been the cause of many painful illnesses and difficulties. It had nearly cost him his life to cut his first set; the gums showed a constant tendency to inflammation, and there were abscesses, which Mamsell Jungmann used to open with a needle at the proper time. Now his second teeth were beginning to come in, and the suffering was even greater.

He had almost more pain than he could bear, and he spent many
sleepless, feverish nights. (417)

Hanno's life is marred by his bad teeth, his ill health, and the cod liver oil
and other foul-tasting remedies poured down his throat in an effort to
strengthen him. Like Thomas, Christian, and Tony, Hanno has a problem
with what he eats. He tries to consume happiness at Christmas time by
eating all the sweets he can at one time, but this of course makes him sick.
Shortly after explaining to his friend Kai why he is unsuited for life, that his
music comes to nothing, that he can never earn his bread with it, he dies.
Hanno, marked from the first by his diseased teeth, struggles with life, finds
a moment of transcendence in his music, but succumbs to death in the form
of a gastrointestinal infection because he does not have the apparatus to
grasp life. With Hanno's death the saga of the Buddenbrook family ends.

Almost in the center of this grim novel there is an anecdote that is
grotesque but ostensibly peripheral to Thomas Mann's account of the inner
decay and destruction of not only a family but also the bourgeois way of life
and its culture:

> James Möllendorpf, the oldest of the merchant senators, died in a
> grotesque and horrible way. The instinct of self-preservation became
> very weak in this diabetic old man; and in the last years of his life
> he fell a victim to a passion for cakes and pastries. . . . They found
> his lifeless body, the mouth still full of half-masticated cake, the
> crumbs upon his coat and upon the wretched table. (334)

What is the significance of this anecdote? In it, we are confronted with the
graphic and grotesque picture of a man, shockingly and literally eating
himself to death. He perhaps mistakes his short-run pleasure for his long-
term good. He eats the food he desires, but it kills him. The senator in this
short, macabre anecdote is in fact emblematic of all the characters—their
eating habits kill them because, in the culture Thomas Mann has portrayed,
life is impossible.

Thomas Mann, both in the text of *Buddenbrooks* and in the text of the
display and consumption of food within that text, renders a cultural critique
portraying the destructive force of the regnant values. Many authors, including Bruch and Bromberg, identify bourgeois society as the milieu in which
eating disorders as we know them originated, and it is within this cultural
environment that the symbolic language of food succeeds in portraying that

persons are themselves consumed when desire is conflated with material success.

Notes

1. Franz Kafka, "A Hunger Artist," trans. Willa and Edwin Muir in *Franz Kafka: The Complete Stories*, ed. Nahum N. Glatzer (New York: Schocken Books, 1946), 268–77.

2. Hilde Bruch, *Eating Disorders: Obesity, Anorexia Nervosa, and the Person Within* (New York: Basic Books, 1973), 3.

3. Numerous authors have described the signifying aspects of food. See, e.g., Joan Jacobs Brumberg, *Fasting Girls: The Emergence of Anorexia Nervosa as a Modern Disease* (Cambridge, Mass.: Harvard University Press, 1988), 4, who remarks: "Food functions as a system of signs and symbols with multiple meanings." Other notable examples of the analysis of the language of food in particular contexts are Mary Douglas, "Deciphering a Meal," *Daedalus* 101 (1972): 61-68, and Roland Barthes, "Toward a Psychosociology of Contemporary Food Consumption," in *European Diet from Pre-industrial to Modern Times*, ed. Elborg and Robert Forster (New York: Harper & Row, 1975), 47–49.

4. Thomas Mann, *Buddenbrooks* (1901), trans. H. T. Lowe-Porter (New York: Alfred A. Knopf, 1946), 230. All subsequent references will be to this edition and cited with page numbers in the text.

5. Bruch, *Eating Disorders*, 20.

6. Ibid., 45.

7. Bruch speaks in terms of the mother when tracing the origins of eating disorders, but the point can be made in terms of general family structures as well: "The important aspect is whether the response to the child's needs was appropriate, or was superimposed according to what the mother felt he needed, often mistakenly" (51).

8. Arthur Schopenhauer, *The World as Will and Representation*, trans. E.F.J. Payne (1958; reprint, New York: Dover, 1969), 1:147.

9. Ibid., 197.

10. For a discussion of refusal of food interpreted in this light, see Brumberg, "Love and Food in the Bourgeois Family," in *Fasting Girls*, 126–40.

11. Mervyn Nicholson, "Food and Power: Homer, Carrol, Atwood, and Others," *Mosaic* 20 (Summer 1987): 47.

DÜRRENMATT'S GASTRONOMIC GROTESQUERIES:
Eating in a Dis-ordered World

Barbara Lide

In his comedy *Der Meteor* (The Meteor, 1966), the Swiss writer Friedrich Dürrenmatt (1921-90) presents as his protagonist a Nobel Prize–winning author, Wolfgang Schwitter, who at one point recalls an extramarital affair of one of his former wives: "At the time, she was cheating on me with a butcher—and I was consuming the best filets mignons of my life."[1] Schwitter's recollection, with its accompanying stage direction, "laughs," shows that he has achieved not only temporal but also comic distance from his wife's betrayal. The second half of the speech, about the filets mignons, serves as a punch line, giving a comic twist to a situation that, except in a bedroom farce, usually is not comic. Even more noteworthy is that Dürrenmatt's punch line accentuates the pleasant compensatory experience of eating and subordinates the painful experience of being betrayed. A marriage can fall into disarray, but food remains a comforting constant.

The bond between food and comfort, perhaps the first bond that human beings establish, is especially strong and ingrained, developing immediately after birth, when infants are cradled and suckled by their mothers; the

German word for nursing a baby, *stillen* (to quiet, appease, calm, soothe, pacify), is strikingly appropriate. Many people continue throughout their lives to turn to food in their search for comfort, for satisfaction of nonphysical hunger, for a means of coping with difficult situations.[2] Frequently, especially in cases of obese people, the fat resulting from such eating serves both symbolically and concretely as a protective layer between the self and the world.[3]

The protagonist of Dürrenmatt's short prose fantasy "Der Tunnel" (The Tunnel, 1952) is representative of those corpulent people who both literally and figuratively bolster themselves with fat in order to ward off their real and imagined fears of the world's horrors. According to Dürrenmatt's biographer Elisabeth Brock-Sulzer, this character also represents the writer himself, in "a kind of grotesque self-portrait," a "caricature" that "might have been written by an amused enemy."[4] Dürrenmatt describes his fictional doppelgänger as "a twenty-four-year-old, fat, so that the horrible things lurking behind the wings, which he saw (that was his ability, perhaps his only one), could not get too close to him, who loved stuffing the orifices of his flesh, since it was through these that the monstrous things could come streaming in."[5] In "The Tunnel," as often in life itself, the protective layer of fat turns out to be inadequate (167).

In drama, the genre with which Dürrenmatt is most closely associated, food traditionally belongs in the realm of comedy. Traditional comic plays culminate in wedding feasts or festivals, usually symbolizing not just a celebration but a reconciliation, in which either a new social order is established or the old social order is reconfirmed. Similarly, the act of eating, of putting food into one's mouth and enjoying it heartily, is the act of a comic character—of a Falstaff, for example, not of a Hamlet. As food is necessary for self-preservation, so comedy is related to the impulse to preserve life. As Susanne Langer notes, "Comedy is an art form that arises naturally wherever people are gathered to celebrate life, in spring festivals, triumphs, birthdays, weddings, or initiations. . . . It is an image of human vitality holding its own in the world amid the surprises of unplanned coincidence."[6] Langer also reminds us that the Comus, from which the term "comedy" derives, was indeed "a fertility rite, and the god it celebrated a fertility god, a symbol of perpetual rebirth, eternal life" (331).

Eating, however, can get out of hand, causing grotesque obesity and such psychophysiologic disorders as bulimia (literally, "ox hunger");[7] comedy, too, can slip over the bounds of the comic into the grotesque and the tragicomic, especially in our contemporary world.[8] Such developments abound in Dürrenmatt's works, arising and intertwining to depict—and create—a grotesque, disjointed world. One can trace these developments from his earliest drama, *Es steht geschrieben* (It Is Written, 1947), with the Anabaptist Johann Bockelson engaging in a culinary orgy, to his last work, the novel *Durcheinandertal* (Valley of Confusion, 1989), in which one of the main characters, Moses Melker, kills his wife Cäcilie, "a Himalaya of fat," by stuffing her with chocolate truffles, which she greedily devours until she dies.[9] My purpose here is first to discuss the relationship between Dürrenmatt's gastronomic grotesqueries and his theory and practice of contemporary drama and then to examine, on the basis of selected Dürrenmatt texts, the role that food and eating, especially bulimic eating, play in depicting and creating Dürrenmatt's dis-ordered world.

Both Karl Guthke, in his study of modern tragicomedy, and Kenneth Whitton, in *The Theatre of Friedrich Dürrenmatt*, quote Novalis's statement "After an unsuccessful war, comedies must be written."[10] Dürrenmatt reflects a similar thought in *Romulus der Grosse* (Romulus the Great, 1949), a historical tragicomedy he wrote not long "after an unsuccessful war." Early in the first act, the Roman emperor Romulus learns that his daughter, in preparation for her acting class, is studying the lament of Antigone before she goes to her death. Romulus advises her, "Don't study this old sad text; practice comedy, it's much more suitable for us. . . . Whoever is at the end of his rope, as we all are, can understand only comedies."[11]

Dürrenmatt elaborates considerably on this idea in his frequently quoted essay "Theaterprobleme" (Problems of the Theatre, 1954, 1955), in which he discusses tragedy, comedy, and the task of art in a post–World War II age. As George Steiner was to declare several years later, Dürrenmatt expresses in "Theaterprobleme" his conviction that tragic drama had died.[12] While Steiner and Dürrenmatt view the demise of tragedy from different perspectives, they see the same fundamental underlying cause: the atrocities visited by human beings on one another during World War II and its aftermath and, especially for Steiner, the apparent withdrawal of a god or gods from the world of mortals.[13] Later, in *Durcheinandertal*, Dürrenmatt came to illustrate the idea of a world from which God has withdrawn by replacing the "God with the beard" from the Old Testament with a worldly and even more powerful "God without a beard."[14] For Dürrenmatt, not only are there no more noble tragic heroes, but the divine element, or the element of fate, that steered the lives of the protagonists in tragic drama and imposed a certain order and justice on their existence is no longer present in our world. Tragedy, according to Dürrenmatt, presupposes a world already formed,

one possessing an established order. For him, therefore, our present world
could not be reflected in the kind of historical dramas that Schiller wrote,
not only because the necessary order is lacking but also because tragic
figures such as those depicted by Schiller do not exist. We no longer have
tragic heroes, but "only tragedies . . . carried out by world butchers and
meat-grinding machines."[15] Comedy, on the other hand—as long as it is not
satirizing an established society, as in the plays of Molière—presupposes an
unformed world, one involved simultaneously in the processes of developing
and of going to ruin, a world that is packing it in, as our own world is doing
(120–21).

Comedy, then, is the mode most in tune with our times, primarily
because, unlike tragedy, which conquers distance and creates empathy, it
establishes the necessary distance and objectivity that enable us to cope
with our present reality (121). Dürrenmatt does not, however, have in mind
using comedy as a coping device in the sense that one uses comic relief, as a
temporary escape from the tragic. On the contrary, his intention is neither to
escape the tragic nor to avoid what he earnestly considers his obligation as a
playwright. For him, the use of the comic mode is a means of fulfilling the
task of drama, which is to give shape to our shapeless world and to create
form out of our chaos (121). Further, Dürrenmatt believes that, although
pure tragic drama is no longer possible, we can achieve the tragic through
the comic (122). To be sure, the very restrictions of the theater necessitate
shaping chaotic subject matter into some kind of form presentable on the
stage. Whether audiences are convinced that Dürrenmatt has given form to
their own chaotic reality is not certain. It is indisputable, however, that he
successfully depicts a chaotic, disordered world, a world he sees as a
labyrinth,[16] well represented by the asylum of *Die Physiker* (The Physicists,
1962) and the madhouse of *Achterloo* (1983). As the German writer
Erich Kästner points out, with reference to Dürrenmatt's comedy *Die
Ehe des Herrn Mississippi* (The Marriage of Mr. Mississippi, 1952),
Dürrenmatt reminds us "that the world is coming apart, despite all the
glue."[17] Indeed, "a universe that is coming apart" apparently has become
the standard expression applied to Dürrenmatt's world.[18] Still, in the midst
of his chaotic and comic world, and by means of his comedic vision and
comic technique, Dürrenmatt does indeed prove he can achieve the tragic,
even occasionally—as in *Romulus der Grosse*—attaining a degree of tragic
nobility. His primary method in achieving tragedy is comic exaggeration,
carrying the comic to the point of absurdity and grotesquerie and, primarily
by contrast, highlighting the tragic elements he wants to accentuate. As

Dürrenmatt himself once explained, "[my method] is dialectical. I show the other side."[19]

What is the role that food plays in all this? We have already seen, in the self-portrait that he presents in "The Tunnel," that Dürrenmatt himself was a fat man who relied on his fat to cushion himself as he made his way through a labyrinthine world. In the same vein, it is noteworthy that in *Weihnacht* (Christmas), a one-page story Dürrenmatt wrote at Christmas time in 1942 and the piece that made him decide to become a writer,[20] the narrator, who finds the body of the Christ child in the snow, eats its halo, which tastes like "old bread," and then grotesquely bites off and eats its head, which tastes like "old marzipan."[21] The theme of eating permeates both Dürrenmatt's life and his literary works, and also the very language he uses to express himself on a variety of topics, language evincing a close and compelling inner relationship between Dürrenmatt and the world of food, with both its pleasant and unpleasant aspects. In declaring that tragic drama is dead, for example, he states that tragic heroes have been replaced by tragedies perpetrated by "world butchers" and "meat grinders," employing the language of animal slaughter and the preparation of meat for human consumption. Even in suggesting a tragicomic scenario about the death of antarctic explorer Robert Falcon Scott, he has Scott freezing to death, not in the snow and ice of Antarctica but trapped by some quirky accident in a meat locker in the middle of a city, where he has gone to buy food for his antarctic exploration.[22] Consider also the language Dürrenmatt uses to explain why he believes Kafka's works are unsuitable for the stage: "The bread he presents to us offers no nourishment; it remains, lying undigested, in the indestructible stomachs of the theatregoers and season ticket holders."[23] In describing the metaphorical bread served up by Kafka, Dürrenmatt consistently turns to food, to the vocabulary of cuisine, in his search for expression. In much the same way, a number of his characters turn to food, not to fulfill a physical hunger but in their search for psychological nourishment in moments of despair.

In *Romulus der Grosse*, Romulus, the historical last emperor of Rome, who becomes ahistorical in Dürrenmatt's interpretation, is one such character. With his empire collapsing around him and the Germanic tribes advancing toward Rome, Romulus retreats to the country to raise chickens, including a hen, the most productive laying hen in his collection, named after the Germanic leader Odoaker. As he explains, he does not want to disturb the course of world history (31).

Romulus appears to be more concerned with eating than with the collapse of his empire. At one point, for example, he reflects on his diminishing power, symbolized by his golden laurel wreath. In order to pay the debts of the empire, he has been forced to pluck out a number of gold leaves, which at the beginning of his reign totaled thirty-six; now, after Romulus breaks off a few more leaves to pay his cook, whom he regards as "the most important man" in his empire (13), a mere five leaves remain. After musing on this for a moment, Romulus puts the wreath back on his head and orders his breakfast of "ham, bread, asparagus wine, a bowl of milk, an egg in an egg cup" (14).

For Romulus, the act of eating is not the communal activity characteristic of comedy, but a solitary act, despite his inviting both his wife and his daughter to join him, ordering breakfast for them, and offering them—in addition to the array of food he eats—cold roast beef and fish. Attempting to entice his daughter Rea to join him, he even uses diminutives, as one does with a child, offering her a *Fischchen* ("fishie") (18). The women decline his invitation, however, and he must eat alone, a solitary, clownlike figure, with others reprimanding him for eating instead of doing his duty as emperor to defend his empire. His wife nags him, shouting, "Romulus, the Germanic soldiers are marching against Rome and you are still eating breakfast!" (25). His daughter's fiancé, Ämilian, addresses him contemptuously as "Imperator of good eating . . . Caesar of chickens and strategist of egg laying . . . whom the soldiers call Romulus the Small" (44), and he tries to shame Romulus into defending his empire by telling him, "You are aware of the suffering of your people and you are eating your meal!" (45).

Romulus has no intention of hindering the progress of the Germanic tribes as they advance toward Rome. On the contrary, he looks forward to the defeat of the Roman Empire, which he describes as "a world empire . . . and at the same time an institution that publicly practiced murder, plunder, oppression, and exacted war contributions at the cost of other peoples, until I came along" (51). The determination of Romulus to avoid any more oppression and bloodshed on the part of his people, even if it means sacrificing his own life, may have been an influencing factor in Dürrenmatt's calling him, not ironically, "Romulus the Great."

Finally, ordering what he believes to be his *Henkersmahlzeit,* or "executioner's meal," Romulus explains: "And I must die. The Germanic soldiers will kill me. Before the day is over" (65). True to historical fact, however, Odoaker does not have Romulus killed. Dürrenmatt, taking the noble gesture of the historic Odoaker a step further, has his Germanic leader not only sparing the life of the Roman emperor but also wanting to subjugate himself and his people to such a wise and just leader (70). Odoaker's kneeling before Romulus, however, does not give rise to the kind of comic irony that could lead to a happy resolution. Dürrenmatt sees here a tragic irony, arising in part from the thwarting of Romulus's plan. All along, there has been method in Romulus's madness; now his wish to sacrifice all he has—his people, his family, even his own life—for the betterment of the world does not come true. His surrender, first to the eggs of his hen Odoaker, then to the Germanic leader himself, leads not to the death of a comic figure who breakfasts contentedly while his empire is conquered, but to the isolation of a noble and tragic figure. As Dürrenmatt explains, "that is the horror of this imperial chicken breeder, this world judge disguised as a fool, whose tragedy lies precisely in the comedy of his end, in his being pensioned, who, however—and only this makes him great—has the insight and the wisdom to accept it" (79).

In *Romulus der Grosse,* Dürrenmatt presents three motifs that recur in his works and are related to eating as a means of coping with a dis-ordered world. The first motif is that of turning to food as an avoidance mechanism (Romulus avoiding the reproaches of his family and his subjects). The second is that of turning to food as a way of gaining strength in order to confront an overwhelming situation (in the case of Romulus, the situation— the advance of the Germanic troops that will lead to the defeat of his empire—is brought on by himself). The third motif is that of the *Henkers-mahlzeit,* or executioner's meal.

The first two motifs, which illustrate typical responses to stress, especially on the part of overweight people,[24] appear to have their counterparts in Dürrenmatt's own life. As mentioned above, Dürrenmatt described himself in "The Tunnel" as a fat man who stuffed food into his body in order to shut out the horrors of the world. There also were occasions on which he apparently ate considerable quantities of food in order to fortify himself in the face of a difficult task. Ernst Schröder, the actor who played Bockelson in the premiere production of *Die Wiedertäufer* (The Anabaptists, 1967)—the comic revision of *Es steht geschrieben*—describes a dinner meeting with Dürrenmatt, who was at the time engaged in revising a scene from the play:

> Today he ordered his food without interest. Meat salad, tossed salad, bouillon, boiled meat—indiscriminately, in no particular order. Before he was finished with one course, he was already writing . . . I am amazed. He lights up his Havana, writes, ladles out soup, writes. Eats boiled meat, writes. Without being aware of it, he

reaches for the bread, tears it apart violently, and sins—forgetting his diabetes. Not one single time this month have I seen him eating bread. I am sure that he doesn't even notice it. Consumption and production are one and the same for him, just as the world and the stage for him are one and the same. With glowing spirits he orders new wine.[25]

It is as if Dürrenmatt needed to consume food in order to produce words, as if the consumption of food provided the strength necessary to write.

Dürrenmatt often transfers this kind of behavior to the characters he creates, exaggerating and enlarging on the eating process to achieve comic and grotesque effects. His last and perhaps most exaggerated character to use food as an avoidance mechanism is the policeman Lustenwyler in *Durcheinandertal,* a man whose very name suggests one who burrows or wallows in the pleasures of the flesh—in his case, eating.[26] Lustenwyler becomes a village policeman simply because he "had not done anything all his life but eat, and . . . had expressed the wish of becoming a policeman or a railroad signal man in order that he might continue to have to do nothing but eat, but since the railroad flatly rejected him, there remained only the police" (69). In his twenty years as village policeman, Lustenwyler manages to convert the police station into a kitchen, its walls hung thick with sausages and hams, in which something is always frying, cooking, grilling, steaming, or marinating, and in which chopped meat, onions, garlic, vegetables, and open tuna, sardine, and anchovy tins are scattered among police reports, photographs of criminals, handcuffs, and a revolver (72). Not once does Lustenwyler appear to concentrate fully on police matters; in one instance he even consumes three bowls of soup while typing a report, after which he slices himself a piece of bacon to chew on while he listens to a complaint. He then turns his attention to making a bacon sandwich, which he eats while he questions the complainant. Finally, in the same breath in which he states that he must report the case, he says, looking around, "I'm sure that I still have a can of beans here somewhere" (75). Lustenwyler, who well serves Dürrenmatt's satirical purpose of showing that a Swiss village policeman has very little to do, exemplifies two types of eaters who are prompted by a hunger other than physical: those who turn to food to avoid action, and those who turn to food so that they might gain the strength they need in order to take any action. On the one hand, Lustenwyler cushions himself from the topsy-turvy world of *Durcheinandertal* in his culinary police station, where little other than gastronomic action takes place; on the other hand, in order even to write up a police report or to listen to a citizen's complaint he must fortify himself by consuming at least three bowls of soup and a bacon sandwich.

A more striking and frequently cited example of a character who turns to food in order to gain strength to deal with a difficult situation is police commissioner Bärlach in the detective fiction *Der Richter und sein Henker* (The Judge and His Hangman, 1950). Bärlach, a man suffering from stomach cancer, and whose doctor predicts that he has but a year to live, begins a veritable binge, as he helps himself to hors d'oeuvres consisting of sardines and crayfish; salads with cucumbers, tomatoes, and peas, covered with a mountain of mayonnaise and eggs; and cold meats, including cold cuts, chicken, and salmon. He manages to consume all this, with bread, washing it down with two glasses of wine and asking that his glass be filled for the third time, while Tschanz, his dinner guest, is still eating the single portion of potato salad he has chosen for his first course. Bärlach then turns his attention to three pastry shells filled with goose liver, pork, and truffles, accompanied by two glasses of red wine, before tackling the main course of veal cutlet, rice, French-fried potatoes, and a green salad, accompanied by champagne. After second helpings of everything except the potatoes, he finally is ready for the cheese course, which includes radishes, pickles, and pearl onions.[27]

What Bärlach engages in here is not only binge eating; he is participating in a culinary duel[28] with his adversary Tschanz, a murderer he has caught in a trap. As he eats, Bärlach, a sick, shrunken old man, acquires a superhuman, demonic strength that enables him to overpower his adversary. He is described as "eating without pause, greedily slinging into himself the foods of this world, crushing them between his jaws, a demon, who was stilling an unending hunger. On the wall, his form cast itself in wild shadows, twice enlarged, the powerful movements of his arms, the sinking of his head, like the dance of a triumphant negro tribal chieftain" (111). Bärlach not only is turning to food to gather strength to cope with the difficult situation of informing Tschanz that he knows Tschanz is the murderer he has trapped; he also is partaking of a *Henkersmahlzeit,* the meal served to those condemned to death for the purpose of providing them with one last pleasure in life before they are executed, for both he and Tschanz are about to die.

The *Henkersmahlzeit* runs like a leitmotif throughout Dürrenmatt's works, from *Es steht geschrieben,* in which Bockelson's description of the meal he has eaten is what Dürrenmatt himself called a "Fressarie" (an aria to gluttony),[29] to *Durcheinandertal,* in which the motif extends even to the policeman bringing a cervelat to Mani, a dog he is supposed to shoot: "Lustenwyler . . . threw the dog a cervelat. It was the proper thing to do, since he, after all, had to shoot him. The parish president reached into his side pocket and also took out a cervelat. All three ate cervelats — the president, the dog, and the policeman. The dog ate the fastest" (94). Here we have, as in *Romulus*, a *Henkersmahlzeit* without an execution: the dog is one of the few characters in the novel (and he is a main character) who survive at the end.

For many of Dürrenmatt's characters, however, the *Henkersmahlzeit* is indeed just that, with the meal occasionally growing to extreme proportions. In *Es steht geschrieben*, Johann Bockelson eats a momentous meal that turns out to be a *Henkersmahlzeit*, for it is not long afterward that he is put to death. Bockelson rhapsodizes on this meal:

> "I have eaten superbly. . . . To be sure, it was a modest meal, as is fitting in difficult times, yet, with the help of God, I was satisfied, and a pleasant feeling is spreading through my limbs. I recollect with deepest pleasure the fish chowder, with the hermit crabs and sea snails, served to me as a first course. Ah, it was exquisite! Also, the giant pike still lingers gently in my mind like a distant lover, poached in red wine and stuffed with trout, ruddles, blue char, sour olives, pickled mushrooms, pearl onions, and pickles. . . . How I lusted after the frog's legs, Valais blind worms, and escargots à la Bourguignonne with soft-boiled swallow's eggs, which were passed to my royal highness on a silver platter. Praised be the goodness of the Lord, who entices such wonders from the dark womb of Nature! . . . He made the precious vines to grow, whose wine I enjoyed. Praised be Nacktarsch and Liebfrauenmilch! Praised, too, be the pork belly in gelée and caviar, the oysters with champagne, the Easter lamb, roasted on a spit and filled with little Strassbourg sausages, roasted larks, and the sweetbreads of prematurely born calves, along with the hearty Burgundy wine. . . . Blessed and glorified be what I have just enjoyed! O Russian salad with tuna! O Steinhäger! O Sauerkraut!"[30]

This lengthy dithyrambic oratory, which Gerhard Neumann calls "a culinary word orgy, obviously modeled on Rabelais,"[31] is a parody of a hymn of praise to God that goes on for two pages, in which Dürrenmatt employs a combination of anachronisms, high-blown language, comic exaggeration, and comic repetition and enumeration. Despite the luxuriance of both the menu and the language with which Bockelson describes what he ate, what he has engaged in is clearly binge eating. And what could be more appropriate for a condemned man, since the binge, despite what might appear to be destructive behavior, is actually a "thrust toward life," a protective mechanism that speaks "the voice of survival."[32]

Dürrenmatt presents his most complex example of binge eating in *Die Panne* (Traps, 1956), in both versions of which, the short story and the radio play, he serves up a veritable gustatory orgy, a "thrust toward life" on the part of the retired judges and lawyers and also a *Henkersmahlzeit* for the main character, Alfredo Traps. I should like to consider here the short story,[33] rather than the radio play,[34] partly because it ends with the *Henkersmahlzeit* turning out to be a true executioner's meal, followed by the suicidal death of the condemned Traps — as opposed to the ending of the radio play, which shows Traps driving away totally unaffected by the events of the night before. More important, however, is that the short-story version contains the more colorful (one is tempted to say "meatier" or "juicier") narrative passages, lacking in the radio play, that describe the food being served, the people who eat it, and the manner in which it is consumed, all of which contribute considerably to the grotesqueness of the Lucullan feast.

Considerable discussion has been devoted to this feast, much of which concentrates especially on the wordplay on *Gericht* (court) and *Gericht* (course served at a meal), on the connection between eating and justice, and on the theme of the *Henkersmahlzeit*.[35] One study in particular, that of Peter Spycher, does mention the grotesqueness of the old men who partake of the feast (250–51). These old retired justice officials who gather together for dinner had been leading a miserable existence before the state's attorney came up with the idea that they play the game of conducting mock trials. As Traps's defense attorney explains to him, the state's attorney lay dying; it was believed that the host, the retired judge, suffered from stomach cancer; Pilet, the executioner, suffered from diabetes; and the defense attorney himself had a serious blood pressure problem (55). The game changed all that. It became a "fountain of health" (55) for these men. Their hormones, their stomachs, their pancreases began again to function; they found themselves with renewed energy, youth, and flexibility; and their appetites returned (56). With the return of their appetites came the elaborate feasts, now an integral part of the game they play to add meaning to the otherwise uneventful and meaningless lives they have been living since they retired to the countryside.

What we have, then, in *Die Panne* is partly a renewed celebration of life, the image described by Langer "of human vitality holding its own in the world amid the surprises of unplanned coincidence" (331). Here Dürrenmatt does indeed present the comic ideal of communal feasting. The old men welcome Alfredo Traps into their midst. He drinks "to good friendship" (31) with his defense attorney; the entire friendly atmosphere gives him a "solemn feeling of happiness, blessedness, and cosmic harmony" (40). Traps is moved by the "touching brotherhood" of the group (64), which extends even to his drinking to brotherhood with his prosecutor, after which "they kissed each other, embraced, caressed each other, drank to one another, and emotion spread over them, the devotion of a beautifully developing friendship" (75).

In the midst of this friendly court (*Gericht*), many a delectable course (*Gericht*) is served. Traps begins with a Campari on the veranda and then is led into the dining room to try the port before enjoying the first course of cold cuts, Russian eggs, snails, and turtle soup (35). The fish course, accompanied by a light, sparkling Neuchatel (36), is followed, served sequentially on fresh plates, by beefsteak tartare; champignons à la crème, accompanied by a Réserve des Maréchaux (40); roast loin of veal, with Pichon-Longueville 1933 (49); a salad (50); chicken, with Château Pavie 1921 (64); eight kinds of cheese (Camembert, Brie, Emmentaler, Gruyère, Tête de Moine, Vacherin, Limburger, and Gorgonzola) accompanied by two bottles of vintage 1914 Château Margaux (68, 70, 78); coffee; a fine Roffignac cognac, vintage 1893 (100); torte (103); and champagne (116).

As important as the meal itself, however, is the fact that such an elaborate meal, so carefully planned and executed, displaying the culinary artistry of the housekeeper, Simone, and accompanied by the finest wines, turns into a gastronomic grotesquerie. One must consider the entire scene presented by Dürrenmatt, beginning with the appearance and behavior of the dramatis personae in this culinary drama. With the exception of Alfredo Traps, they are old men, ranging in age from seventy-seven to eighty-seven. The host, a former judge, is described as a little old man, scarcely higher than his garden gate (17–18), almost foppish, with his few remaining hairs carefully brushed and in his exaggeratedly oversized frock coat (24). Among the others who fill the veranda "like monstrous ravens" (24) are Pilet, a former executioner, completely bald, who in keeping with the conventions of his former profession wears a bushy black-dyed mustache and a white carnation in his buttonhole and behaves with overcorrectness (25); Kummer, a former lawyer and Traps's appointed defender, described as "fatter than

Pilet, immense, as if put together out of rolls of fat," with a "very red face, powerful drunkard's nose, jovial goggle-eyes behind a gold pince-nez," and, because of an oversight, wearing a nightshirt under his black suit, the pockets of which are stuffed with papers (26); and Zorn, the state's attorney, tall and thin, an "apparition from yesteryear," with a monocle, duelling scars on his face, a hooked nose, a snow-white mane, and a sunken mouth, a man who buttons his vest the wrong way and wears socks that do not match (26).

At the beginning of the evening, these men are reserved, polite, and discreet. As the meal progresses, they become less inhibited, and the smiles and polite laughter they exhibited while drinking their aperitifs turn to giggling, crowing, cackling, squealing, and shouting. By the time the chicken is served, they are smacking their lips, eating with their hands, praising the culinary masterpiece, drinking, toasting everyone's health, and licking the sauce from their fingers (65). At one point, the state's attorney roars out Greek and Latin verses and then cites Schiller and Goethe; the dwarflike judge blows out all the candles but one, which he uses to make hand shadows on the wall of goats, bats, devils, and goblins, all the while grumbling and hissing; and Pilet bangs on the table, calling for a death sentence (69–70). At a later point, general tumult breaks out: while Pilet embraces and kisses Traps, the judge and state's attorney dance around the room, banging on walls, climbing on chairs, and smashing bottles (87). By the time the sentence is announced, the judge is so drunk he can hardly speak (114–15), and Pilet, attempting to lead Traps up to his room on all fours, falls asleep on the stairs (25–26).

It could be argued that it is the wine, and not the food, that promotes the grotesque behavior on the part of the men. But when one considers the immense quantities of food they consume, along with the fact that they begin even the first course with unembarrassed slurping (35), one would have to agree that, even without the wine, the gastronomic grotesqueries would be present. Traps, the younger man who considers himself to be a stouthearted eater, is amazed at the vitality and the gigantic appetites, at the sheer gluttony of these men (77), who even after consuming the many courses of the meal are able to "plunge into the torte" when it is served sometime after midnight (103).

With comic exaggeration Dürrenmatt brings his communal celebration of life, with its harmless game played by four harmless old men, from the realm of the comic into that of the tragicomic. As the extravagant dinner deteriorates into a gustatory orgy, Dürrenmatt reveals a topsy-turvy world in which psychic murder can be committed without any feeling of guilt on the part of the murderer, a world that four old men can illuminate with what they consider to be the "pure rays of justice," however grotesque and whimsical that justice may seem (114). At least in the short-story version, Traps, after acknowledging his guilt, carries out his own execution by hanging himself. The ending of the radio play version, which has Traps driving off with no clear recollection of his "trial," is perhaps more poignant, for it illustrates that the clear-cut justice of the old men, unencumbered by the confusion of the official legal system (51), does not matter and that these men are indeed powerless, reduced to playing games and feasting.

The old men in *Die Panne*, along with Romulus, Bockelson, Bärlach, and Lustenwyler, exemplify Dürrenmatt's characters who turn to food for reasons other than satisfying a physical hunger. Whether they use eating as an avoidance mechanism, or in order to gain the strength they need to deal with a difficult problem, or whether they resort to binge eating as a means of clinging to life, they are all using food in order to cope with their difficult, and often helpless, situations. In some cases, as has been pointed out, their eating behavior reaches grotesque proportions. This may be a consequence of Dürrenmatt's comic exaggeration. The ultimate result, however, is that by having his characters indulge in unnecessary, even bulimic, eating as a means of coping with a world that "is coming apart, despite all the glue," Dürrenmatt not only depicts a dis-ordered world; he also creates such a world, inhabited by characters who are themselves exemplary of that world and its grotesqueness.

Notes

Unless otherwise indicated, all translations into English are the author's.

1. Friedrich Dürrenmatt, *Der Meteor* (Zurich: Verlag der Arche, 1966), 27.

2. See Geneen Roth, *Feeding the Hungry Heart: The Experience of Compulsive Eating* (New York: New American Library [Signet], 1982), 17, 94; Hilde Bruch, *Eating Disorders. Obesity, Anorexia Nervosa, and the Person Within* (New York: Basic Books, 1973), 128; and Susie Orbach, *Fat Is a Feminist Issue II: A Program to Conquer Compulsive Eating* (New York: Berkley Books, 1982), 53–58.

3. Theodore Isaac Rubin, *Forever Thin* (New York: Gramercy Publishing Co., 1970), 47.

4. Elisabeth Brock-Sulzer, *Friedrich Dürrenmatt: Stationen seines Werkes* (Zurich: Diogenes Verlag, 1986), 317.

5. Friedrich Dürrenmatt, "Der Tunnel," in *Die Stadt* (Zurich: Verlag der Arche, 1952), 151.

6. Susanne K. Langer, *Feeling and Form: A Theory of Art* (New York: Scribner's, 1953), 331.

7. David M. Stein and William Laakso, "Bulimia: A Historical Perspective," *International Journal of Eating Disorders* 7 (1988): 201.

8. See Wolfgang Kayser, *Das Groteske: Seine Gestaltung in Malerei und Dichtung* (Oldenburg and Hamburg: Gerhard Stalling Verlag, 1957), 11.

9. Friedrich Dürrenmatt, *Durcheinandertal* (Zurich: Diogenes Verlag, 1989), 137.

10. Karl S. Guthke, *Die moderne Tragikomödie: Theorie und Gestalt* (Göttingen: Vandenhoeck & Ruprecht, 1968), 120; Kenneth S. Whitton, *The Theatre of Friedrich Dürrenmatt: A Study in the Possibility of Freedom* (London: Oswald Wolff, 1980), 20.

11. Friedrich Dürrenmatt, *Romulus der Grosse. Ungeschichtlichte historische Komödie* (Zurich: Verlag der Arche, 1958), 19.

12. Friedrich Dürrenmatt, "Theaterprobleme," in *Theater-Schriften und Reden* (Zurich: Verlag der Arche, 1966), 119.

13. George Steiner, *The Death of Tragedy* (New York: Oxford University Press, 1961), 351-53.

14. Dürrenmatt, *Durcheinandertal*, 7-9.

15. Dürrenmatt, "Theaterprobleme," 119.

16. Friedrich Dürrenmatt, *Stoffe I-III* (Zurich: Diogenes Verlag, 1981), 77.

17. Erich Kästner, "Die Ehe des Herrn Mississippi," in *Friedrich Dürrenmatt, Werkausgabe in dreissig Bänden*, ed. in cooperation with the author by Daniel Keel (Zurich: Diogenes Verlag, 1980), 149.

18. Friedrich Dürrenmatt and Charlotte Kerr, *Rollenspiele: Protokoll einer fiktiven Inszenierung und Achterloo III* (Zurich: Diogenes Verlag, 1986), 153.

19. From an interview with Violet Ketels, *Journal of Modern Literature* 1 (1970): 92-93.

20. Dürrenmatt and Kerr, *Rollenspiele*, 51.

21. Dürrenmatt, "Weihnacht," in *Die Stadt*, 9.

22. Friedrich Dürrenmatt, "Dramaturgische Überlegungen zu den Wiedertäufern," *Die Wiedertäufer: Eine Komödie in zwei Teilen* (Zurich: Verlag der Arche, 1967), 101.

23. Dürrenmatt, "Theaterprobleme," 98.

24. Lynn Cattanach and Judith Rodin, "Psychosocial Components of the Stress Process in Bulimia," *International Journal of Eating Disorders* 7 (1988): 81-83.

25. Ernst Schröder, *Das Leben, verspielt* (Frankfurt a.M.: S. Fischer Verlag, 1978), 189-90.

26. *Lusten-* suggests *Lüste*, or the pleasures of the senses or the flesh; -*wyler* suggests someone from a settlement ending in the common Swiss place name -*wil*, as in the town Wil, formerly spelled Wyl. The -*wyler* in Lustenwyler, however, is also a homonymn of *Wühler*, or one who burrows or rummages.

27. Friedrich Dürrenmatt, *Der Richter und sein Henker* (Hamburg: Rowohlt, 1955), 110-13.

28. See Gerhard Neumann, "Friedrich Dürrenmatt: Dramaturgie der Panne," in G. Neumann, J. Schröder, and M. Karnick, *Dürrenmatt, Frisch. Weiss: Drei Entwürfe zum Drama der Gegenwart* (Munich: Wilhelm Fink Verlag, 1969), 56.

29. Dürrenmatt and Kerr, *Rollenspiele*, 86.

30. Friedrich Dürrenmatt, *Es steht geschrieben*, in *Komödien II und frühe Stücke* (Zurich: Verlag der Arche, 1959), 79-80. I am indebted to Renate Usmiani for the translation of *Röteln* (ruddles) in her article "Justice and the Monstrous Meal in the Work of Friedrich Dürrenmatt," *Canadian Humanities Association Bulletin* 20 (1969): 10-11.

31. Neumann, "Friedrich Durrenmatt," 56.

32. Susie Orbach, *Hunger Strike: The Anorectic's Struggle as a Metaphor for Our Age* (New York: W. W. Norton & Co., 1986), 144; see also Roth, *Feeding the Hungry Heart*, 16-17.

33. Friedrich Dürrenmatt, *Die Panne: Eine noch mögliche Geschichte* (Zurich: Verlag der Arche, 1956).

230   Barbara Lide

0

34. Friedrich Dürrenmatt, *Die Panne: Ein Hörspiel* (Zurich: Verlag der Arche, 1961).

35. See, e.g., Peter Spycher, *Friedrich Dürrenmatt: Das erzählerische Werk* (Frauenfeld and Stuttgart: Verlag Huber, 1972), 231-71; Hans Bänziger, "Die Gerichte und das Gericht von Alfredo Traps in einer ländlichen Villa," in *Friedrich Dürrenmatt: Studien zu seinem Werk*, ed. Gerhard P. Knapp; Gerhard Neumann, *Friedrich Dürrenmatt: Dramaturgie der Panne* (Heidelberg: Lothar Stiehm Verlag, 1976), 218-32; Timo Tiusanen, *Dürrenmatt: A Study in Plays, Prose, Theory* (Princeton, N.J.: Princeton University Press, 1977), esp. 82, 100, 127; and Renate Usmiani, "Justice and the Monstrous Meal in Dürrenmatt."

THE FORBIDDEN FRUIT
AND FEMALE DISORDERLY EATING:
Three Versions of Eve

Gunilla Theander Kester

The production of disorderly eating in literature combines body as text and text as body, and it reveals the common trait of both as symptom. In discussing the case of Anna O, Dianne Hunter explains the anorexic symptoms of her hysteria as "her way of literalizing through her body her felt psychic condition."[1] In Gayl Jones's disturbing second novel, *Eva's Man,*[2] the female narrator literalizes her felt psychic condition when she poisons a man with rat poison and castrates him with her teeth—an expression, I believe, of her longing for a lost female community and oral culture. Even though Eva literally literalizes somebody else's body, she produces an act of symptomatic disorderly eating that is both textual and sexual, both book and body.

Eva's Man is an African-American narrative of *Bildung* constructed as a kind of psychoanalytic process or a postmodernist detective story in which the narrating subject wants to understand what happened to the narrated subject, the protagonist.[3] The story of Eva Medina Canada is produced in the space between these two halves of the divided subject, which, using the concept of the semiotic sign as a model, could be called "the subjectifier" and "the subjectified." In an attempt to negotiate a healing of the rift within the divided subject, *Eva's Man,* among other strategies, presents a powerful revision of the eating-of-the-forbidden-fruit story, a revision that inscribes both a female perspective and an African-American perspective. On the one hand, Gayl Jones's novel illustrates the feminist agenda to, in the words of Susan Rubin Suleiman, "reappropriate, by means of ironic rereadings—and rewritings—the dominant cultural productions of the past."[4] On the other hand, it exemplifies what Henry Louis Gates describes as African-American "Signifyin(g)," or troping—that is, a "use of repetition and reversal (chiasmus)," which, still according to Gates, "constitutes an implicit parody of a subject's own complicity in illusion."[5] I will argue that, produced by the divided subject and her own complicity in illusion, the disorderly eating in *Eva's Man* takes place on two levels. On the level of story, or *fabula,* Eva the cannibal represents one kind of disorderly eater. On the level of discourse, or *sjuzhet,* the reader, involved in a futile search for truth, becomes a disorderly eater who must eat the dish that Eva serves.[6] The subjectifier creates a structure that makes the reader expect the truth, but when the moment comes for Eva to reveal what actually happened to her, she instead feeds the reader an intertextual allusion to the biblical story of the apple and the fall of humankind.

The literary production of female disorderly eating has a long and renowned tradition. One of its earliest and most well-known formulations is in the book of Genesis in the Old Testament where Eve's refusal to comply with God's commands produces an early example of female disorderly eating. When Eve eats of the forbidden fruit she breaks a patriarchal taboo and as a result is punished by death. God had said, "You may freely eat of every tree of the garden; but of the tree of the knowledge of good and evil you shall not eat, for in the day that you eat of it you shall die" (Genesis 2:15–17). This early example illustrates the link between a patriarchal taboo, the female subject, and eating as a criminal act. It also exemplifies the deadly consequences of such behavior: as a result of her disobedience, Eve is quickly criminalized and sentenced to death.

The connection between the female subject and the act of eating as a criminal act—a breaking of the law that deserves capital punishment—is deeply ingrained in Western culture. The biblical account of the fall of man and woman in Genesis and Milton's version of that same story both link eating and death. In Milton's *Paradise Lost,* God sends his Son to judge Eve and Adam after they have eaten the forbidden fruit. Eve is sentenced to procreate in sorrow and to remain inferior to her husband:

> "Thy sorrow I will greatly multiply
> By thy conception; children thou shalt bring
> In sorrow forth, and to thy husband's will
> Thine shall submit, he over thee shall rule."[7]

In a slightly different version, Adam too receives both a personal death sentence and one that applies to the whole human race.

> "Because thou hast hearkened to the voice of thy wife,
> And eaten of the tree concerning which
> I charged thee, saying, 'Thou shalt not eat thereof,'
> Cursed is the ground for thy sake; thou in sorrow
> Shalt eat thereof all the days of thy life;
> Thorns also and thistles it shall bring thee forth
> Unbid, and thou shalt eat th' herb of the field;
> In the sweat of thy face shalt thou eat bread,
> Till thou return unto the ground, for thou
> Out of the ground wast taken; know thy birth,
> For dust thou art, and shalt to dust return."[8]

The Son's pronouncement indicates that, in Milton's view, the fall of man and woman is a fall into sorrowful eating. It is also a fall into linear time and toward death. The punishment of Eve is to have mortal children; her death takes place in a kind of Kristevan "future perfect."[9] Adam's lot, in contrast, is focused on the origin of man and on death, which can be seen in the formulation "Know thy birth / For dust thou art, and shalt to dust return." In that sense his fate is history. Signifying or troping on this story, Gayl Jones provides a powerful revision of all the elements of this narrative: female disorderly eating, the forbidden fruit, and death.

Eva's Man

Eva's Man (1976) tells the story of a woman who, in spite of many brutal experiences of male abuse and molestations, tries to build a sense of self through sexual and textual transgressions that, in one fashion or another, relate to the production of disorderly eating in literature. Her life story begins when she is five years old and her family moves from Georgia to New York City, and ends in a psychiatric prison. Her act of mutilation of the male body represents a somewhat unusual form of disorderly eating; it also reverses the common trope of a man writing on a female body as on a blank page.[10] Eva's way of narrating her experiences of this moment when body and book—love and law—intersect produces an intertextual portrayal of female disorderly eating.

Eva's life story splits into two realms of experiences. On the one hand, she is repeatedly violated by men and responds passively to them. On the other hand, she refers to a catalog of interesting women who nurture her responses and her imagination. Eva's story is shattered and often confusing, but through the many fragments, she presents an underlying chronological pattern that begins in the new neighborhood where Eva experiences her first physical violation. A boy named Freddie Smoot sticks a dirty popsicle into her and forces her to fondle him. She is five years old. With this story the subjectifier starts an early association between men and food to which she consistently returns. Men are consumers of food and women; they eat and they have sex. Her final act of revenge on Davis reflects her attempt to imitate this behavior as she presents it.

This semiotic system of male appetite and consumption is repeated in the following sections, and Eva's crime is presented as a counterpoint throughout. This way the text emphasizes a division of experience: while women get punished for a certain behavior, men go free.[11] When Eva is about twelve years old, her mother's young lover, the musician Tyrone, age twenty-two, repeatedly assaults her. Presumably as a kind of payment and consolation, he starts bringing her "things like popcorn and potato chips, doughnuts, cookies, candy, stuff like that" (31). Tyrone never suffers any consequences for his treatment of Eva. The next man to exploit Eva sexually is her married cousin Alfonso, who moves to New York from Kansas when Eva is seventeen years old. Alfonso questions Eva about her sexual experiences and teaches her an expression for intercourse that fits well into the semiotic system of male consumption established in the text. He asks Eva if she's "been getting it."

> "How old are you?" he asked.
> "Seventeen."
> "And ain't had the meat? Most girls your age had the meat *and* the gravy." (57)

The meat-and-gravy image reinforces the way men teach Eva that she is a sexual dish. Talking to Davis ten years later, she shows that she still thinks of herself as food: "I feel like an egg sucked hollow and then filled with raw oysters" (66). Alfonso also introduces Eva to Moses Tripp, a consumer of bourbon and pigfeet who will later assault her. Through a casual association Eva links her childhood memories to her situation in the psychiatric prison. She mentions in passing that her psychiatrist has the same last name as the little boy with the dirty popsicle stick, Smoot. He also has a soft voice, which Eva describes as "cotton candy" (76).

Eva's childhood memories form a gender-divided pattern in which men consume food and women but in which female consumption may be deadly. When Eva finishes school, her mother takes her to North Carolina to visit Miss Billie and her daughter Charlotte, a not-so-young woman who refuses to marry and have children. In the African-American literary tradition, the return to the South often signifies the subject's understanding of his or her past in America and a link to black culture and heritage.[12] But Eva's return to the South does not give her a sense of her heritage and history. Rather, it reaffirms the gender division within the tradition. Charlotte tells Eva a story of a little girl who ate a buckeye and consequently died, suggesting that female consumption can be deadly. The story implies that for women geography holds no freedom; they have no country or region where they are safe. To women, consumption of foreign objects and male bodies carries a death sentence no matter where they do it.

Within Eva's system, Davis becomes the crowning example of man as a consumer of food and women. While the other men Eva meets eat, Davis is the first to make the explicit identification between women and food. Melvin Dixon argues, "Davis makes the connection between himself and food—'you eat food as if you're making love to it'—only to suffer the consequences."[13] According to the system Eva constructs, when she kills and mutilates Davis she attempts to erase the difference between their bodies and their positions in language; she desires to make him similar to her. In so doing, she also makes herself similar to him; she behaves like a man. First she objectifies him, and then she attempts to consume him. She dispossesses him, and she changes the grammar of the story. She is no longer "Davis' whore"; instead, he becomes "Eva's man," a nomination that shows the grammatical lack of an equivalent term for a male prostitute.[14] Many critics see Eva as a kind of "avenging angel" who reaches a climactic and existential moment of freedom as she takes the life of Davis and treats the body as she pleases.[15] But the grammatical change she gains through her act of violence only supplies the title for her story. Her true pursuit of freedom lies not in imitating male behavior but in writing her own subjectivity. In order to do that, she must reconnect with a female textual history that goes all the way back to Eve and the apple.

Eva's Man is structured as a kind of archeology of being, an undigging of the origin of selfhood, a search for the birth of the female subject. It links this event to a moment of female disorderly eating and to Eva's unusual mutilation of the dead male body. This structure makes the reader antici-pate a final version of the main event, a wish that is ultimately thwarted because the intertextual reference to the biblical story has a double function: it establishes a context for the eating-the-forbidden-fruit motif, while simultaneously erasing the possibility of a final and subjective truth. Further, the tension between the subjectifier and the subjectified creates an appetite for truth, a desire to rescue and to restore the presence of a female subject. Eva systematically evokes a series of different versions of and reactions to her criminal act. For example, she quotes the newspaper article about it and relates the reactions of the policemen, her landlady, and her fellow prisoners. These reflections heighten the archeological fervor and increase the longing for a decisive *arche*-version, an *Ur-Bild*, which will be not a mirror or a reflection but the real thing. When Eva begins to formulate her sensations and memories of her violent act, however, she offers no factual, historical summary, but instead begins an intertextual and comparative play on the story of Eve and the forbidden apple: "I opened his trousers and played with his penis. My mouth, my teeth, my tongue went inside his trousers. I raised blood, slime from cabbage, blood sausage. Blood from an apple. . . . My teeth in an apple. A swollen plum in my mouth" (128). The food images connect Eva's act with the male code of consumption, while at the same time they acknowledge the difference between the male organ and the fruit. During the castration, Eva transfers the male body from one code to another, from sausage to apple and plum, from the male sphere to the female. Eva's intertextual allusion to the biblical Eve is not ironic in Suleiman's terms. Her repetition of Eve's act—eating the forbidden fruit—presents a powerful rewriting of the biblical story. This new Eva wants to recreate the myth. This time she desires a solitary, manless Eden where she can eat the fruit (and the snake), invent a new language, and clear a space for a different and female knowledge.

In prison Eva meets a new group of women and slowly rejoins a female community. The novel ends with Eva and Elvira making love, Elvira asking Eva to tell her when it tastes sweet and Eva responding "Now," the last word in the book (177). That moment of eternal presence revises linear time, history, and the patriarchal death sentence carried out through women's mortal children. It also cures female disorderly eating since the other female body is not a foreign substance that will kill the consumer. Eva's experience of women is an alphabet and, as the etymology of that word indicates, these women begin a different knowledge, the alpha and beta that can inscribe female subjectivity.

Notes

1. Dianne Hunter, "Hysteria, Psychoanalysis, and Feminism: The Case of Anna O," in *The (M)other Tongue: Essays in Feminist Psychoanalytic Interpretation,* ed. Shirley Nelson Garner, Claire Kahane, and Madelon Sprengnether (Ithaca, N.Y.: Cornell University Press, 1985), 95.

2. Gayl Jones, *Eva's Man* (Boston: Beacon Press, 1982). Hereafter, references to Jones's work are in parentheses.

3. Alison Lee details some uses of detective stories in postmodernist novels in her study *Realism and Power: Postmodern British Fiction* (London: Routledge, 1990).

4. Susan Rubin Suleiman, ed., *The Female Body in Western Culture: Contemporary Perspectives* (Cambridge, Mass.: Harvard University Press, 1985), 18.

5. Henry Louis Gates Jr., *Figures in Black: Words, Signs, and the "Racial" Self* (Oxford: Oxford University Press, 1987), 240; idem, *The Signifying Monkey: A Theory of African-American Literary Criticism* (Oxford: Oxford University Press, 1988).

6. The distinction between *fabula* and *sjuzet* comes from Russian formalist Boris Toma-shevsky's "Thematics," printed in *Russian Formalist Criticism: Four Essays,* trans. with an introduction by Lee T. Lemon and Marion J. Reis (Lincoln: University of Nebraska Press, 1965), 61–95. His ideas are further discussed by Seymore Chatman in *Story and Discourse: Narrative Structure in Fiction and Film* (Ithaca, N.Y.: Cornell University Press, 1978), 17–22. See also Wallace Martin's *Recent Theories of Narrative* (Ithaca, N.Y.: Cornell University Press, 1986), 107–26, and Robert Scholes' *Structuralism: An Introduction* (New Haven, Conn.: Yale University Press, 1974), 77–91.

7. *Paradise Lost,* 10.193–96, in *The Complete Poetical Works of John Milton,* ed. Douglas Bush (Boston: Houghton Mifflin Co., 1965).

8. Ibid., 10.198–208.

9. See "Women's Time," in *The Kristeva Reader,* ed. Toril Moi (New York: Columbia University Press, 1986), 187–213.

10. See Susan Gubar's " 'The Blank Page' and the Issues of Female Creativity," in *Writing and Sexual Difference,* ed. Elizabeth Abel (Chicago: University of Chicago Press, 1982), 73–93. Gubar argues that this "model of the pen-penis writing on the virgin page participates in a long tradition identifying the author as a male who is primary and the female as his passive creation—a secondary object lacking autonomy, endowed with often contradictory meaning but denied intentionality" (ibid., 77). Gubar also discusses how "one of the primary and most resonant metaphors provided by the female body is blood, and cultural forms of creativity are often experienced as painful wounding" (ibid., 78). Eva's preoccupation with blood and

bleeding, as well as her description of her mutilation of Davis' body, fits in this pattern; her transgression is cultural and textual, and it takes the shape of a terrible wounding. See also "Defiance: The Body (of) Writing/The Writing (of) Body," chap. 7 in Elizabeth A. Meese's *Crossing the Double-Cross: The Practice of Feminist Criticism* (Chapel Hill: University of North Carolina Press, 1986), 115–32. It is also worth noting with Barbara Johnson that "the very equation of the woman's body with the blank page implies that the woman's body is white (indeed, of a whiteness no actual bodies possess)." See Barbara Johnson, "Is Female to Male as Ground Is to Figure?" in *Feminism and Psychoanalysis,* ed. Richard Feldstein and Judith Roof (Ithaca, N.Y.: Cornell University Press, 1989), 267.

11. Keith E. Byerman, "Intense Behaviors: The Use of the Grotesque in *The Bluest Eye* and *Eva's Man,*" *CLA Journal* 25 (1982): 447–57, emphasizes the gender difference regarding what is considered criminal and/or acceptable behavior. He maintains that Eva's experiences and the stories of the queen bee only reinforce "the view that women are by nature sinful, that they are responsible for the evil in the world. Original sin, in some cosmic way, has attached itself to the female gender. Eva is thus further encouraged to believe that a woman can never be innocent, even if she has done nothing" (ibid., 454). This view reflects that of Eva's psychiatrist at the end of the novel. His analysis of Eva's behavior is simplistic: "You thought you were a bad woman, so you went out and got you a bad man" (*Eva's Man,* 174). Eva responds by getting violent. Her reaction could be a sign of two things: either his interpretation is correct and she resents the mirror image, or, more believable, her version of "the truth" is so far removed from his that she resents his attempts at "writing her script." Other African-American authors explore the same theme. In an interview with John O'Brien, Alice Walker explains that in writing *The Third Life of Grange Copeland* she wanted "to explore the relationship between men and women and why women are always condemned for doing what men do as an expression of their masculinity. Why are women so easily 'tramps' and 'traitors' when men are heroes for engaging in the same activity?" (*Interviews with Black Writers* [New York: Liveright, 1973], 197).

12. See Jean Toomer's *Cane* (spatial return) or Ralph Ellison's *Invisible Man* (psychological return), to mention two well-known examples.

13. Melvin Dixon, "Singing a Deep Song: Language as Evidence in the Novels of Gayl Jones," in *Black Women Writers, 1950–1980: A Critical Evaluation,* ed. Mari Evans (New York: Anchor/Doubleday, 1984), 246.

14. The word "gigolo," with its associations to dance and lovemaking, does not give the male prostitute the suppressed and humiliated role that the word "whore" gives to a woman.

15. Byerman, "Intense Behaviors," 452.

AFTERWORD

Peter W. Graham

This is an afterword but not a conclusion. Perhaps Byron, of all the writers considered in this volume, has most memorably articulated the perils of closure: "Nothing so difficult as a beginning / In poesy, unless perhaps the end." The problem of how to finish is as real for the critic as it is for the poet, and in the fifteen essays here collected, each author has had to conclude her argument or end his account as seemed best in the individual case. Now that the sequence of essays, diverse in tone, method, and scope and ranging widely through genres and times, is complete, a reader might wish for some valedictory remarks from the editors. New territory has been explored: what about a bird's-eye view of the ground covered? We have traveled widely over time and place: would it not be desirable to highlight the pattern of similarities underlying the cultural differences? Or what about some brief discussion of roads not taken here but well worth following in subsequent studies? The editors resist the temptation to answer such questions — to conclude — precisely because this collection is open-ended by design. Its essence is to be suggestive, not comprehensive. Taken together, the fifteen essays are meant to enact an innovative mode of reading: envisioning texts in light of contemporary perceptions of disorderly eating. This volume's subject lies at the nexus of nature and culture, where much remains to be seen and said—where, to borrow the metaphorical commonplace that serves as title to Louis Marin's recently translated study, there is abundant "food for thought." We believe that what these essays truly invite is continuance rather than summation.

Contributors

PAULA MARANTZ COHEN is Associate Professor of Humanities and Communications at Drexel University. Her book *The Daughter's Dilemma: Family Process and the Nineteenth-Century Domestic Novel* has been published by the University of Michigan Press.

LILLIAN CORTI, who holds a Ph.D. in Comparative Literature from the City University of New York, has taught at various academic institutions, including CUNY, the University of Tulsa, and Marien Ngouabi University in Brazzaville, the Congo, where she was supported by a Fulbright grant in 1990. She currently teaches English and World Literature at the University of Alaska in Fairbanks.

The literary black sheep in a medical family, LILIAN R. FURST is Marcel Bataillon Professor of Comparative Literature at the University of North Carolina. She serves as a Contributing Editor for *Literature and Medicine,* has published numerous books and articles on eighteenth- and nineteenth-century European literature, and is presently engaged in a study of realism.

An assistant professor of theater arts at Cornell University, J. ELLEN GAINOR holds a 1991–92 NEH fellowship to write a critical study of the plays of Susan Glaspell. Her book *Shaw's Daughters: Dramatic and Narrative Constructions of Gender* will be published by the University of Michigan Press.

JOANNA B. GILLESPIE, Affiliated Scholar at the Pembroke Center for the Study of Women and the John Carter Brown Library, Brown University, publishes essays on eighteenth- and nineteenth-century Anglo-Protestant women's autobiographical writings. She is completing the life-and-times of one such woman, Martha Laurens Ramsay, and a book of interviews with twentieth-century churchwomen titled *Women, Congregations, and Change.*

A founding editor of *Literature and Medicine,* PETER W. GRAHAM is Professor of English at Virginia Polytechnic Institute and State University. His latest work on Byron is *"Don Juan" and Regency England* (Virginia), and his most recent project is a collaboration with Fritz Oehlschlaeger, *Articulating the Elephant Man* (Johns Hopkins).

NANCY A. GUTIERREZ, Associate Professor of English and Women's Studies at Arizona State University, is author of *English Historical Poetry: 1476–1603* (Garland) and numerous articles on English Renaissance literature. She is currently working on a book on adultery and witchcraft in Renaissance drama.

GUNILLA THEANDER KESTER, a native of Sweden, completed an M.A. in English at the Pennsylvania State University and a Ph.D. in Comparative

Literature at the University of North Carolina. She has received a Fulbright grant and a Sweden-America Foundation Fellowship.

Co-editor of two international anthologies of poetry by women, DEIRDRE LASHGARI teaches World Literature and Women's Literature at California State Polytechnic University at Pomona. She is currently completing a book on narrative strategies in nineteenth-century novels by women and is working on a second book, *Violence, Silence, and Healing Anger in Twentieth-Century Writing by Women.*

BARBARA LIDE is Associate Professor of Languages and Comparative Literature at Michigan Technological University. Especially interested in modern German and Scandinavian literature and modern drama, she has translated, and published extensively on, Strindberg. She is currently writing a book on Strindberg and irony.

Assistant Professor of English at Bryant College, PAULO MEDEIROS is author of "The Cannibalistic Text," forthcoming in a special issue of *Mosaic* devoted to the topic of food and literature. His current projects include a study of the problematics of literal bibliophagy as well as an inquiry into Nietzsche's consumption imagery in *Die Frohliche Wissenschaft.*

ELSA NETTELS, Professor of English at the College of William and Mary, is the author of *James and Conrad* (Georgia), which won the 1975 SAMLA Studies Award, *Language, Race, and Social Class in Howells's America* (Kentucky), and a number of articles on American writers.

MERVYN NICHOLSON is Chair of the Department of English at University College of the Cariboo in British Columbia. Interested in the Romantics, the logic of visualization, and cosmology, he has published more than twenty articles in a range of journals including *The Journal of the History of Ideas, Women's Studies, Mosaic, College English, The Wordsworth Circle, Children's Literature,* and *Comparative Drama.*

RAYMOND ADOLPH PRIER is an independent scholar whose works include *Archaic Logic: Symbol and Structure in Heraclitus, Parmenides, and Empedocles* and *Thauma Idesthai: The Phenomenology of Sight and Appearance in Archaic Greek.* He edited *Countercurrents: On the Primacy of Texts in Literary Criticism.* The piece on Huysmans' *A Rebours* is a base essay for a projected volume on phenomenological narrative from Goethe through Durrell.

Assistant Professor of English at Southern Methodist University, MARTHA SATZ has published essays on such diverse topics as Jane Austen, Mary Wilkins Freeman, Kafka, Thomas Mann, Richard Wright, and the Holocaust. She is now at work on a manuscript entitled *What Can a Woman Know? What Should a Woman Do?: Representations of Female Epistemological and Ethical Paradigms in Fiction.*

Printed in the United Kingdom
by Lightning Source UK Ltd.
108432UKS00001B/70